TECHNOLOGY IN WORKING ORDER

Within the social sciences there is growing interest in the contribution that can be made to the uses, design, operation, and implementation of technology. Much funding and research has gone into empirically based field-work enquiries which have led to important developments in a range of industrial and practical settings.

Sociology has had a long-standing interest in technology, but it has only recently begun to address the social foundations of technology. This development coincides with an interest that has been shown by the sciences of computer systems development in the contribution that sociology can make to systems development. By principally stressing issues that have been developed within ethnomethodology and conversation analysis, this book clearly demonstrates how sociology can address the ways in which technology is a socially organised domain of activity.

The volume brings together new and original research and looks at how it can be of direct relevance to developments in industry. Subjects covered range from introducing technology into the lives of air traffic controllers and the police, to studies of simulated human–computer interaction and the use of 'intelligent machines' in medical settings.

Many of the contributors have worked at Xerox's Palo Alto Research Centre and Rank Xerox's Cambridge EuroPARC: both centres at the forefront of research in the area. This volume is the first to bring their work together, and will make a lasting and original contribution to the field.

Graham Button is Principal Lecturer in Sociology at the University of Plymouth and Visiting Senior Scientist at Rank Xerox, Cambridge EuroPARC.

TECHNOLOGY IN WORKING ORDER

Studies of work, interaction, and technology

Edited by Graham Button

London and New York

First published in 1993 by
Routledge
11 New Fetter Lane, London EC4P 4EE

Simultaneously published in the USA and Canada
by Routledge
a division of Routledge, Chapman and Hall Inc.
29 West 35th Street, New York, NY 10001

Typeset in Baskerville by LaserScript Limited, Mitcham, Surrey
Printed and bound in Great Britain by
Biddles Ltd, Guildford and King's Lynn

British Library Cataloguing in Publication Data
A catalogue record for this book is available from the British Library.

Library of Congress Cataloging in Publication Data
Technology in working order: studies of work, interaction, and
technology/edited by Graham Button.
p. cm.
Includes bibliographical references and index.
1. Computers and civilization. 2. Technology – Social aspects. Methods
engineering. I. Button, Graham.
QA76.9.C66T36   1992
303.48′34 – dc20   92-10514
CIP

ISBN 0–415–06839–8

CONTENTS

ILLUSTRATIONS

CONTRIBUTORS

Bob Anderson, Director, Rank Xerox EuroPARC, Cambridge.

Douglas Benson, Principal Lecturer, Department of Applied Social Science, The University of Plymouth.

Graham Button, Principal Lecturer, Department of Applied Social Science, The University of Plymouth and Visiting Senior Scientist, Rank Xerox EuroPARC, Cambridge.

Harry Collins, Professor and Director, Science Studies Centre, School of Social Sciences, The University of Bath.

Norman Fraser, Research Scientist, Logica Cambridge Ltd, Cambridge, and Visiting Research Fellow, Social and Computer Sciences Research Group, Department of Sociology, The University of Surrey.

Richard Harper, Research Scientist, Rank Xerox EuroPARC, Cambridge.

Joanne Hartland, Graduate Student, Science Studies Centre, School of Social Sciences, The University of Bath.

Christian Heath, Senior Lecturer, Department of Sociology, The University of Surrey.

John Hughes, Professor, Department of Sociology, The University of Lancaster.

Kathleen Jordan, Research Fellow, Department of Sociology, Boston University.

Paul Luff, Research Fellow, Department of Sociology, The University of Surrey, and Research Fellow, Rank Xerox EuroPARC, Cambridge.

Michael Lynch, Associate Professor, Department of Sociology, Boston University.

CONTRIBUTORS

Wes Sharrock, Reader, Department of Sociology, The University of Manchester.

Lucy Suchman, Principal Scientist, Xerox, Palo Alto Research Centre.

Robin Wooffitt, Research Fellow, Social and Computer Sciences Research Group, Department of Sociology, The University of Surrey.

PREFACE

This book is a collection of sociological studies that investigate the way in which computer systems technology is ordered and produced in the interactional work of participants in its design, its construction, its implementation, its use, and by those who talk and write about it. In this respect it is primarily aimed at sociologists, developing what we hope are sociologically interesting issues about the social production of this form of technology. However, it has been written at a time when the disciplines associated with computer systems development, such as computer science, software engineering, human–computer interaction, psychology, ergonomics, and design, have shown an interest in sociological issues. This is particularly true for the development of a new field of study, computer-supported cooperative work (CSCW) and at the last *European CSCW* conference in Amsterdam in 1991 sociologists were included amongst some of the major speakers. Also, at Lancaster University, a new centre for CSCW has been opened which is the product of the collaboration between the departments of computer science and sociology.

However, it is not only the field of CSCW that has shown an interest in sociological studies. Within human–computer interaction the contribution that sociology can make to interface design has been actively pursued, and in this respect not only have sociologists figured on the list of major speakers at the prestigious *CHI 91* conference in New Orleans but also the *American Association of Artificial Intelligence* has held a workshop on the contribution that ethnomethodology and conversation analysis could make to systems development at its 1990 meetings in Boston. This followed on from an extended workshop held at the University of Surrey into computers and conversation, which resulted in the publication of the well-regarded volume (also called *Computers and Conversation*) edited by Paul Luff, Nigel Gilbert, and David Frohlich (1990) which brought together researchers in HCI and sociology.

Further, sociologists have been involved in the exploration of

xi

problematic issues within computer systems development. Thus the Oksnoen symposia that are in part sponsored by the Norwegian, Swedish, Danish, Finnish, and Icelandic governments as well as private industry, have brought together computer scientists and sociologists in discussions of 'formalisation' and 'customisation'. In addition, the Oxford University Computing Laboratory and British Telecom workshop on *Requirements Capture and Analysis* in 1991 explored the contribution that sociology could make to the development of methods for apprehending user requirements. Also, systems designers who have been rethinking the methodology of design and championing the idea of user-centred and participatory design have had occasion to review sociological methodology.

Lastly, in this list of interests, industrial research establishments are exploring the relationship between sociology and computer systems development. Thus Xerox's Palo Alto Research Centre (PARC) and its European partner, Rank Xerox's Cambridge EuroPARC, have long-term interests in examining the contribution that sociology can make to various computer systems development issues, particularly design.

I have selected the above for mention because, although sociologists are involved in many discussions of, symposia on, and institutions to do with computer systems technology, they have been mainly motivated or organised by researchers in the disciplines associated with computer systems development, rather than by sociologists themselves. I have also selected the above because, although some of them have involved a variety of sociological positions, all of them are united by the interest that has been shown in one area of sociology in particular, that of ethnomethodology and conversation analysis.

With a couple of exceptions, the chapters in this book are framed by an ethnomethodological interest in the ordering and organisation of practical action and interaction. In the light of that interest, technology is viewed as ordered in the work through which that action and interaction are organised. These are interests that ethnomethodologists and conversation analysts would wish to share with other sociologists, and it is this audience that this book is primarily aimed at. However, in as much as the various disciplines associated with computer systems development have thought fit to invoke ethnomethodological and conversation-analytic studies in their enquiries, I would like to use the opportunities afforded by a preface to invite them to share the interests articulated through the studies that make up this volume. It must be remembered, though, that, should this invitation be taken up, and although some of the studies are written with this invitation in mind, difficulties that disciplines have in reading and understanding the writings of other disciplines will be encountered.

Graham Button

GENERAL INTRODUCTION

The studies included in this book are concerned with the details of the interactional work involved in the social ordering and production of technology. Accordingly, they reveal an analytic heritage which is common to most of them, though there are one or two exceptions. They address technology from within the programme of ethnomethodological studies of work and the programme of conversation analysis. This means that they are interested in the details of the work of technology as a social achievement and in the social practices through which participants recognisably and accountably orientate themselves to technology in the course of its design, construction, development, implementation, and use, and in talking and writing about it. They are thus concerned with issues such as the situatedness of work practices, the local deployment of knowledge, the assemblage of context, interactional contingencies, praxis, and the sense that these matters have in the accountable occasions of their investigation. In a variety of ways the studies pursue the ordering of technological work as that is displayed in participants' activities and interactions. The studies are united in two other respects. They are mainly empirical studies of particular work settings, and the technology involved is mainly computer technology.[1]

The studies also cluster around a number of themes, and in order to reflect this the book has been organised into different parts, each part containing chapters that address one of the themes. The first theme is epistemological. It is concerned with exploring a way of making technology sociologically interesting without at the same time losing the very content of technology in practices of sociological theorising. The second theme is concerned with the introduction of technology into work settings and with how that technology fits into the organisation of established working practices. The third theme addresses the use of technology in work settings that are organised around technology and how technology is built into the interactions of those who use and consume it. Fourth, the design of

1

computer systems and their implementation is, from a sociological point of view, practical action and interaction in its own right and this theme examines how design and implementation can be investigated as, and also as grounded in, social praxis. The fifth and last theme is that of human–computer interaction, and is concerned with how sociological studies of the sort presented in this book may reorientate traditional ways of thinking in this field of study.

As each theme makes up an individual section of the book, with its own introduction, I will not here either 'introduce' the themes or summarise the studies that make up the sections as is often traditional in an intro-duction, leaving those tasks to the section introductions. However, I will say something about the sociological nature of this collection and its possible interest to disciplines other than sociology, since, in a way, this constitutes a sixth theme which is not given explicit attention elsewhere, although it is implicit in a number of the studies found in different parts of the book.

It is important to stress that all of the studies are *sociological studies* and are primarily involved in developing descriptions of the work of ordering technology for sociologists. Thus the studies are concerned with making points that, hopefully, sociologists will find interesting. However, there have in recent years been a number of newly emerging interests within the sciences of computer systems development that might make sociological studies a fruitful resource for these disciplines. Computer-supported co-operative work (CSCW); the rethinking of design philosophies as exampled in the idea of 'participatory design'; a reflection on design methodologies such as those involved in requirements capture; issues of power and control in computer systems; re-conceptualising models of the user; these and other matters all involve the activities and interactions of people with technology and thus all involve some understanding of the social grounds of human conduct and thought, and the social grounds of technology. In this respect a covert sixth theme is that it is hoped that this collection will not only appeal to sociologists, but that, in as much as it is grounded in the social practicalities of technology, it will hold some interest for those involved in the various sciences of computer systems development, be that computer science, software engineering, psychology, ergonomics, or design.

NOTE

1 There are exceptions to all of this but even these are interleaved into these general concerns. Thus, although Harry Collins may not, at least on the basis of his previous work (see, for example, his critique of Garfinkel, Lynch, and Livingston's investigation of the discovery of a pulsar (Collins 1990), be fully persuaded by the programme of ethnomethodological studies of work and conversation analysis, and although his study is a 'thought experiment' nevertheless he shares an interest in practical action which is common to all the

studies in this book. Further, as happens in the other empirically based studies in Section V, he explores how the grounding of human–computer interaction in practical action has implications for certain ambitions in computer systems development. In this respect, although he may not wish to be associated with ethnomethodology as a programme of study, the interests of his chapter sit alongside the others in this section on human–computer interaction. This is also true for Joanne Hartland's study. Again, although she may not see her work as influenced by ethnomethodological concerns, nevertheless, her interests in the local, occasioned interpretative practices of electrocardiograph operators and their use of 'interpretative' machines are aligned to the other studies in Section II. The last exception is that the investigation of 'implementation' in Section IV is done through a new technology that is aligned to computer systems technology, biological engineering. This topic is, however, a generic one for 'new technology', be that biological or computational technology, and the processes described in this chapter are relevant to computer systems development.

Part I

ANALYTIC ORIENTATIONS

INTRODUCTION

The chapters making up this book are all studies of practical actions and interactions which are orientated towards technology. In the main they are empirical investigations of the social production of technology and are concerned with the way in which activities and interactions order technology. In this respect they differ from other sociological interests in technology. The chapter in this section explores the reasons for this difference and, by so doing, the analytic auspices framing most of the ensuing investigations are revealed.

Two other sociological schools of thought on technology are utilised to frame the arguments: i) *'the social shaping of technology'* and ii) *'the social construction of technology'*. They are given prominence because in different ways they represent a new turn of thought in sociology with respect to technology that, on the face of it, appears similar to the studies and arguments presented in this book.

Arguments about the 'social shaping of technology' were forged around the mid-1970s to mid-1980s and are represented in MacKenzie and Wajcman (1985). They contrast with previous sociological interests in technology in two ways. First, they question the view of the relationship between the technical and the social that was prevalent in the social sciences. This was that technology determined, even caused, the development of social structures, the classic exemplification being that technological change determines/causes social change. By stressing how technology is shaped by social forces such as economics and gender, an attempt was made to ground the technical in the social. Thus, technology was to be thought of through and through as a social phenomenon.

The second distinctive feature about the arguments concerning the 'social shaping of technology' is that they sought to develop an interest in the organisation of the technology itself rather than subsuming technology under the auspices of other sociological topics. For example, an important sociological preoccupation with the nature and organisation of 'work' at the time that the 'social shaping of technology arguments' were developed was 'the labour process'. Braverman's (1974) influential *Labour and Monopoly Capital* had revived a popular sociological interest in how work is organised under capitalism. The labour-process thesis is, however, uncompromisingly a thesis about the organisation of work under monopoly capitalism, which is applied equally to workers in technology as it is to workers in, say, education. It says nothing about the actual work or content of technology as such. As Friedman and Cornford's (1989) labour-process analysis of computer systems development bears witness, this order of sociological interest in technology has not disappeared. However, with the development of arguments concerning the 'social shaping of technology', an interest in the actual content of the technology, what it is that differentiates it from other activities, came to be seen as a sociologically interesting issue in its own right.

An example of this concern is the interest that has been shown in the *history* of a technological development: how the details of a particular technology can be located in the history of *its* development (where history is understood to involve socially organised processes). Thus, with arguments about 'the social shaping of technology', a sociology of technology emerged that sought to ground technology in the social by making the content of technology a phenomenon for sociological analysis.

The second school of thought, 'the social construction of technology', has also attempted to show that technology is a socially organised phenomenon and to develop an interest in the content of the technology. There are a number of different groupings within the social constructionist camp which have sharp disagreements with one another, the result of them having translated their various and often different concerns with science into concerns with technology. However, for the sake of brevity, they will be considered in terms of their common interests. The distinctive contribution that the social constructionist argument made to the sociological study of science was, at least to the satisfaction of its proponents, to show that scientific knowledge is socially organised and socially constructed. This overturned previous sociological interests in science which had been less concerned with the organisation of scientific knowledge and, on the constructionist argument, more concerned with science as a form of social institution. The social constructionists saw themselves as shaking the epistemological foundations of science, and, through the application of arguments initially influenced by Wittgenstein and in later years by arguments drawn from semiology and literary theory, they sought to recast the nature of sociological enquiry.

The 'social constructionist' arguments concerning technology have also been at pains to break from traditional sociological interests in technology. Thus they have attempted to found technology in the social by stressing its 'interpretative flexibility', or by casting technology as 'text' or as the outcome of the association of elements in an 'actor-network'. As were their arguments concerning science, their arguments about technology are radical departures for a sociology that is still wedded to its structural, mathematical, political, and policy-orientated foundations.

Thus both schools of thought turned around the sociological interest in technology by grounding technology in the social and by addressing the content of technology. However, at the same time and separately from these developments, ethnomethodology was examining technology under the rubric of its studies of work. The ethnomethodological interest in technology is, as is its interest in science, in the interactional work through which science and technology are ordered. It is ethnomethodology's contention that it is in the details of the unique interactional work through which technological work is organised *as* technological work as opposed to other forms of work that it becomes possible to address the social production of technology and to pitch the relationship between the social and the technical at the appropriate epistemological level. From an ethnomethodological point of view, despite the seeming interest in the content of the technology in the studies of 'the social shaping of technology' and 'the social construction of technology', the technology disappears from view in their arguments. This is due to their insistence on subduing the articulation of technology in technical and mundane discourse to a sociological theory of reality. In contrast, ethnomethodological studies have tried to recover technology in the work of participants to its ordering. In this manner an attempt has been made to give substance to the idea that technology is a socially organised phenomenon without at the same time having to deny the understandings of those who are engaged in its production. That organisation is sought in their ordinary and mundane work activities.

The chapter that follows is concerned to show that, despite their arguments that they are interested in the organisation of the technology itself (its 'content' as some describe it), if sociologists are not careful, there is a danger of obscuring the very topic of interest: the social production of technology. It is this aspect that the remaining chapters in the book mainly address through the analysis of the activities and interactional work of ordering technology.

1

THE CURIOUS CASE OF THE VANISHING TECHNOLOGY[1]

Graham Button

Sociologists interested in the social constitution and organisation of technology have rallied to the cry 'address the content of technology'.[2] This reveals the extent to which an embryonic new 'sociology of technology' is juxtaposed against traditional sociological interests in technological phenomena which, it is argued, ignore the social foundations of technology.[3] The general run of sociological interest in technology is said to be less concerned with questions about the constitution and organisation of technology than it is with using technology as a platform from which to observe the constitution and organisation of the structural arrangements of society.

Posed against a technological determinist position, the argument that technology is constrained by social considerations may seem a powerful enough way of sustaining sociological concerns in the social character of technology, for it motivates an examination of how it is constrained.[4] The sociologist can thus develop an understanding of the various mechanisms through which the social world impinges upon and shapes technology. However, on close inspection the constraining mechanisms that have been posited often turn out to be very familiar to sociologists from other domains of study. For example, MacKenzie and Wajcman's (1985) collection of studies of technology emphasises the role of economics and gender in the shaping of technology, forces that have been recognised to be at work in other domains of activity as well. There is, though, a fine line to tread between developing an interest in the shaping mechanisms and an interest in the phenomenon that is said to be shaped. In emphasising what might seem to be generally operative forces such as economic and gender forces, there is a danger that the argument that technology is socially constrained and shaped may run the risk of losing the very 'content' of technology it wishes to address. Instead of examining what it is about human activity and human interaction that makes technology the recognisably distinct phenomenon it is understood to be by those who design it, make it, use it, write and talk about it, an analysis of the posited shaping forces can end up taking precedence, and technology itself can thus become merely another incidental arena in which to observe them at work.

For some, however, the emphasis upon the *social construction of technology*[5] augurs both the possibility of breaking free from traditional understandings of technology as a determining influence upon society and of developing an understanding of the very constitution of technology unconstrained by sociological categories of analysis: categories concerned more with the social by-play of technology than with the content of the technology itself.[6] Thus, the ideas associated with the social construction of technology may have an initial appeal to those sociologists who are dissatisfied with more traditional arguments over the relationship between structure and action.[7] Given its pedigree in the sociology of scientific knowledge (SSK),[8] the social construction of technology promises actually to address the technology itself, without transforming technology into yet another phenomenon in the determination of social arrangements.

However, it will be suggested here, along with Woolgar (1991), that the translation of constructionist positions in the sociology of scientific knowledge for a sociology of technology is not without its dangers. The argument behind this conclusion differs from Woolgar's though. It will be contended that the emphasis upon the *social construction* of technology obscures the fact that the concept of technology is intelligibly used in our culture to orientate to a particular domain of social life; the facticity of technology is displayed, accounted for, and testified to in participants' activities. In short, the argument here is that technology is a *social production*. Recognising that technology is a socially produced phenomenon directs attentions to the details, the haecceties[9] of its production and allows the work through which technology is socially produced to be inspected for its distinctive character. For these reasons ethnomethodologists have tended to examine technology under the rubric of ethnomethodological studies of work, enquiring into the specifics of technological work, asking what it is about that work that comprises its technical character. In other words, an ethnomethodological thrust at technology is concerned with how technology is produced in the specifics of the ordering of work activities.

In what follows I want briefly to explore the reasons why examining technology in this way makes the rather obvious fact that technology is a socially grounded phenomenon interesting. I will do so through a consideration of other, particularly social constructionists' attempts to address the socially constituted nature of technology. This is not intended to be a criticism of these positions.[10] However, the analytic auspices of this collection diverge from those of social constructionism, even though on the face of it they may seem, to those not versed in the respective arguments, very similar. It is hoped that in distinguishing the different arguments the reasons why the majority of studies in this book are empirical

11

studies of social actions and interactions through which technology is ordered can be revealed and underscored. In short, the questions that will be addressed in this chapter are: i) how do we preserve the sense of technology as an achieved domain of social life that is orientated to and produced in the details of the activities and interactions of people who plan, design, construct, make, and use it, and who talk and write about it? and ii) how do we address and reveal the details of that achievement?

SOCIOLOGY AND TECHNOLOGY

The revival of interest in technology amongst sociologists can be accounted for by relatively new developments within both technology and sociology. Within technology, the advent of 'the micro-chip revolution', the growth of 'information technology', and the dawn of what is generally referred to as 'new technology' beckon sociologists with the implicit promise of the emergence of a new form of society, and because they have spawned yet further topics on which to ply the sociological trade.[11] Within sociology, the broad social constructionist position, flushed with success in revitalising the sociology of science, has recognised that technology would seem to be amenable to the sorts of considerations that it brought to bear on science.[12] Thus, whilst in the years since it was first broached in the 1920s Ogburn's ambition for a sociology of technology has been at times becalmed by the winds of sociological interest, it is currently in full sail, though perhaps under a different flag to the one it flew when launched.

However, whilst an interest in developing a 'sociology of technology' may have fluctuated, sociology has nevertheless steadfastly nurtured an interest in technology. There is no contradiction here, just the recognition that there is a difference between a sociology that treats 'technology' and 'technological knowledge' as sociological topics in their own right and a sociology which uses technology as a platform for viewing the constitution and structural arrangements of society in general. It is the fortunes of the first that have varied whilst the fortunes of the second are, in part, the fortunes of sociology itself.

Throughout its history, sociology has had occasion to invoke technology in its description of the way in which the structural arrangements of society have been constituted. The idea that technology plays a constitutive role in the organisation and reproduction of social relationships can be found in the very foundations of sociology. It has also been a feature of the subsequent emergence of sociology as a distinctive discipline, and continues to inhabit the new moments of contemporary sociological thought. For example, Marx recognises the importance of technology for understanding class relationships in his examination of the relationship between labour and technological production in the form of automated and powered machinery. Also, technology is invoked in discussions of social change, the

12

favoured example being White's argument that the development of feudalism as a social system was the product of the stirrup (White 1978). Further, technology also figures in recent post-modernist descriptions of society; Poster (1990), drawing from the works of Baudrillard, Foucault, Derrida, and Lyotard, argues that new forms of social reality and social life are emerging due to the increasing mediation of communications by electronic machinery.

Obviously these examples differ from one another in various ways, but they do display a similar interest in the relationship between technology and society. For Marx, the technology of production plays a role in the constitution and the reproduction of class relationships in capitalist society in as much as technological-based production is characteristic of the mode of production in capitalist society. Further, for White, the new form of combat made possible by the stirrup necessitated a reorganisation of society that would sustain a new warrior elite. Finally, for Poster, technology has changed the nature and the consequences of communication: 'the new level of interconnectivity afforded by electronic media . . . heightens the fragility of social networks' (Poster 1990: 3).

As these three examples show, sociology has pursued an interest both in technology as an agent in the constitution and transformation of social relations and in describing the mechanisms through which technology impinges upon the organisation of society as a whole. The strongest statement about the order of the mechanisms involved has been posited by 'technological determinists', those such as White who argue that technology *causes* social development. It cannot be argued that this extreme deterministic understanding is a feature of Marx's and Poster's arguments or that it is a feature of the general run of sociological interest in technology. However, it has been the influence of technology upon social structure rather than the social constitution of technology that has held the interests of sociology, technological determinism being just an extreme formulation of the general conception of the relationship.

In contrast to the general run of sociology, however, it is the argument that technology is a socially constituted phenomenen that has assumed a predominant place amongst the ideas of a small group of sociologists who have attempted to develop the study of technology as a *particular* rather than a diffuse topic. The relationship between technology and society that is promoted by this attempt is summed up in the title of MacKenzie and Wajcman's (1985) reader *The Social Shaping of Technology*. They argue in their introduction that through economic and gender mechanisms the social is constitutive of technology and technological development. Thus they quote approvingly Hughes's (1985) study of Edison's development of the light bulb, arguing that the economic forces at work that he describes display the efficacy of the social. Further, they invoke Cockburn's (1985) study of compositors in the printing trade to show how the gender

13

mechanism has resulted in technology becoming the *property* of men through the exclusion of women from technological jobs. The general outline of 'the social shaping of technology' was drawn against a background of sociological interest in technology as an arena in which traditional interests in issues such as labour relationships were played out. Thus, as will shortly be examined, the argument was that in as much as the technology could be viewed as socially shaped, then the content of technology was amenable for sociological scrutiny.

The argument that technology is *socially shaped* however, constitutes only one wing within the sociological camp that has generally argued that technology is a socially constituted and organised phenomenon. Another wing has gone further than saying that technology is *shaped* by social factors and has argued that technology is *socially constructed*. Drawing upon the branch of constructionism within the sociology of scientific knowledge that calls itself 'the empirical programme of relativism', Pinch and Bijker (1987) argue that there are a number of parallels (which we will shortly examine) that may be drawn between studies of the social construction of scientific knowledge and the social construction of technology. However, the term 'social constructionism' is a broad one and it cannot be represented as if it were all of a piece. The differences between the factions in the field of SSK have spilled over into the new constructionist interest in technology. Thus Woolgar (1991) questions the epistemological value of turning to the empirical programme of relativism as advocated by Pinch and Bijker because they construe technology as an immutable object, immune from the forces of reflexive practice.[13] In order to build in reflexive practice, Woolgar argues that technology can be understood to be 'reflexive text'.

There are obviously keen differences between the various constructionist concerns that have been brought to bear upon technology, as indeed, there are between the constructionist positions and the positions of those who argue that technology is shaped by economic and gender factors. However, in considering the relationship between sociology and technology it is the similarities between the various positions that are more interesting for the purposes of this chapter. A first similarity is their mutual desire to overturn a deterministic position and reverse the relationship that has been posited between technology and the social, arguing that technology is grounded in and constituted by socially operative forces.[14] The second similarity, and the one I want to concentrate upon, is that they argue that traditional sociological concepts, theories, and methods are inadequate for the job of capturing the constituting forces of technology.

This latter argument manifests itself in a common complaint that sociology does not examine the composition and the content of technology. Thus, MacKenzie and Wajcman underscore the fact that technology is not just about objects but about human activities as well: '"Steel making", say, is technology: but this implies that the technology includes what steelworkers

14

do, as well as the furnaces they use' (MacKenzie and Wajcman 1985: 3). Pinch and Bijker (1987) argue that, whilst, in examinations of technological innovation, there are discussions of the influences that are brought to bear upon technology, there is no discussion of the content, no discussion of what makes up the technology in question: 'the technology itself'. In arguing for a reflexive version of technology, Woolgar suggests that the following question is asked: 'How is the reality of the technology itself created, described and sustained, and, in particular, how do the effects and capabilities of the technology relate to the effects and capabilities of the other entities in the text in which they are inscribed?' (Woolgar 1991: 42). Callon (1986) emphasises how his idea of 'translation' allows the mechanisms through which actor-worlds are constructed to be brought to the fore and how these mechanisms cannot be taken for granted: 'whether they are fuel cells, catalysts, users, or industrial firms, translated entities could in theory follow other routes or be brought onto other projects' (Callon 1986: 36). Law (1987), in his study of Portuguese expansionism in the fifteenth century, stresses how technology is an '*emergent phenomenon*' requiring associative activities: 'The galley builders associated wood and men, pitch and sailcloth, and they built an array that floated and that could be propelled and guided' (Law 1987: 115).

Therefore, the idea that technology can be viewed as a socially constituted and socially organised phenomenon leads its various advocates to argue that it is the content of technology itself that is the sociologically interesting issue because it is socially shaped or socially constructed. Thus, although they may have their differences, the various arguments associated with the idea coalesce around an interest in the 'social content of technology'.

But it is here that we encounter a profound problem. If studies done in terms of this announced interest in the content of technology are examined, it seems that the content of technology, far from being visible, has mysteriously vanished in the course of the investigation. We can begin to illustrate this with respect to two of the gender-orientated studies found in MacKenzie's and Wajcman's collection. In Cockburn's (1985) examination of compositors it seems that, despite her declared interest in the skill and technology of compositing (which can be regarded as aspects of the technology itself), the details of the work practices of compositing and the details of the use of the technology are glossed over. Instead of a description of what the work consists of as the embodied skilful practices of the compositors, we are offered an account of the construction of gender differences and hierarchy at work, reinforced by the concept of patriarchy. The account actually given is an overhaul of descriptions of sexual relationships at work.

Similarly, Barker and Downing's (1985) account of the introduction of word processing in the office is not an account of the actual use of

15

technology in terms of, for instance, the work practices of using word processors or how that technology sits beside existing organisations and work practices. These are issues involving 'the content' of technology. Instead, it is an account of 'how a form of control which embodies the social relations of men's dominance and women's subordination is being replaced by a technology which isn't "neutral" but embodies the social relations of capital's dominance over labour' (Barker and Downing 1985: 163).

These studies would suggest that, despite the claims, it is *not* the technology that is the interest but *gender relationships*. Technology is merely one of many arenas in which to view the playing out of gender relationships in society at large. It is 'power in society', 'the capitalist mode of production', 'the reproduction of and resistance to gender relationships' that are the real topics of enquiry, not the technology itself. Now, and importantly, I am not proposing that in themselves these topics of analysis are illicit or that technological arenas should not be used to explore them. Indeed, if an interest in gender relationships is being pursued then the office or other work-places provide an obvious context in which to explore them. However, it is necessary to face squarely just what the interest is and to be honest about that interest; in these examples it is not, as might be supposed from the claims made by MacKenzie and Wajcman, the quiddity of technology. Again, in these studies which stand testimony to the idea of the 'social shaping of technology', the technology seems to vanish from view. This is a worry if, as has been argued, the social shaping of technology is supposed to stand in contrast to traditional interests amongst sociologists in technology.

Part of the problem here might be that the proponents of the social shaping of technology argument are utilising traditional sociological categories of analysis such as economics and gender. The social constructionist school of thought has, however, in part developed in opposition to the use of these categories. It is then more surprising to find that, within constructionist examinations, technology it is still found to be subservient to sociological theories and categories of analysis.[15]

THE SOCIAL CONSTRUCTION OF TECHNOLOGY

Pinch and Bijker (1987) argue that the developments in the sociology of scientific knowledge that have taken place in the last decade may be productively translated into studies of technology. Taking one particular strain of thought in SSK, the 'Empirical Programme of Relativism' (EPOR), they argue that a 'social construction of technology' (SCOT) can be developed that parallels the analytic and descriptive stages of the EPOR. They identify three common stages. In the EPOR the first stage is to demonstrate that science is open to different interpretations (interpretative flexibility of scientific findings) which is paralleled in SCOT by demonstrating that technological artifacts are socially constructed and interpreted. The second stage of the EPOR is to map out the mechanisms through which debate is closed; this is paralleled in SCOT by the stabilisation of the artifact by not only 'solving' the problems but having relevant groups see that the problems have been solved. The third stage is exactly the same for both – to see how the content of the artifact (scientific or technological) is related to the social. With respect to SCOT this can be done by examining the meanings that are given to technological artifacts by relevant social groups.

Woolgar (1991), however, takes Pinch and Bijker to task for promoting this wholesale translation of SSK concerns into concerns for SCOT. His main objection is that this translation loses the epistemological bite of SSK because it replicates for studies of technology what he describes as an analytic ambivalence in relativist-constructionist approaches such as the EPOR. One relevant feature of this argument is that the EPOR is a form of 'realism'.

This might seem to be a strange problem to lay at the door of a group of people who espouse a relativistic point of view. However, in their ironicising of scientific accounts and, in the move to technology, their ironicising of technological accounts, they take an intentionally and distinctly opposi- tional position to the understanding of technology displayed both by the people they study and in the various disciplines that make up the fields of science and technology. Thus, for example, as opposed to reality being an objective phenomenon, as it is conceived within the natural sciences, an alternative conception of reality is provided by the relativist- constructionists which is that reality is the culturally dependent social construction of the natural sciences. They use this understanding to under- mine the claims of science and technology, and confront scientific and technological practice as engaged in and orientated to by those whose work testifies to its factual status, utilising the theoretic predisposition to view reality as socially constructed.

Although I am not sure that Woolgar would want to put the argument in this way,[16] I am sure that he would recognise the contradictory upshot of the relativist-constructionist position for he writes: 'The relativist argument ironically depends upon a practical (that is "discursive" or "textually embedded") realism, both with respect to the purportedly extant reality underlying scientists' constructions and with respect to the antecedent circumstances recruited as explanations. We thus see that the program- matic relativism gives way to a realism in practice' (Woolgar 1991: 24–5).

However, there is a further issue which also emerges from what Woolgar calls this 'analytic ambivalence'. It is that in these studies of science and technology the status of science and technology as *worldly cultural objects* vanishes. That is, how science is known as and in science and how technology is known as and in technology, and, indeed, how they are both encountered in the everyday world of cultural experience, is lost to the sociologist. Through an act of theoretic fiat a whole domain of human activity, as it is understood by those who produce it and those who live in the culture in which its practices are manifest and attested to, is lost. The orientations of scientists, the orientations of technologists, the orientations of persons at large in society are lost by ironicising them through relativist-constructionist theoretical practices. Consequently, the practices of scientists and of technologists, as they are known to those who engage in them, are lost to a sociology intent upon pushing and championing its version of social reality.

This is not to say that we should credulously believe everything scientists or technologists say to us, or to say that we should thoughtlessly believe in the renditions of science and technology we encounter in the street. Far from it. However, if, as the relativist-constructionist position announces, it is necessary to attend to the beliefs and sayings of scientists and technologists, we also have to find a way of maintaining an analytical indifference to those beliefs in addressing their manifestation in the activities of science and technology. Otherwise we would not be able to understand their role in the production of scientific or technological knowledge because we would be in continual dispute with the people we study. However, we hardly maintain an indifference to them if we wish to replace the theories and beliefs of scientists and technologists with the theories and beliefs of sociologists.

Despite all that is said about the differences between the relativist-constructionist position and the positions taken in sociology at large with respect to issues of 'reality' and 'knowledge', it turns out that there is a common interest in juxtaposing the sociological descriptions of activities with the description that the people who engage in those activities would give, though without any notably intense concern for ensuring that the descriptions of those involved in science and technology are properly and cogently identified, described, and understood. Thus, the professional speaking and writing of scientists is often construed by the constructionists as a form of realism, and as a naive form of it at that, without their even considering the possibility that this is an inadequate way of understanding that speaking and writing. That constructionists may share this proclivity with their realist opponents does not justify their dependence on it. Like sociologists at large the relativist-constructionists want to describe what is *really going on* in contrast to what the people involved in the activity think they are doing. They want to tell us, and scientists, what scientists are *really* doing regardless of what they may themselves say about it. Harvey Sacks once remarked on an old sociological formula that he felt was played out in most of the major works in the social sciences: they suggest that people think they know about the things that they do, then argue that they do not really know about such matters, and finally suggest that the current sociological text will show them what they are really doing. In the relativist-constructivist argument it is possible to view yet another version of this old formula at work.

One of the self-proclaimed virtues of the relativist stance is said to be that it does not privilege particular accounts of reality, for example that it does not privilege accounts given by scientists or technologists. Before pursuing this further it should be noted, however, that this is not a particularly new turn of thought. It has been previously espoused by labelling theorists of deviance who balked at the idea that deviance was an inherent quality of an act or a person and instead lodged the reality of deviance in social processes and social negotiations.[17] The contradiction in this argument has, however, long been recognised. Coulter (1973) made the point that it strips people of their ability to assess their own activities; people are precluded from recognising their private activities as deviant because 'the reality of deviance' resides in its social construction; deviance is constituted only in the negotiation and consensus organised in the publicly successful labelling process. Inevitably, then, labelling theorists are not only denying people their own version of reality, denying their ability to reflect upon their private activities utilising the cultural resources at hand, but also the utility of those very resources themselves. The upshot of labelling theory was that, contrary to its claims, it was yet another sociological theory attempting to demonstrate that sociologists have a keener insight into the true nature of social reality than others.

The relativist-constructionist position does not seem very different to that espoused by labelling theorists in this respect, for their argument is that the reality projected by science is to be displaced by the reality projected by sociology, and the meaning which scientists give to their own actions is to be transformed by the sociologists' reinterpretation. For example, against the picture of 'discovery' that is abroad in science which depicts discovery as the outcome of the application of scientific procedure, the relativist-constructionists pitch a description of discovery as the outcome of 'consensus formation'. There is a danger here of losing hold of both science and technology not only by absorbing individual sciences or technologies into an undifferentiated 'science' where it is not possible to distinguish one science from another (genetics from physics say) but also by drawing the very domain of science into other domains in which the process of closure occurs. The problem here is that in our culture there *are* distinguishable and recognisable 'domains' of activity. The way in which they are distinguished is what tells us about them, for in our culture their possibility *is* something that is recognised as the work of (the) science and the work of (the) technology. We can, without too much difficulty, speak of people being 'technical' and people being 'non-technical', and can recognise someone as doing technical work as opposed to 'just messing about'. If we want to make science, scientific knowledge, technology, and technological knowledge phenomena available for sociological investigation in such a way that we actually address the science or the technology, i.e. their 'contents', then constructing an alternative version of reality would not seem to get us very far. There is, as Woolgar rightly remarks, an 'analytic ambivalence' here.

As a result of this ambivalence something is missing in relativist-constructionist accounts. This is the interactional work through which the specifics of the technology are produced. In merely rendering a sociological theory of reality, the interactional *practices and processes* through which technological work is organised and the technology itself is produced are missing. The common recognisability in our culture of the phenomenon of science or the phenomenon of technology is lost to the relativist position; just what is involved in doing scientific work and just what goes into the production of a piece of technology is certainly blurred in their accounts, and thus the ordinary distinctions that exist in our society are disregarded in the name of a sociological theory of reality. People are being asked to give up established distinctions without it being clearly understood what they involve, on the basis of a sociological theory which has only the most ambiguous relationship to the meaning of their activities. Consequently, the methods through which phenomena are distinctively produced and recognised are missing from these accounts. '*What*' it is to be doing science or technology, the interactional specifics of the work of (the) science and of (the) technology are ignored, and hence the science and the technology vanish from view.[18]

Woolgar's solution to the 'analytic ambivalence' that he associates with the relativist-constructionist position is to examine technology as *reflexive text*. In the light of the above argument we can ask if this reintroduces the 'missing what' of technology, the specifics of the interactional work of ordering technology. To both address this point and to understand his argument it is necessary to recall the thrust of a reflexive turn in the sociology of scientific knowledge. Previously Woolgar (1988) argued that the phenomena of investigation are the discursive and interpretative practices through which scientific accounts of physical phenomena and sociological accounts of scientific practices are constructed. In this account the idea that science is practical action and even the idea that science could be construed as an object are considered to be less viable sociological topics than the actual *sociological accounting practices* themselves. In other words, his sociological interests are aimed at the practices of sociological description. Woolgar preserves this argument in his opposition to the relativist-constructionist position: 'Under this rubric, what we apprehend as technology is to be construed as text, the production and consumption of which is on a par with our own writing and reading practices' (Woolgar 1991). He gives a demonstration of what such an orientation might then look like by referring to Winner's account of the Moses Bridge.

Winner (1985) argues that 'technology can have politics' because the Moses Bridge which connects Long Island to Jones Beach was built in such a way that it physically precluded the use of public transport. In as much as this form of transportation was normally used by Black people, Winner argues that the technology excluded Blacks from prime recreational territory, leaving it for the almost exclusive enjoyment of Whites. Woolgar argues that the technology can thus be *read* in two ways: as a way of transporting people or as a way of playing out racial prejudice. Woolgar's interest is in the persuasiveness of the text, with what it is that makes one reading of the text more persuasive than another reading. Now the object of interest is both an ontological one and an epistemological one. It is ontological in the sense that he is interested in how the reality of the technology is constituted through the inscription process, and it is epistemological in the sense that he asks how, given the fact that texts may be variously interpreted, technology is factually constituted. Woolgar's reflexive understanding of the phrase that 'technology is text' is, he argues, 'an attempt to integrate in the web of associations through which our apprehension of technology is ordinarily constrained' (Woolgar 1991).

However, far from providing for the ways in which technology might be ordinarily constrained, juxtaposing the two readings of the bridge in this way obscures those ordinary constraints. The reason for this is that the two readings of the bridge are placed alongside one another as if they were different and independent readings. However, even upon light reflection it can be recognised that one reading is necessarily dependent upon, even requires the other. That is, the reading or description of the bridge as a means for playing out racial prejudice is dependent upon the very description of the technology *as* a bridge and an understanding of the way it works in transporting people. The account of the bridge as an agent of social control is then a *re-description*, the intelligibility of which is dependent upon the prior description 'bridge'.[19] One account is tied to and embedded in the other, indeed has to be preceded by the other description. In this respect one reading of the bridge does *not* replace the other.[20] The sociological account of the bridge as an agent of social control is irremediably tied to the ordinarily constrained description of the technology 'as a bridge' and the whole understanding of its relation to racial prejudice hinges upon the understanding that bridges are constructions which supposedly enable people to make crossings. To pursue the persuasiveness of one reading over the other is then to direct our attention away from the ordinary constraints involved in describing some technology 'as a bridge'. It focuses upon the sociological re-description as opposed to the descriptions that people ordinarily give of the world and the objects in it, it directs attention away from the 'ordinary constraints', as Woolgar puts it, involved in the recognition and description of technology. Yet, these 'ordinary constraints' are a feature of the intelligibility of technology. Consequently,

21

in the reflexive turn in constructionist studies the technology also seems to vanish in misconceived problems of sociological description.

What of the other constructionist argument that Woolgar does not address, 'the actor-network' position? This idea and its corollary 'translation' are associated with with Latour (1987, 1988) and Callon (1986) and have been elaborated on by Law (1987). It was, in part as Callon argues, conceived in order to abandon the 'constricting framework of sociological analysis with its pre-established social categories and rigid social/natural divides' (Callon 1986: 34). Borrowing from a semiological heritage which has more of an interest in concepts such as 'textual signifier' than it has in 'meaningful action', it allows animate and inanimate phenomena to be associated in ways that are not traditionally provided for in professional (and we might add, lay) sociology, for the actor network is an amalgam of elements. 'I use "actor", "agent", or "actant" without making any assumptions about who they may be and what properties they are endowed with . . . they can be anything – individual ("Peter") or collective ("the crowd"), figurative (anthropomorphic or zoomorphic) or nonfigurative ("fate")' (Latour 1987).

The idea of an actor-network is also found in studies of technology. For example, Callon's (1986) study of an electric car (VEL) in France invokes fuel cells, electrons, Renault, and users as actants; and in his study of the stabilisation of objects, artifacts, and technical practices built around a case study of Portuguese expansion, Law (1987) describes actants such as wood, men, pitch, and sailcloth. The idea of 'network' is also reworked. Callon (1986) argues that 'network' is not used in the traditional sociological sense, for it is not a stable assemblage of elements, rather it is a contingently linked series of heterogeneous elements which can at any moment redefine themselves and their relationships.

A further element in the actor-network version of constructionism is the idea of 'translation'. In Latour's account *The Pasteurization of France*, Pasteur's laboratory, the microbes, and the routine of the laboratory through which they had been displayed '*translate*' narratives about diseased animals and humans, about public health and sanitation into scientific accounts of the effects of microbes (Latour 1988). Again with respect to technology, Callon describes how EDF is a point of passage for characterisations of Renault, fuel cells, and consumers and translates them into the entities they become. What they become is not fixed but is the achievement of the translation endeavour. They are constructed or constituted in the activities of translation.

Notwithstanding the difficulties that may be associated with the assignment of the same ontological status to animate and inanimate elements associated in an actor-network, the previous difficulties encountered in different forms of the constructionist argument may seem to recede. This is because in the actor-network approach, with its emphasis upon the *association* of elements, it might be possible to find the specifics of the interactional work involved in the production of technological artifacts. In emphasising association the actor-network proponents might actually direct attention to the work involved in the production of technology as opposed to becoming entangled in debating reality with societal members.

However, in a telling piece, Law (1987) reveals the analytic motivation behind detailing the association of elements in an actor-network. 'I am arguing, in common with Callon . . . that *stability and form of artifacts should be seen as a function of the interaction of heterogeneous elements as these are shaped and assimilated into a network*' (Law 1987; original emphasis). On this account the artifacts are the result of the elements that go into a network, and thus the reason for examining actor-networks would seem to be to satisfy the question 'How does an artifact emerge?' or, to put it another way, to answer the question 'Why are things as they are?'

But surely this is the age-old question of sociology? Have not sociologists traditionally addressed the elements that have 'caused' a particular state of affairs to be as we perceive it? To be sure, the proponents of the actor-network approach are attempting to be as comprehensive as they can, to broaden the accounting base, to introduce as many 'causes' as they can when they invoke the various 'actants' involved. In itself this may not be problematic. However, it is problematic in another respect, for once again the technology vanishes in a quest for its sources. All that has been done is that more and yet more elements are added, thinking that in adding them we will better know of what an artifact consists. However, in questing for the elements, the actual assembly, the details and processes of, to use their terminology, 'association' is, curiously, never addressed.

This point can be made a little bit more concrete by examining a particular study done in the actor-network mould. In his examination of Portuguese expansionism in the nineteenth century Law describes the Portuguese galley as an emergent phenomenon which is the product of the galley builder's association of wood, men, and sailcloth. However, we should presumably also say of air (because the men must breathe), of food (because the men must eat), of microbes (because during the course of these things people would be sick), of the earth (because people must sometimes have something to stand on), of daylight (because people have to see), and so eternally on and on. Any list of 'actors' in their sense is likely to be only a very short and – given their approach – quite arbitrary selection from the effectively infinite list of actors involved. So, lest the strange rhetoric of the argument obscures its point or, on the one hand, the litany of, but on the other, the arbitrary selection of 'actors' stupefy the analytic senses, we should recognise that what we have here is no more nor less than a traditional issue: how to account for a particular state of affairs by combining various elements. The new move that is seen to distinguish it from previous sociological interests in technology is that, instead of emphasising just one 'cause' or 'source', the social, there are multiple 'causes' or 'sources, a 'pattern of forces'.

However, what is missing in his description is an account of *the details of the associating*, an account of the interactional work, the particular embodied practices of the galley builders, even though it is in those details that the galley as an artifact emerges, or is produced. The galley, as Law recognises, did not just emerge from the elements, it emerged from the *association* of the elements. But in Law's actor-network argument, although we have a description of all the things that went into the galley's production, including the fact of their association, we are given no understanding of what that association consists of in the production of the particular object 'the galley'. This is because, in using the term 'association', Law has abandoned the idea of *actions* in favour of *processes*. Association becomes a process not an account of the work activities of constructing the galley. But the galley did not emerge from the fact that there was some wood lying around, men standing and looking at it, and some sailcloth flapping on a line. It also did not emerge from some unspecified processes of the association of these elements. Rather, it was produced from out of the specifics of the embodied work of the galley designers and builders using an assemblage of materials. The galley is a product of their working order, the activities and interactions of their work. Without an account of those work practices the technology again vanishes in a puff of theoretical zeal.

A further consequence of arguing that artifacts are a function of the association of the elements in a network is that the artifact is then merely used as a means for viewing the clash or conflict of elements in that network. If the technology is seen as the function of the interaction of elements it becomes a way of addressing those elements. In this respect it is the pattern of forces that is the object of analysis and the technology merely assumes the role of a platform from which to watch the associative and disassociative forces at work. It does not require much imagination to see that here again is the very problem that positions such as the actor-network approach with its supposed emphasis upon the 'content' of technology might be expected to have addressed.

TECHNOLOGY IN WORKING ORDER

The order of problems that we have discussed above has made ethnomethodologists wary of talk of constructionism.[21] In an exchange between Harold Garfinkel and Norbert Wiley (Garfinkel and Wiley 1980), Garfinkel expressed his worries about the social constructionist bent in sociology, which at that time was rampant in interactionist studies. The major thrust of his argument was that in a variety of ways the idea of 'construction' takes the phenomenon out of the realm of the social world. For example, it ignores the cultural 'worldliness' of objects and instead renders them as, for instance, either mentalistic or negotiated phenomena. In order to explore this cultural worldliness of phenomena ethnomethodologists have tended to stress the idea of *production* in their studies. This has, in turn, lent an emphasis to the *work* involved in the production of cultural objects and artifacts, the work of the occupations involved. Ethnomethodological studies of work[22] have thus addressed the details of the interactions and actions engaged in by occupations' members. The attempt has been to describe what it is about what people do that organises the accountability of their activities and interactions as the work of the occupation. So, for example, ethnomethodological studies of science[23] have tended to be approached under the rubric of ethnomethodological studies of work. Ethnomethodological studies of science have thus attended to the 'missing what', the haecceties, the 'thises and thats' of scientific practices. 'How science is displayed in and testified to by the ordering of its work, and, importantly, the ordering of the *specific* science's work' has been the ethnomethodological question.

It is this question that is asked with respect to technology. However, it is not a question that ethnomethodologists try to answer abstractly or theoretically. Given that ethnomethodologists are interested in the interactional specifics of the work, in its haecceties, its 'thises and thats', ethnomethodologists engage in the observational and empirical study of the interactional work. What they find is bounded by those studies and it would only gloss the details of the interactional work to discuss it outside the context of its investigation. In this respect the ethnomethodological programme of work is quite simple: it recommends that sociologists engage that work and explicate its order. Having said that this order is locally produced, it follows that its explication must also attend to the local features of its production and in this respect it is now an appropriate juncture to hand this volume over to the specific studies of the ordering of technology around which it has been built. In this chapter I have merely attempted to lay an analytic foundation. Considering those positions that on the face of it may seem to be quite close to ethnomethodology provides for the distinctiveness of the proposition that technology is socially achieved in the social practices through which people recognisably and accountably orientate to technology in the course of its design, construction, development, implementation, its use, and in talking and writing about it, as these matters are accountably located in the specifics of their achievement in the local circumstances of their display.

CONCLUSION: FINAL WORDS FOR THE SCIENCES OF COMPUTER SYSTEMS DEVELOPMENT

Throughout this chapter I have been exploring ways of addressing technology from a sociological point of view. Rather than taking technology as a determining feature of social structure, the idea that technology is, in part, a socially organised phenomenon has been taken seriously. However, recent developments in this respect are problematic, for technology as a worldly phenomenon seems, like the bottom of the rainbow, to move on even as we reach for it. Part of the reason for engaging in this examination has been to reveal the analytic grounds for the majority of studies in this collection. These studies are attempts to address the work of ordering technology and thus preserve for sociology the ordinary, mundane, and routine practices involved in the social production of technology.

However, I am very aware that some researchers within the sciences of computer systems development have recently been attracted to sociology. With developments such as computer-supported cooperative work, human interaction, and participatory design, it would appear that knowledge about the work practices that the technology may be integrated into, knowledge about the organisational context into which systems are placed, and knowledge about how human beings interact with one another might prove to be fruitful resources for their own activities. Nevertheless, it may be that the relationship between sociology and the sciences of computer systems development is not just a simple matter of transferring 'knowledge' from one domain to another. This is because 'knowledge' about social arrangements has often been developed within sociology under the auspices of sociologically generated analytic categories and these categories may have little appeal to the sciences of design. It may be difficult for them to see the relevance of sociology's analytic categories for their problems. For example, an interest in playing out existing sociological categories of analyses for the domain of technology may seem irrelevant for those in the practical world of technological production, and thus the concerns that we have associated with arguments from the 'social shaping of technology' camp of sociologists may be a long way from their practical interests.

Thus a sociology that actually addresses 'the technology' may seem to beckon them more forcefully, and in this respect the initial calls from the constructionist camp in sociology may fall more softly upon their ears. However, the constructionist viewpoint that has formed the vanguard of sociological interests in the 'content of technology' would, at least in terms of the brief explorations that have been made here, seem just as problematic for the sciences of computer systems development. On the basis of these arguments, this group of sociologists would, despite their disdain for much of sociology, seem intent on playing the same old sociological game.

Now I hope that I am not to be heard as proposing that in ethno-methodological studies of work an answer resides to the embryonic and problematic relationship between sociology and design. I hope I have not been that careless and foolish in my arguments. Nevertheless, ethno-methodological interests in the organisation of working practices and in

26

the methods through which technology is built into working life by those who use it – interests in: interactional details; organisation; and practices of design (to mention some of the issues to be found in this collection) – are all interests that, albeit in different guises to those manifest in ethnomethodology, are shared by those in the various sciences of computer systems development. Thus it is to be hoped that, if the sciences of design are intent upon pursuing a relationship with sociology, then a sociology that is interested in the working order of technology, a sociology of work, interaction, and technology may seem to them to be a place to begin to mark out the boundaries of that relationship.[24]

NOTES

1 Details of many discussions that I have had with Wes Sharrock and Bob Anderson have made their way into this chapter. It would become tedious to keep marking them out even if I could remember where it would be relevant to do so, thus the simplest way of acknowledging my debt is to say that these discussions have helped to forge the arguments presented here. I am also grateful to Wes Sharrock, Paul Luff, and Elisabeth Tribe for their comments on earlier versions which I have, in the main, incorporated.

2 See the following collections for examples of this exaltation: MacKenzie and Wajcman (1985), Law (1986), Bijker, Hughes, and Pinch (1987), and Fyfe and Law (1988).

3 See, the introduction by MacKenzie and Wajcman (1985) to their influential reader on *The Social Shaping of Technology*.

4 See MacKenzie and Wajcman (1985).

5 The phrase 'the social construction of technology' is used generically, and covers different and often conflicting interests in the construction and constitution of technology. For an appreciation of the main arguments involved see contributions to Callon, Law, and Rip (1986), Bijker, Hughes, and Pinch (1987), Fyfe and Law (1988), and Woolgar (1991).

6 See Woolgar (1991) who accuses MacKenzie and Wajcman (1985) of an analytic indifference in their argument over the social shaping of technology.

7 See Sharrock and Button (1991) for a detailed examination of the issues involved here.

8 Despite its age, Knorr-Cetina and Mulkay's (1983) collection still remains a good example of the range of the sorts of sociological interests in science of which SSK is a part.

9 This is a term used by Harold Garfinkel (1991) to direct attention to the practices that go to make an object what it uniquely is, the 'just thisness' of an object. Consequently, to pursue the social production of technology is to pursue the practices that make technology uniquely recognisable and accountable. The issue is one of finding, in the details of its production, the practices that make it up *as* technology. In his excellent forthcoming book, Mike Lynch examines what is involved here in much more detail that I now have the space for.

10 This is not to say that they cannot be found wanting, but to do so would require much more space than is available for the arguments presented here. For such an examination, see Mike Lynch's consideration of the social construction of scientific knowledge and ethnomethodological studies of science (Lynch forthcoming).

11 See, for example, Murray and Woolgar's (1991) review of the range of socio-logical interests that have been generated by the advent of general and wide-spread software production and distribution.

12 See, for example, contributions to Callon, Law, and Rip (1986), and Bijker, Hughes, and Pinch (1987).

13 This argument is drawn from what Woolgar's understanding of 'reflexive sociology' (see Woolgar 1988), an issue that will be taken up below.

14 I have to be careful here because the actor-network argument that will shortly be turned to asserts the similar ontological status of animate and inanimate 'actants', and thereby would resist privileging the social elements in the associ-ation of technology.

15 The remainder of this chapter explores the various constructionist positions. These are considered in greater length then the arguments about the social shaping of technology because they may seem to be closer to the ethno-methodological arguments around which most of this book revolves.

16 In the past Woolgar himself has shown little reticence in lambasting the portrayals of reality in the natural sciences; see, for example, Latour and Woolgar (1979).

17 See Schur (1971) and Becker (1973).

18 The idea of the 'missing what' is a corner-stone of ethnomethodological studies of work (Garfinkel 1986). It remains, however, implicit in those studies, though it has been explicitly attended to in many of Garfinkel's public lectures. The absence of a coherent account of what is involved here has been more than made up for in Mike Lynch's description of ethnomethodological studies of work that makes up chapter seven of his forthcoming book, *Ethnomethodology and the Sociology of Science: Toward a Post-Analytic Ethnomethodology.*

19 For a fuller understanding of the issues involved here, see Sharrock (1991).

20 It was just this point that Winch (1958) was trying to make with respect to descriptions of Azande magic. It is not that Evans-Pritchard's description com-peted with the Azande's description, it was that it was dependent upon that description for its intelligibility.

21 It might be pointed out that the title of Coulter's (1979) influential ethno-methodological text was the *The Social Construction of Mind.* However, even a cursory reading will show that the idea of construction is not articulated as the constructionism in both interactionism and in the various constructionist positions in the sociology of scientific knowledge and the social construction of technology.

22 See Garfinkel (1986).

23 See Garfinkel *et al.* (1989); Lynch, Livingston, and Garfinkel (1983); Lynch (1985a).

24 See Anderson's remarks on 'practical sociology as a hybrid discipline' for the exploration of links between sociology and the sciences of computer systems development.(Anderson *et al.* forthcoming).

Part II

INTRODUCING TECHNOLOGY INTO THE WORK SETTING

INTRODUCTION

The chapters that comprise this section are studies of the introduction of new forms of technology into various work settings: the office environment, hospitals, the different arenas of police work, and a manufacturing company. The technology is also various. In the office environment, video and audio links have been used to mediate the interactions of administrative staff who, although spatially separated, nevertheless need to be in frequent interpersonal communication with one another. Machines that can 'interpret' electrocardiograms have been introduced into some hospitals either to supplement or to replace trained human operators. Within the police forces in the United Kingdom, computer systems can be found in many levels of police work and range from large databases to systems involved in control and command. Routinely, the accountancy systems in the manufacturing industries have been computerised, firms being sold customised and tailored packages that are supposed to fit their particular requirements.

The studies in this section of the book are all concerned with how the various technologies fit into the various work settings. In particular, they are concerned with how the technology fits into the contextual exigencies of working practices and organisational life manifest in the settings and with how participants' understanding of that fit is built into and becomes a feature of its use. They are concerned with the practical actions and interactions that make up the work of the participants in those settings and with how the characterisability of those settings is in part achieved by reference to that work. Thus, the work settings are construed as the achievement of the organisation of the work of participants as constituted in their actions and interactions.

This understanding has a consequence for the way in which the investigation of the introduction of technology is conducted. Distinct from other sociological interests in technology and the work-place, the emphasis that these studies place upon the details of the action and interactions through which the work of the setting is achieved means that they are concerned with how the technology fits and is fitted into those practical actions and interactions. Thus, although the introduction of technology into work settings is a familiar sociological topic, the particular way in which the studies in this section understand 'work' and 'settings' means that their investigations of this topic are somewhat different from more traditional sociological investigations of the introduction of technology which have been conducted through an examination of issues such as 'union reaction', or 'de-skilling', or 'changes in the labour process'.

As discussed in the previous section, 'work' here is understood as the distinct interactional contingencies and details that make accountable the various and characterisable jobs, occupations, and business of participants in work settings, and thus also make accountable these distinct and characterisable settings. Consequently, the interest that these studies display in the introduction of technology into the work setting is in questions concerning the relationship between the technology and those actions and interactions. For example, it can be asked whether the technology supports the routine actions and interactions that constitute the work of the participants or requires a reorganisation of those actions and interactions and thus a reorganisation of the work of participants. Further, if it does not support the work practices of participants and requires a reorganisation of that work, how is that reorganisation accomplished, and what are the effects of that reorganisation for the characterisable work of the setting? How is technology accommodated to the work of the setting in the actual practices of its use?

These are sociological questions, and answers to them are intriguing for those sociologists who are interested in human action and interaction, and for all the familiar reasons that sociologists have to be interested in these matters. However, in answering these sorts of questions the studies in this section may also hold some interest for those who design and implement systems such as the ones described. This is because all of the studies describe how the technology that was introduced was, in different ways, insensitive to the actions and interactions that make up the work of the setting and how this was consequential for the way in which the systems were used.

Thus, Christian Heath and Paul Luff describe how the introduction of video and audio equipment to mediate the interactions of office personnel was insensitive to their 'normal' ways of interacting. The interactional asymmetries that were created disrupted the work of the office personnel. Joanne Hartland describes how the 'interpretative' electrocardiograph machines do not mirror or match the procedures and practices through which human operators assign normal and abnormal characterisations to readings. The idea of improvised conduct that is implicit in her account is drawn out and underscored by Doug Benson's account of the way in which the formalisation of police work by the various systems that have been introduced into the police forces is disjunct from the actual *ad hoc* practices of police work 'in the field'. In the last chapter in this section, Graham Button and Richard Harper show how the introduction of a new accountancy system into the division of a foam cut manufacturer for the furniture industry cut across the production processes.

The fact that the various systems were not aligned to the actions and interactions involved in the work of the settings described, and in some cases actually cut across and disrupted those actions and interactions, affected the way in which the systems were used and built into the work of the participants. Thus, the office workers had to engage in bizarre forms of activity in order to attract one another's attention. The electrocardiograph operators would turn off the 'interpretative' capabilities of the machine. The hoped-for increase in control and command by police management over the work of police officers has not materialised, and both production and accounts workers in the foam cut division worked around the accountancy system and eventually refused to work with it at all.

In two respects the studies in this chapter thus paint a pessimistic picture of working with technology. First, the technology does not, in the settings considered, support the work of the participants and, second, the reaction to this by those who have now to work with the technology in the settings examined may undermine the effectiveness that technology can have in those work settings. For example, to computerise the accounts of the foam cut division in the company examined by Button and Harper was an obvious step; however, the problems that system introduced because it did not support existing production practices and which eventually led to its abandonment, may jeopardise the introduction of other systems in the future, for the adage 'once bitten twice shy' has a added poignancy when tens of thousands of pounds are involved.

However, it should not be thought that this pessimistic picture is a contrived outcome of carefully selecting the studies that make up this section nor that it is the result of striking an anti-technology posture. Rather, it suggests that the sciences of design are perhaps in the same boat as sociology in their understanding of human conduct. Both sociology and the sciences of design lack an appreciation of the details of human action as actual, situated, embodied conduct. In sociology the disjuncture that exists between the formalisations of human conduct (as embodied in sociological descriptions) and human conduct-in-practice has resulted in some sociologists rethinking what is involved in sociological description in order to found sociological description in human praxis as opposed to sociological theory. In the sciences of design the disjuncture between the formalisations of human conduct (as embodied in systems) and human-conduct-in-practice may result in an attempt to found systems in a better appreciation of human conduct. On the bases of the sociological arguments presented in this book this later ambition may coincide with the former ambitions to found sociology in human praxis. Thus, it is interesting to speculate that in studies of work interaction and technology it might be possible to explore how to develop solutions to dilemmas that exist both for sociology and for the sciences of design.

2

DISEMBODIED CONDUCT

Interactional asymmetries in video-mediated communication

Christian Heath and Paul Luff

What of the hands? We require, promise, call, dismiss, threaten, pray, supplicate, deny, refuse, interrogate, admire, number, confess, repent, confound, blush, doubt, instruct, command, incite, encourage, swear, testify, accuse, condemn, absolve, abuse, despise, defy, flatter, applaud, bless, humiliate, mock, reconcile, recommend, exalt, entertain, congratulate, complain, grieve, despair, wonder, exclaim . . . . There is not a motion that does not speak and in an intelligible language without discipline, and a public language that everyone understands.

(Montaigne 1952: 215–16)

Over the past thirty years, there have been numerous attempts to develop audio-visual technologies which provide real-time access between geographically dispersed individuals (cf. Egido 1990). As yet however, these attempts have met with relatively little success. The videotelephone and conferencing systems were early precursors of such developments, and in more recent years we have seen the ways in which audio-visual technologies can support a range of computer-based tools, such as shared meeting spaces (e.g. Watabe *et al.* 1990), shared text editors (e.g. Olson *et al.* 1990), and shared drawing tools (Bly 1988; Tang and Minneman 1991). These extraordinary technological innovations have been accompanied by a growing body of research concerned with the potential contribution of audio-visual technologies to cooperative work (including Abel 1990; Egido 1990; Gale 1989; Fish *et al.* 1990; Smith *et al.* 1989). Despite this work, we still have relatively little understanding of the character of interpersonal communication mediated through video technologies or the extent to which the media facilitate collaboration in the work-place.

At EuroPARC, Rank Xerox Research Laboratories in Cambridge, we have been developing a media space to support cooperative work and informal sociability between physically distributed individuals within a single building. As part of these developments we have been exploring the ways in which personnel within the organisation utilise and communicate through a ubiquitous audio-visual infrastructure that provides for free-flowing accessibility between individuals in different physical locations. Preliminary observations suggest that, whilst the technology provides real-time audio and visual access between personnel, it transforms the visual conduct of the participants which in turn can be consequential for the delivery and receipt of talk. In particular, interpersonal communication through the media space appears to introduce certain asymmetries into the interaction which, as far as we aware, are not found in more conventional settings. In this chapter, we wish to explore these asymmetries and briefly discuss their implications for developing a technology to support real-world collaborative work.

BACKGROUND AND SETTING

An important element in EuroPARC's recent initiatives is the development of an audio-visual infrastructure in its Cambridge offices. The infrastructure allows scientists and administrative staff to establish visual and audible contact with each other or to view public areas such as a commons area and the conference room. EuroPARC's offices straddle three floors and in part the technology was introduced to facilitate informal contact between organisational personnel. The system basically consists of a camera and 14-inch monitor in each office, with larger monitors in the public areas. There is some variation in the way in which members of the laboratory position their monitor and camera in relation to their workstation and within the overall environment of their office. Typically however, the monitor with camera seated on top is positioned to one side, roughly at a 120-degree angle, of their workstation and the flat PZM *multidirectional* microphone is normally positioned on the desk by the workstation. It is operated by a footpedal.

Over the past three years the infrastructure has become increasingly sophisticated and we have experimented with various additional facilities which might enhance contact and cooperation between EuroPARC's personnel. A number of these developments have been designed to provide 'users' with more delicate ways of scanning the local environment or establishing connectivity (see, for example, Borning and Travers 1991). Despite these technological developments, the most prevalent use of the system within the EuroPARC is to maintain an open video connection between two physical domains, typically two offices. These 'office shares' are often preserved over long periods of time, weeks and sometimes months, and simply provide two physically distributed individuals with a sense of co-presence. Audio connections are normally switched off until the two colleagues specifically wish to speak with each other.

As part of the introduction and development of the system, we undertook selective audio-visual recording of particular connections between individual offices. To diminish the potential influence of recording on the way individuals used the system, and to enable us to gain an overall picture of how frequently and for what purposes individuals used the connection, we undertook 'blanket' recording of particular connections for up to two or three weeks. This data corpus was augmented by field observation both of connections and of discussions in the laboratory concerning the system. We also collected audio-visual recordings of experimental systems and the use of related technologies in environments other than EuroPARC, for example the Xerox Television (XTV) link between Britain and the USA.

The analytic framework of the research draws from conversation analysis and cognate approaches. It focuses on the *in situ* or contextual character of human conduct and in particular the sequential and socio-interactional organisation which informs the production and intelligibility of social actions and activities. In the project at hand, the analysis was simultaneously driven by a range of substantive concerns which in part derived from the growing body of research concerned with the interactional organisation of visual and vocal conduct (for example, Kendon 1990; Erickson and Schultz 1982; Cosnier and Kebrat-Orecchioni 1987; Goodwin 1981; Heath 1986). The corpus of findings within these and related studies provided a heuristic with which to compare some features of the organisation of interaction in video-mediated presence, and through detailed case analysis began to reveal some curious features of communication though audio-visual technology.

VIDEO-MEDIATED COMMUNICATION

We will begin by briefly discussing how audio-visual connectivity can contribute to collaborative work and informal sociability between physically distributed individuals and then proceed to reveal the way in which the technology can transform the significance of both visual and vocal conduct.

Gearing conversational initiation

Unlike a telephone or audio connection, video provides the opportunity for individuals visually to assess the availability of a colleague before initiating contact. More precisely, the video channel not only allows one individual to discern whether a colleague is actually in his or her office, but also to assess more delicately the state of his or her current activity and whether it might be opportune to initiate contact. At EuroPARC, we have recently introduced facilities into the infrastructure which further support the possibility of momentarily glancing at a colleague before deciding whether it is opportune to establish engagement. In this way, video makes an important contribution not only to the awareness of others within a physically distributed work environment, but also to one's ability to respect the territorial rights and current work commitments of one's colleagues.

It should be added that video technology also provides the possibility of unmotivated encounters, that is, colleagues happening to encounter each other by, for example, one person noticing another noticing them and initiating conversation. In this way the technology can begin to support the range of informal sociability which would normally be associated with an open office environment, whilst avoiding some of its obvious disadvantages.

Coordinating talk with concurrent activity

Once individuals have established contact with each other, video provides participants with the ability to coordinate talk with a range of other activities in which they might be simultaneously engaged. This aspect of video's contribution is particularly important to Computer-Supported Cooperative Work (CSCW) where individuals are frequently undertaking screen-based activities whilst speaking with colleagues. Mutual visual access provides individuals with the ability to discern, to a limited extent, the ongoing organisation and demands of a colleague's activities, and thereby coordinate their interaction with the practical tasks at hand. Moreover, mutual visual access provides individuals with the ability to point at and refer to objects within the shared local milieu.

Such facilities have become increasingly important in recent years as scientists have begun to develop shared real-time interfaces (cf. Bly 1988; Olson et al. 1990). Recent experiments by Smith et al. (1989) and Olson and Olson (1991) have demonstrated the importance of providing video for participants to coordinate simultaneous screen-based activities. Curiously, the studies by Smith et al. (1989) tend to suggest that the video channel is employed during periods of talk about the task, or as they describe it 'metatalk', rather than featuring within the coordination of the activity. The system's design, and facilities such as individual pointers, providing the necessary distinctions and referents for the participants jointly to accomplish the task.

Speaker recognition and turn transfer

As part of our data collection, we gathered recordings of the use of multi-party audio-visual connections both at EuroPARC and the Xerox Video Conferencing facility at Welwyn Garden City. Analysis of these materials reveals that participants are relatively insensitive to much of each other's visual conduct, and yet the video channel does seem critical to the organisation and flow of the meetings the systems support. The key contribution of video within these multi-party interactions appears to be the way in which it provides participants with the ability to recognise who is speaking and to coordinate speaker change systematically. In particular, video provides the possibility of participants utilising more flexible and informal procedures for coordinating speaker turns. In contrast, audio or telephone conferencing necessitates relatively 'formal' arrangements for allocating and exchanging the floor between multiple participants.

Despite the important contribution made by video to support collaborative work between physically dispersed individuals, it is important to note that the technological medium provides a communicative environment which differs markedly from actual physical co-presence. In the following we will sketch some of the more significant differences between human conduct performed through audio-visual media and actions and activities undertaken in face-to-face settings. These differences can raise certain problems for users, but these problems can, ironically, provide a strong foundation for screen- or document-based collaborative work. We will begin by discussing the way in which a look, and gaze, is transformed when performed through video and go on to discuss the articulation of talk and production of gesture in and through media space.

Looking through video

> When one perceives another is looking at one, one perceives that the other intends something by one, or expects something of one. In a word, one is being taken account of by another. It seems reasonable to suppose that this will have marked arousing consequences, but what line of action it arouses another to take will depend upon the context in which the look is perceived.
>
> (Kendon 1990: 51)

In many ways personnel in EuroPARC who maintain open video connections treat the visual availability of a colleague on the screen as if the other is co-present, though perhaps at some distance. They presuppose that they are able to exchange glances with each other, wave to initiate contact, and remain sensitive to one another's conduct. They assume that the medium provides mutual accessibility and the ability to initiate contact, to move from disengagement to conversation, as they might if they were actually co-present. For example, in the following fragment, drawn from a recording of a video connection between a scientist and a member of the administration, we find Maggie, the scientist, attempting to initiate contact with Jean by looking and waving.[1]

Maggie turns towards Jean and then waves. For more than ten seconds she stares at Jean but receives no response. Finally, Maggie looks away to her phone and dials Jean's number, summoning Jean to the telephone. Only when Jean replies to Maggie's greeting do the parties establish visual

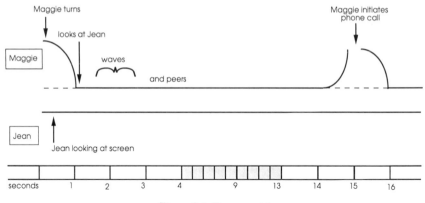

Figure 2.1 Fragment 1

contact. In attempting to contact Jean, Maggie assumes that their mutual visual accessibility provides the possibility of attracting the other's attention in the way she might if she were physically co-present. Despite the failure of her initial glance to engender a response from her colleague, Maggie presupposes that various visual actions will eventually serve to attract attention. By recycling her shift of gaze towards Jean, gesturing, and even staring, Maggie presupposes that her visual conduct will be effective in the way that it might if they were in a similar socio-spatial arrangement in co-presence. Even the shape of her gesture, the waving hand criss-crossing her line of regard and forming a potentially noticeable element within the mutual domain, not only fails to engender a response, but actually passes unnoticed.

In this and numerous other instances in the data corpus, we find participants presupposing the effectiveness of the resources they might ordinarily use to establish mutual engagement, even after their actions have met with successive failures. They assume that a glance or wave will have the impact it might if they were co-present with the other, and will systematically upgrade their attempts to engender a response from a colleague despite the other's apparent insensitivity. In video-mediated presence, personnel at EuroPARC initially assume that the medium provides an environment akin to co-presence, in which relatively insignificant features of bodily comportment, such as looking at another, can serve to gain another's attention and provide for the progressive movement into a state of talk and interaction. However, presence mediated through video appears to interfere with the ability of a look, or even a wave, to engender response from a potential co-participant. Though users assume that the technology will support delicate ways of moving from a state of incipient talk to mutual engagement, they discover that these forms of visual conduct are not necessarily supported by the technology.

40

In the following instance drawn from a recording of the same connection a couple of days later, the users face similar problems establishing mutual contact through video.[2]

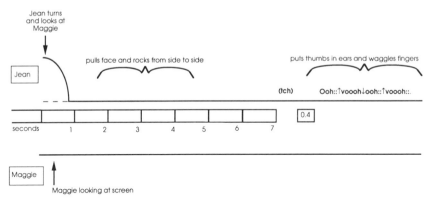

Figure 2.2 Fragment 2, transcript 1

Prior to the beginning of this fragment Jean returns to her desk. As she sits down in her chair, she turns and acknowledges Maggie, in the way she might if she were re-establishing co-presence. Neither her re-emergence within the scene nor her initial glance serves to engender any response from her colleague and in consequence she begins a series of gestures through which she attempts to gain Maggie's attention. She turns to her colleague, places her thumb on her nose, and, rocking from side to side, waggles her hand at her colleague. This elaborate performance fails to attract notice and, continuing to look at her colleague, Jean places both thumbs in her ears, waggles her hands and utters 'Ooh::↑voooh↓ooh:: ↑voooh::'. Finally, thrusting her face towards the monitor (the other), she abandons her attempt to initiate contact, uttering 'No, she wo<u>n't</u> look at hhme'.

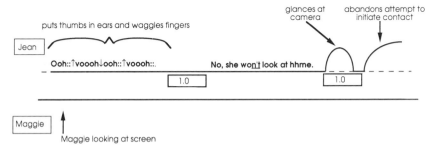

Figure 2.3 Fragment 2, transcript 2

41

It is interesting to note that the gestures used by Jean in her attempt to establish mutual contact allow her to exaggerate her visual orientation towards Maggie. The waggling fingers balanced on the end of her nose that flicker across her line of regard, coupled with movements from side to side, exaggerate her bodily and visual alignment towards the other. Similarly, the hands to the side of the head, and the moving fingers, underscore her orientation towards her colleague, broadening the visual appearance of her head and its particular alignment. Despite her theatrical movements, Jean's attempts to gain her colleague's attention fail and a few moments later she abandons her efforts to initiate contact.

As in fragment 1, the user presupposes the effectiveness of their visual conduct through the media, assuming that a glance and then, more dramatically, a series of gestures will 'naturally' engender a response from the potential co-participant. However, the glances, their accompanying gestures, and the power of the look ordinarily to attract the attention of another appear to be weakened when performed through video rather than face to face. In neither these, nor the many other instances we have examined, is there evidence to suggest that the potential co-participant is deliberately disregarding the attempts to attract their attention. Rather, the looks and gestures of their colleagues simply pass unnoticed as if their appearance on a screen rather than in actual co-presence diminishes their performative and interactional impact. The sequential and interactional significance of such actions is undermined by the medium. In consequence, the relatively delicate ways in which individuals subtly move from disengagement to engagement in face-to-face environments, especially when they are in a 'state of incipient talk', appear to be rendered problematic in video-mediated co-presence.

The relative impotence of a look or gaze when mediated through video is also consequential to the ways in which individuals preserve privacy. In co-presence, the interactional significance of a look, coupled with our ability to remain sensitive to the actions of others, even though they may be outside the direct line of our regard, constrains our looking at others and their opportunity to look at us. Privacy relies upon the power of the look to engender action and peripheral awareness, even amongst individuals who may be co-present yet disengaged. By undermining the performative impact of a look and our ability to remain peripherally sensitive to the conduct of the other, as it appears on the screen rather than in co-presence, audio-visual technology can interfere with constraints and competences, the socio-interactional organisation, which provide the foundation of privacy in 'public' domains. As we saw in fragment 1, the failure of a look to engender a response, can inadvertently lead an individual to stare at a colleague, to watch another's actions where the other is unaware that they are receiving the attentions of their colleague.

As individuals have become accustomed to the technology and its fallibilities, they have become increasingly sensitive to such problems and in some cases have developed a range of practical solutions to enable them to preserve each other's privacy. Even so, by posing a threat to the ordinary ways in which we maintain privacy in 'public' domains, the technology, at least as it is currently configured, can continue to generate a range of difficulties and make people uneasy about using the media space. In this light we have recently been exploring technological solutions to some of the problems which derive from the ways in which video can undermine relatively minor, yet significant, aspects of our socio-interactional organisation.

The articulation of talk and recipient insensitivity

The relative ineffectiveness of gaze and other forms of visual conduct in video-mediated co-presence is not only consequential for the ways in which users are able to establish mutual engagement. It can also generate 'difficulties' for the articulation of talk and for the communication of information embodied in gestures and other forms of bodily movement. The following example is drawn from an extensive collaboration between two scientists over a period of a few weeks. In it we find that the relative inability of looking and gesturing to have an impact on the co-participant is consequential for the delivery of an extensive answer. The collaboration was supported by an open video and audio connection between two offices at EuroPARC. We join the action as Ian initiates contact with Robert by enquiring what he should tell Marty to do.

Fragment 3, transcript 1 (AB 41:5, 17:51:52)

```
 1  I:   What I shall I tell Mar::ty^ to do(hh).
 2       (1.2)
 3  R:   Er:°m::
 4       (1.2)
 5  R:   Let's see:: well first > first off I'd (.2) what I did
 6       las: t night which seemed to (work) was send it tw::ice
 7       under different names:: < an then she did a (di::p:).
 8       (1.6)
 9  R:   en then she: could clean up the er::: (.8) line
10       noi:se.
11       ( .... )
12       (2.3)
13  R:   °thhh
14       (.3)
15  I:   O.k ay
16  R:   (Such a hack)
```

At the outset it can be noticed that Robert delays his reply to Ian's question firstly by pausing, then by producing 'Er:°m::' (line 3), and then once again by pausing (line 4). Even when he does begin to reply, the actual answer is not immediately forthcoming. It is as if the speaker is deliberately delaying the gist of his response. The gist of the reply is delayed, postponed from the beginning of the speaker's turn, by virtue of the preface 'Let's see::' and various forms of speech perturbation, including a sound stretch ('see::'), a 0.2-second pause (line 5), and consecutive restarts 'well first > first off I'd (.2) what'. The speaker's actions and his apparent difficulty in beginning his reply may be systematically related to the conduct of the (potential) recipient, and particularly to Robert's inability to secure his co-participant's gaze. A more detailed transcript might be helpful.

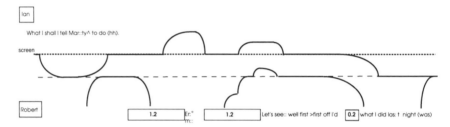

Figure 2.4 Fragment 3, transcript 2

Ian's original question is produced as the two colleagues are independently engaged in individual screen-based activities. As he initiates contact by asking the question, Ian momentarily glances at Robert and then turns back to his screen. By the time Robert reorientates, he finds Ian engaged in dealing with some text. In the light of having a potential recipient who is apparently engaged in another activity, Robert uses an utterly conventional device for attempting to secure co-participant alignment; he delays the delivery of the reply and produces an object which projects more to follow but withholds the actual reply (cf. Goodwin 1981; Heath 1986).

Withholding the reply fails to engender any reorientation from Ian, and, following 'Er:°m::', Robert begins progressively to shift his gaze towards Ian, as if attempting to encourage a reorientation whilst avoiding actually staring at his potential recipient. Both the withholding of the reply and the subtle shifts in Robert's orientation fail to encourage any display of recipiency from the co-participant. Robert begins the preface 'Let's see::' and looks directly towards his colleague. The alignment of gaze towards the co-participant, the preface, the sound stretch, the pause, and the restarts are all devices which are regularly used to secure recipient alignment at the beginning of a turn. Finally, the pause appears to engender a response from Ian, and, following his realignment of gaze from the screen towards his colleague, the speaker begins the gist of his reply with little evident perturbation or difficulty.

It is apparent therefore that in fragment 3 the respondent has various difficulties in securing the relevant form of co-participation from the potential recipient, ironically the party who initiated the interaction in the first place. The potential recipient displays little orientation to the speaker's successive attempts to secure his gaze. It is possible that the difficulties faced by the speaker in attempting to secure a realignment from the recipient derive from the relative ineffectiveness of his visual conduct and, in particular, the apparent inability of the co-participant to notice the successive shifts in orientation undertaken by the speaker. Elsewhere (Goodwin 1981; Heath 1986), it has been demonstrated that a realignment of gaze by a speaker towards a potential recipient can be a critical element in utilising perturbations in talk or even gestural activity to engender a co-participant's reorientation. In video-mediated interaction, the relative scale and presentation of a speaker's more delicate shifts in orientation on a TV screen may pass unnoticed and thereby undermine the performative impact of conventional devices to elicit gaze.

In passing, a further point should be mentioned. To provide individuals with the ability to vary their position whilst speaking with colleagues through the media space, we deliberately used multidirectional microphones (PZM) to provide audio connections. These multidirectional microphones are designed to conceal relative changes in the direction of a sound within a circumscribed domain. In consequence, they mask changes in the sound level of a speaker's voice which ordinarily allow a potential recipient to infer when a speaker is realigning their gaze. Thus, the relative ineffectiveness of a speaker's shift of gaze to engender a response in video-mediated interaction may not only derive from the relative inaccessibility of visual conduct, but also from the absence of changes in tone and loudness of the voice.

The visibility of gesture

It is often suggested that one of the important contributions that video can make to interpersonal communication derives from the way in which it can convey gestures and other forms of bodily movement. It has been found, for example, that participants do coordinate relatively subtle elements of their bodily comportment (Smith *et al.* 1989; Olson and Olson 1991) and that the technology allows individuals to discern information conveyed through gesture and such like. In our own research, we have found inter-actants using gestures as they would in face-to-face interaction, not only to convey information but to organise how a recipient should participate during the delivery of turns at talk. In the following fragment, for example, Robert is attempting to deliver an extensive description of an interface to Ian. As he delivers the description Robert produces a series of gestures which appear to illustrate certain features of the interface whilst simultaneously attempting to engender some form of response from Ian.

```
 1   R:   there's: two degrees of freedom you can
 2        move it in X an Y::                        ◄——   side to side
                                                             gesture
 3        (0.3)
 4   R:   if there are more than two degrees of
 5        freedom you can select which variables
 6        were to be manipulated:                    ◄——   open palm
                                                             movement
 7        (0.5)
 8   R:   which (will) remain fixed                  ◄——   flat palm
                                                             movement
 9        (0.3)
10   R:   an then manipulated at (.)
                                                     ◄—    glance
11        two::(.) <three variables by                     towards Ian
12        the control: icon.                         ◄—    finger
13        (1.2)                                              movement
14   R:   er:: is: this correct
15        (1.0)
16   I:   Well:: (.) not quite.
```

Figure 2.5 Fragment 4

The series of gestures which accompany and embody the description are designed to illustrate certain features of the interface and to circumscribe certain segments of information within the description itself. The gestures are shaped to provide a visual portrayal of the objects or events mentioned in the talk (see, for example, Birdwhistell 1970; Bull 1983; Ekman and Friessen 1969; Schegloff 1984b). There is little evidence, however, that, despite looking at the speaker throughout the delivery of the description, Ian is able to retrieve relevant information from the visual conduct of Robert. Part of the difficulty in utilising the gestures to elaborate the talk and provide the gist of Robert's description, derives from the way in which the gestures disappear out of camera range and leave the recipient with the speakers' outstretched arms but little indication of how they form part of the overall gesture. However, even where the gesture remains largely within the screen, there is a certain way in which the movement appears to be

46

disembodied from the talk it is illustrating. For whatever reason, the illustrative and iconic elements of the gesture appear to lose their performative impact as they are articulated through the medium.

The gestures are also designed perhaps to shape the way in which the potential recipient should participate during the course of the description. Indeed, the movements accompanying the utterances, for example the open palm gesture with 'an then manipulated at . . .' (lines 10–12) and the thrust towards the recipient with the flat palm at 'fixed' appear to designed to elicit some form of acknowledgement. Even the illustrative gesture with 'x an y' might be designed to elicit some form of response from the recipient whilst simultaneously elaborating the talk with which it occurs. The gestures fail to engender either a visual or or vocal response from the recipient either during each utterance or immediately post its delivery. Indeed, curiously, despite Ian's orientation towards the monitor, the gestures seem to pass unnoticed, failing to elicit any form of response from the recipient. It is as if the gestures lose their performative impact. The recipient is not simply withholding response to the speaker's actions, but rather the gestures themselves appear to lose their ability to engender sequentially relevant action from the 'co-participant'.

The relative inability of the speaker's visual conduct to effect some response from the recipient during the production of turns at talk is found elsewhere, amongst different users within the data corpus. Even relatively basic sequences that recur within face-to-face interaction tend to be absent from the materials at hand; for example, when a speaker uses a movement to elicit the gaze of a recipient and coordinates the production of an utterance with the receipt of gaze. Speakers continue to gesture and produce a range of bodily behaviour during the delivery of talk in video-mediated communication, yet their visual conduct fails to achieve sequential and interactional significance. The recipient remains un-affected, and in the light of an apparently recalcitrant recipient, speakers systematically upgrade their demands, their gestures and movements becoming more theatrical as they fail to shape the relevant forms of co-participation within the production of the activity. In the case at hand, fragment 4, the movements are relatively gross even though the recipient is actually looking towards the speaker, but even here gestures and visual reorientation prove ineffective; the speaker's conduct is visible, but impotent.

MEDIATED CONDUCT AND CO-PRESENT ACTION

Communicative asymmetries in video-mediated presence

Video-mediated presence reveals asymmetries in interpersonal relations which, as far as we are aware, are found neither within face-to-face interaction nor in other technologically mediated forms of communication such as telephone calls. Indeed, even in the light of the growing corpus of literature concerned with asymmetries within various forms of institutional language use and interaction, such as the news interview (Greatbatch 1988), the courtroom (Atkinson and Drew 1979), or the medical consultation (West 1985), the distribution of communicative resources is peculiar in video-mediated presence. In institutional environments we find the incumbents of pre-established roles, such as doctor and patient, having differential access and influence to activity types throughout the course of an event. By contrast, in video-mediated communication, the asymmetries tend to parallel the categories 'speaker' and 'hearer' and are in continual flux during the conversation. The asymmetries interfere with the very possibility of accomplishing certain forms of conduct.

The technology provides the participants with mutual visual access and yet undermines their ability to perform gestures and other forms of bodily conduct successfully. A speaker, for example, is able to monitor the visual conduct of a co-participant and remain sensitive, even during the production of a single turn at talk, to the behaviour of the recipient. However, the resources the speaker might ordinarily use to shape the way in which the recipient should participate, gestures and the like, are unreliable when performed through the medium. It is as if the technology undermines their sequential force and thereby their impact within the interaction and, as we have seen, it is not only whilst people are speaking that their visual conduct may be ineffectual. The relatively subtle glances through which individuals can ordinarily re-establish mutual engagement, even gross attempts to attract the attention of another, can be undermined by the medium through they are performed. So, on the one hand, video-mediated presence provides individuals with the ability mutually to monitor each other's visual appearance and conduct, but, on the other hand, fails to provide a reliable medium for the production and recognition of non-vocal actions and activities. The technology appears to interfere with the local, sequential significance of a range of visual actions, revealing an alternating imbalance between the participants as they shift between the roles of speaker and of hearer.

Incongruent environments of action

As yet it is still unclear why audio-visual technologies may fail to support visual conduct and whether it is possible to develop a system which would deal with the difficulties that we have discussed. However, it is possible that the asymmetries we find in video-mediated interaction derive from the incongruent environments in which the participants' conduct is produced and received.

Much of the work performed through gesture and, more generally, body movement is accomplished on the periphery of the visual field; indeed, visual conduct and the ways in which it organises co-participation rely upon its being 'seen but unnoticed'. It 'glosses' or masks its own operation and is frequently designed to work on the margins of the perceptual field of the recipient. In the case of video-mediated communication, the recipient's access to the other's gesture or bodily activity is their appearance on a screen. The gesture is either viewed directly, within the totality of the screen's contents or, if the recipient is looking to one side, constitutes one element of the screen's overall image. In the first case, seeing the image as a whole destroys the relative weighting of gesture or bodily activity in relation to the rest of the speaker's appearance. In the second, it is found that recipients are largely unable to differentiate various elements of a speaker's bodily comportment if they are viewing the screen on the periphery of their vision. Only occasionally are relatively gross movements, such as the other standing or blocking the screen, noticed and 'noticeable'. In consequence, much of the delicacy which features in the design and performance of certain forms of bodily activity is lost to the recipient.

These difficulties become more severe when one considers that the camera and monitor inevitably distort visual conduct. The technology transforms the spatial and temporal organisation of a movement. So, for example, the graduated progression of a gesture, designed perhaps to elicit the gaze of a recipient, its movement towards the periphery of the other's visual field, is transformed when it appears on the screen of the co-participant. The object received is not the object produced.

The way in which the technology transforms our ability to monitor the conduct of the other peripherally and distorts the appearance of bodily conduct might also explain why video-mediated gaze or looking is often ineffectual. Unless the recipient is looking directly at the screen, it is unlikely that he or she is able to discern relatively small changes of head and eye movement of the co-participant. Moreover, it is possible that the relative inability to discern changes in another's gaze direction may well explain why conventional devices for securing recipient alignment, such as pauses, sound stretches, and other forms of speech perturbation, seem to lose their impact when performed though video. Various studies (Goodwin 1981; Heath 1986) suggest that, in face-to-face interaction, these devices sometimes rely upon the accompanying visual orientation of the speaker to engender the relevant responses from the co-participant. The technology renders the look ineffective by virtue of the recipient's inability to dis-criminate peripherally small changes in bodily orientation of the other when it appears on a screen rather than face to face.

It is also worthwhile to consider the way in which an action is produced and the problems faced by, for example, a speaker in communicating through video. In video-mediated presence, the camera and monitor inevit-ably delimit and distort access to a co-participant. An individual's view of the other is from a particular angle and precludes access to a large part of their body or local environment. In consequence the ability to design a bodily movement such as a gesture so that it, for example, operates on the periphery of the visual field of the co-participant becomes extremely problematic. It is not only that a participant has 'limited' access to the other and their current conduct, but also the access the participant has is distorted by the camera. Moreover, the limited access to the other also means that a participant is relatively unaware of changes within their local environment with which their visual conduct may well be competing. For example, it is not unusual in the materials gathered within EuroPARC to find individuals undertaking screen-based activities as they speak to a colleague through the media. The inability of the co-participant to see the other's screen, or perhaps more importantly the other's involvement within the activity in which they are engaged (which might, for example, be embedded in the use of a workstation), undermines the ability to design contextually relevant actions and activities. These problems become more severe when one recognises that, in contrast to physical co-presence, the individual cannot change their own bodily orientation in order to adjust their perception of the recipient or his local environment.

Perhaps, however, the foundation to many of these difficulties derives from the participant's inability to discern how their own conduct appears to the other. In consequence, it is difficult to envisage how an individual can attempt to modify their conduct in order to achieve the relevant impact. So, for example, if a gesture is unsuccessful, in say eliciting the gaze of the co-participant, the speaker is unable to discern how the movement might have appeared to the other in order to redesign the action to accomplish the relevant performative impact. It is not surprising therefore, that, in reviewing the data corpus, one finds numerous instances of individuals upgrading, even exaggerating particular gestures so as to achieve impact on the conduct of the recipient. Unfortunately, these attempts inevitably transform the action the speaker is attempting to accomplish and frequently fail to engender any response from the co-participant.

The technology therefore, at least as it is currently designed and configured, provides physically distributed individuals with incongruent environments for interaction. Despite this incongruity, individuals presuppose the effectiveness of their conduct and assume that their frame of reference is 'parallel' with the frame of reference of their co-participant. Participants presuppose, for the practical purposes at hand, an interchangeability of standpoints, a reciprocity of perspectives. Schutz in his classic studies of the phenomenology of the social world suggests that such a presupposition is a keystone of socially organised conduct.

> Now it is a basic axiom of any interpretation of the common world and its objects that these various co-existing systems of coordinates

50

can be transformed one into the other; I take it for granted, and I assume my fellow-man does the same, that I and my fellow-man would have typically the same experiences of the common world if we changed places, thus transforming my Here into his, and his – now to me a There – into mine.

(Schutz 1962: 315–16)

In video-mediated presence however, camera and monitor transform the environments of conduct, so that the bodily activity that one participant produces is rather different from the object received by the co-participant. The presupposition that one environment is commensurate with the other undermines the very production and receipt of visual conduct and explains perhaps why gesture and other forms of bodily activity may be ineffectual in video-mediated presence. The very presupposition which underlies socially organised conduct generates a range of difficulties for individuals who are attempting to produce and coordinate social actions and activities within the media space.

DESIGN CONSIDERATIONS

The observations above raise a number of issues for the design and development of technologies which provide individuals within a dispersed physical environment with virtual access to each other.

At EuroPARC, we have begun by attempting to address the issue of privacy in video-mediated co-presence whilst preserving the ways in which technologies can support informal access between colleagues within the dispersed office environment. One development has been the introduction of a complex configuration of sounds which conventionally signify to others particular forms of action. For example, colleagues can be alerted to afternoon tea in the 'commons' through the sound of cups and saucers rattling and tea being poured. More relevantly, when one party chooses to glance at another, or even scans through the building via video, glancing to see who is present, individuals who have agreed to making themselves accessible to the colleague in question, hear the sound of a door opening as they momentarily appear on the other's monitor. In order to introduce symmetry into these fleeting interactions, recipients can themselves return a glance and look at the person who is looking at them. However, it is extraordinarily difficult to simulate the delicacy and range of actions that individuals ordinarily employ in initiating mutual contact with each other, even if it consists of no more than a passing glance, and we are still some distance from achieving the subtlety and non-incursiveness of the various ways in which colleagues momentarily establish contact with each other in an open environment. It is critical however that we explore ways in which we can preserve a balance between the privacy of the individual and mutual accessibility in the office environment, without being led to develop increasingly formal solutions to support informal sociability. To this end, systems that incorporate even restricted forms of video access, such as the video snapshots of the Polyscope system described by Borning and Travers (1991), have incorporated features to provide for mutual availability and visibility.

The asymmetries within video-mediated presence may not necessarily be detrimental to the accomplishment of certain tasks and activities; indeed, the relative insensitivity to another's conduct may have important advantages over office environments in which employees are physically co-present. In an open office environment employees can find themselves continually subject to the demands of colleagues and sensitive to relatively small changes within the local environment of 'goings on'. In contrast, video-mediated presence and the asymmetries it introduces, allows individuals who are in one sense co-present to distance themselves from each other and thereby concentrate on individual tasks and activities. Even when individuals are mutually engaged, video-mediated presence allows the participants simultaneously to undertake a variety of more or less related tasks and activities whilst co-ordinating their actions with each other. Audio-visual technologies may make a particularly important contribution in computer-supported cooperative work where participants need to coordinate a range of screen-based activities whilst simultaneously accomplishing specific tasks and activities. Video-mediated presence allows the individual to distance himself from the moment by moment demands of his colleagues whilst preserving mutual availability, allowing users to witness and coordinate tasks and activities whilst remaining relatively insensitive to the potential demands and interruptions of a shared physical environment.

Taking into account the potential advantage of certain asymmetries in video-mediated presence for collaborative work, we have been undertaking a number of small experiments which attempt to deal with the relative ineffectiveness of visual conduct. We were interested in exploring ways in which we might at least increase an individual's sensitivity to the visual conduct of a colleague, to see if this might help solve the problem of privacy. In one experiment we replaced the standard 14-inch monitors with 26-inch screens placed on their sides for several of the staff in the laboratory. This was to see whether the relative increase in the size of the image of the other would have a corresponding effect on the individual's sensitivity to the visual conduct of another. Preliminary analysis of the materials suggests that, during periods of disengagement, individuals are more sensitive to relatively gross movements of the other, such as joining or leaving the scene. Occasionally an individual might notice another turning towards them and there is evidence to suggest that during conversation the gaze of a participant becomes more noticeable and effectual. In contrast, there is little evidence to suggest that the performative impact of gestural activity and other forms of body movement is more secure with the larger, reconfigured monitors. Given that the users' environments remain incongruent, it is unlikely that a simple adjustment to image size will solve the difficulties which arise in both the design and the receipt of visual conduct.

The relative increase in mutual sensitivity with the introduction of larger monitors can however generate problems for users. It has been found that individuals become increasingly conscious of the conduct and changes within the environment of their colleagues, and yet, unlike in co-presence, are unable to differentiate the status of such movements and find themselves unavoidably drawn to look at a whole range of largely irrelevant actions and activities. The larger images of the other and their local environment do not necessarily allow the user to monitor peripherally and assess the significance of changes in the screen's contents. The technology, or rather the other and their local environment, becomes increasingly obtrusive within the user's milieu, providing a stronger sense of co-presence yet undermining the individual's ability surreptitiously to monitor and discriminate the actions and activities of their colleagues. Coupled with the obtrusiveness of the other with larger monitors, is a certain self-consciousness as users appear to become increasingly sensitive to their own appearance in the local environment of their colleague.

In developing audio-visual technologies to support collaboration between physically dispersed individuals, we have tended to establish systems which provide a form of mutual access which is relatively invariable. However, when one considers the extraordinary range of tasks and forms of sociability that the technology might support, it becomes increasingly apparent that we need to provide users with the ability to vary their mutual accessibility systematically. For example, consider the forms of screen-based collaboration reported in the experiments undertaken by Smith *et al.* (1989). For accomplishing many of their tasks users do not need visual access to each other, and yet, at critical moments when they are discussing the problem they are trying to solve, a face-to-face orientation seems to be particularly useful. Or consider the ways in which an individual delicately shifts the orientation towards a colleague as they mutually collaborate on some plans or drawings. It is precisely this issue that is addressed by recent developments in shared drawing tools at PARC. These offer particularly novel approaches to varying the accessibility of a video-projected collaborator (Tang and Minneman 1991).

The technology will support formal and informal collaboration, despite its potentially inherent problems, if users can systematically control, even in the developing course of an activity, their audio and visual accessibility to each other and local environments of action. The success of the technology, its ability to facilitate rather than undermine a range of tasks and forms of communication, will depend upon whether we are able build a virtual presence which supports the delicate and systematic processes of interpersonal coordination found in real-world, everyday work environments.

NOTES

We should like to thank Robert Anderson, Victoria Bellotti, Paul Dourish, Bill Gaver, Marina Jirotka, Allan MacLean, Tom Moran, Gary Olson, and Judy Olson for their comments on earlier versions of this paper and also thank colleagues and numerous visitors to EuroPARC for discussions on some of the issues it raises. Part of the research reported here was undertaken under the auspices of an ESRC/MRC/SERC Research Grant concerned with the Social Organisation of Human–Computer Interaction.

1 For the purposes of presentation in this paper it is useful to map an individual's visual conduct relative to the other 'video partner'. Turning towards the other is indicated by an arc moving towards the dashed line, turning away, by an arc moving away and gaze towards the other is indicated by a continuous line along the dashed line.

2 The transcription system for talk was developed by Gail Jefferson; details of the system can be found in various monographs and collections, including Atkinson and Heritage (1984), Goodwin (1981), and Heath (1986).

3

THE USE OF 'INTELLIGENT' MACHINES FOR ELECTROCARDIOGRAPH INTERPRETATION

Joanne Hartland

The ability to interpret electrocardiograph (ECG) traces is not a widespread skill. Even within the medical community some staff are unable to give accurate interpretations. A machine that could accomplish this task, disseminate the knowledge to a wider audience, and reduce the work-load on human interpreters would be a welcome addition to many clinical departments. The machines currently available are designed to take detailed measurements of the ECG trace, make statements about the rhythm and the morphology, classify the ECG as normal or abnormal, and produce an overall interpretation of the ECG.

Expert human interpretation of ECGs is a complex process and the way humans go about categorising a trace as 'normal' or 'abnormal' is not straightforward. The differences between these human processes and the strategies adopted by interpretative ECG machines will be explained and shown to account for the misinterpretations that the machine sometimes produces. Examples of these misinterpretations are presented and the way that the human practitioners deal with them are described.

Some staff are aware of the possibility of the machine producing inaccurate interpretations, and this affects the way that they react to the machines and deal with their shortcomings. But in some institutions human expertise in this area is not available 'on tap', and the machine interpretation is the only available source of information. In such establishments the machines appear to offer a solution to the skills shortage. Even medical units where expertise is available find the machines attractive for other reasons and use them regularly. There is a danger that the machines' interpretations, which in some instances can be shown to be inaccurate, are taken at face value. In the light of the growing popularity of automatic ECG analysis it is essential that their disadvantages as well as their advantages are made clear. Based on participatory field-work carried out in two hospitals in Wales my conclusion suggests that these machines are not suitable as replacements for human interpreters, but can be employed as useful tools under experienced supervision. Before turning to the bulk of the study however, it is necessary to provide some basic cardiological concepts and terminology.

CARDIOLOGY: CONCEPTS AND TERMINOLOGY

Heart attacks (infarcts), high blood pressure (hypertension), and episodes of chest pain on exertion (angina) are commonplace in the developed Western world. Cardiology is the branch of medicine that deals with these problems and one of the simplest cardiac tests is an electrocardiograph (ECG). This is a record of the electrical potentials produced in association with the contraction and relaxation of the cardiac muscle. The electrical activity is detected by electrodes attached to the surface of the body and it is presented either on a VDU or as a permanent record on paper. An ECG is an essential part of preliminary diagnosis of cardiac abnormalities because irregularities in the timing (rhythm) of the heart's complexes as well as in the shape (morphology) of the complexes are evident on an ECG trace. These cues enable an experienced practitioner to ascertain the condition of the cardiac muscle and the electrical conduction mechanism which triggers the heart's contractions, and to tell whether a previous infarction has occurred.

Ten electrodes are positioned on the body during the recording of an adult ECG: one on each arm and leg, and six more on the chest. Various combinations of these ten electrodes produce a 'twelve lead' ECG. This is a chart showing twelve sections of cardiac rhythm, which offers an all-round view of the heart. Most recordings have a long 'rhythm strip' printed beneath the basic twelve leads which allows detailed examination of the predominant cardiac rhythm.

Each time the heart beats, one 'cycle' is produced on the graph. A schematic cycle is shown in Figure 3.1. The p wave corresponds to atrial

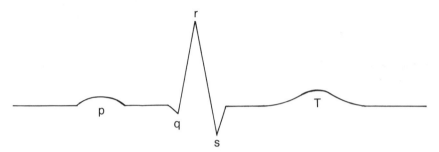

Figure 3.1 Normal sinus rhythm

p wave = atrial depolarisation
qrs = ventricular depolarisation
T wave = ventricular repolarisation

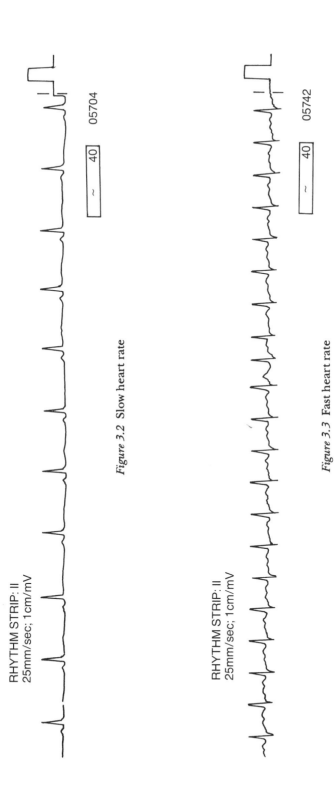

RHYTHM STRIP: II
25mm/sec; 1cm/mV

~ 40 05704

Figure 3.2 Slow heart rate

RHYTHM STRIP: II
25mm/sec; 1cm/mV

~ 40 05742

Figure 3.3 Fast heart rate

contraction, the qrs complex to ventricular contraction and the T wave to ventricular relaxation. In normal sinus rhythm each p wave is followed by one qrs complex and one T wave. Deviations from this pattern signify an unusual rhythm.

Routine ECGs are recorded on all types of patients, even those without obvious cardiac problems. Most patients requiring a general anaesthetic can expect to have an ECG taken in advance to check for cardiology problems, and to determine whether they are fit to withstand anaesthetic and surgery. These 'pre-op' ECGs become more likely with increased age, when the patient is a heavy smoker, or falls into some other high-risk category. If a long stay in hospital is anticipated, a series of ECGs may be recorded, so that changes in cardiac condition can be monitored. ECGs are quick and easy to perform, painless and inexpensive, and it has been estimated that over two-hundred million ECGs are recorded annually worldwide (Banta, Dorwood, and Scampini 1985: 23).

Some writers believe that 'ECG interpretation [is] a complex and hard learned profession' (Doue and Vallance 1985: 29). However, some conditions are easier to identify than others, and certain ECGs can be interpreted by utilising knowledge about the expected normal physiology of the heart and the conduction mechanism. Great use is made of the 'rhythm strip' at this level of analysis.

The 'rhythm strip' is used to determine the heart rate by calculating the number of ventricular complexes per minute. For example, a slow heart rate – usually less than 60 beats per minute (bpm) – is described as bradycardia, and a fast rate, of more than 100 bpm, is described as tachycardia (see Figures 3.2 and 3.3).

Identifying rhythm abnormalities is also relatively straightforward. The most common aberrant beat is the ventricular ectopic. In this case the qrs complex is replaced by a misshapen premature ventricular ectopic beat (Figure 3.4). Similarly, an aberrant atrial contraction is represented by a premature atrial ectopic in place of a normal p wave (Figure 3.5). *Atrial ectopics are easily distinguished from ventricular ectopics. These interruptions to the rhythm are quickly identified, even by novices.*

Analysis of the p wave is also a relatively simple procedure. As described above, the p wave represents atrial contraction, and, by studying the appearance, duration, and position of the p waves, various hypotheses about the atrial chambers and the atrial conduction mechanism can be made. The delay between the p wave and the qrs complex (the pr interval) indicates the amount of time that the electrical impulse takes to travel from the sino-atrial node at the top of the atria, to the Purkinge fibres, which line the inner surface of the ventricles. If this delay is unusually long, first-degree heart block is diagnosed. If the electrical impulses do not conduct to the ventricles, p waves appear without qrs complexes following them.

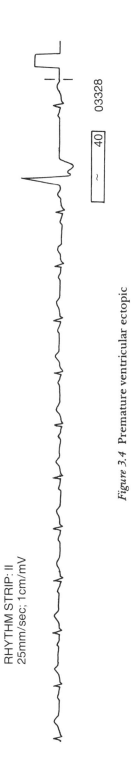

RHYTHM STRIP: II
25mm/sec; 1cm/mV

40 ~

03328

Figure 3.4 Premature ventricular ectopic

Figure 3.5 Premature atrial ectopic

This is second-degree heart block. If the failure of conduction is prolonged the ventricles will begin to beat spontaneously and independently of the atria at an intrinsic rate of about 35 bpm. This is third-degree heart block or complete heart block.

Other abnormal ECGs are, however, less easy to interpret. The patterns associated with new, old and established infarctions, ischemia or muscle hypertrophy, supra-ventricular tachycardias, and axis deviation may occur alongside the rhythm disturbances described above. Analysing traces of this nature involves *more* than utilising a basic knowledge of the physiology and conduction mechanism of the heart. Complex criteria have to be utilised and delicate patterns and trends distinguished. Rather than analysing the rhythm strip, all twelve leads of the ECG must be studied together.

This can tax medical staff for a number of reasons. When presented with these complex traces many medical staff are unable to offer an interpretation and, even if they once understood the traces, nurses, medical students, and doctors working in specialities other than cardiology can easily become 'rusty'. Some staff may never have even mastered ECG interpretation because of a lack of available expert tuition, and in any case the standards of ECG analysis vary widely between institutions. To add to the confusion, it has been admitted that the parameters used to interpret ECG information are not standardised throughout the medical world. As Ginzton and Laks acknowledge, 'Cardiologists do not apply criteria consistently when reading ECGs' (Ginzton and Laks 1984: 40).

AN OPPORTUNITY FOR A MACHINE?

Manufacturers of cardiac monitoring equipment have recognised the esoteric nature of ECG interpretation skill but they see a machine which can accomplish ECG interpretation and disseminate the information to a wider audience as commercially feasible. The initial ECG analysis programs, developed in the 1960s, were greeted with excitement. Each new generation of improved machines has been hailed as a step in the right direction. Ginzton and Laks (1984) suggested that computerised ECG analysis was advantageous because of its speed, consistency, and the reduction in turn-around time (the time between taking the ECG, getting a report, and initiating the appropriate action) that it engenders. Other authors believe that 'these analysis programs are attaining widespread acceptance as a means to help contain the cost of health care', and that they make the physician's job easier, eliminate much of the drudgery involved in ECG analysis, and allow the physician more time to concentrate on patient care (Banta, Dorwood, and Scampini 1985: 23–4).

The justification for introducing interpretative ECG machines is that they can reduce the work-load of the physician by performing some of the more tedious aspects of routine ECG analysis. However, there are two problems associated with this. The first concerns the nature of the knowledge involved in ECG analysis and the second concerns the way in which the interpretative ECG machines are employed in clinical practice.

THE INTERPRETATION OF ECGS BY HUMANS AND MACHINES

In order to approach the first of these problems we will ask the question: 'What sort of knowledge is involved in analysing ECG traces and what strategies are employed?'

Human experts usually approach ECG interpretation in two stages: first they decide whether the trace is normal or abnormal; this is termed 'screening'. Second, they engage in full interpretation of abnormal traces. The first stage would, on the face of it, appear to be one in which a machine could be usefully employed. Indeed, a recent study on the efficacy of interpretative ECG machines concluded that 'the machines tested appear to have a place in sorting electrocardiograms into normal and abnormal [screening]' (Lack, Morris, and Marshall 1989: 24). This is a point that is emphasised by companies manufacturing the machines. The screening function is considered to be the major advantage of the interpretative machines; it allows physicians the luxury of over-reading only those traces deemed 'abnormal' by the machine and gives them more time to do other more interesting things. This view, that the machine can carry out the 'screening' function, is echoed by some cardiologists. For example, one registrar specialising in cardiology suggested that:

> An ECG is just a line on a piece of paper, so all you are doing is describing what you see, based on a background of what you believe to be normal, and only then deciding whether it's abnormal or not . . . given the technology, a machine should be able to say whether a black line on a white piece of paper is normal or not.
>
> (B: 24 April 1989)

As long as the machine limited itself to describing the ECG in relation to what it is programmed to define as normal, he foresaw few problems. Referring to the distinction between normal and abnormal ECGs creates the impression that a definite dividing line can be drawn between the two, with ECGs falling either into one category or the other. It is then seen as unproblematic for interpretative ECG machines to distinguish normals from abnormals. On the whole, users seem largely to agree with this assumption. As a second expert (C) stated; 'I think that you can clearly get a machine that will tell you if an ECG is normal – I don't think that's any problem at all' (C: 24 April 1989).

Most people are willing to rely on machines to carry out the screening function, and a consensus has emerged along the lines of 'in cases where the machine says it is normal, then fine, I think we can rely on that' (D: 17 April 1989).

These comments support the idea that screening is a process that a machine can mimic. However, they ignore the fact that in practice 'normal' is an *achieved* rather than a given characteristic of an ECG. Categorising an ECG as 'normal' involves negotiations performed in the light of prevailing circumstances. This can be seen in three ways. First, when doctors or technicians classify an ECG as normal a number of different contextual factors are taken into account, such as the age, race, medical history, and body size of the patient. Thus, what is 'normal' for one population would not be 'normal' for another. What is 'normal' for an 18-year-old would not be 'normal' for an 80-year-old. Attributions of 'normality' are thus based upon the medical practitioner's experience of the relevant catagories that can be assigned to a patient and the contextual relevance of their information.

Second, rather than being a statistical term, related to the exact morphology of the complexes, 'normal' may refer to a state in which the patient is fit and healthy. An asymptomatic patient may present an ECG that is statistically abnormal, but which experienced practitioners count as 'normal' in that particular case.

Third, disagreement about the criteria for an abnormal ECG is widespread. Similarly, what constitutes a normal ECG is a source of debate amongst medical practitioners. As one cardiologist put it: 'There are as many definitions of what's normal as there are cardiologists' (E: 4 July 1989).

These three points suggest that a definition of normal can only be 'for all practical purposes' and that any blanket formalisation of normal has to be moulded to fit the circumstances in which it is used. A consequence of this is that the meaning of normal and the position of the normal boundaries may be negotiated; thus, when human analysts disagree, considered discussion leads to a consensus interpretation. This suggests that a 'correct' interpretation of an ECG and the normal or abnormal decision are the achievement of the participants, for example the physicians and technicians involved.

The difficulties involved in articulating what constitutes a normal trace also extend into the second stage of analysis – the interpretation of abnormal ECGs. When experts were asked about the strategies that they used to interpret abnormal ECGs, they often found it difficult to express them. The cardiology registrar (B) said:

I look at the rhythm, I look at the rate, I look at the axis, I do this, I do that, but sometimes I just pick it up and say 'my God, complete heart block' and put it down again, or say 'left bundle branch block', and you don't say much more about it.

A senior chief cardiac technician (F) believed that:

> There are so many manoeuvres . . . . that one doesn't even have to think about it. Anyone with a significant amount of experience in ECG interpretation can interpret them with little thought.

Further, a cardiac consultant, C, stated that:

> ECG analysis is such an incredibly complex thing. It's not just what you learn in the books, it's the twenty years of experience, knowing which T waves which are inverted are the ones that are likely to be troublesome and the ones that are not. So that experience side of things is very difficult to verbalise and very difficult to programme.

Thus, it seems that human experts rely on past experience to interpret ECGs. However, whilst they know how to do it, they cannot always explain how they do it. That is, experts find it difficult to specify the characteristics of their knowledge. Verbalising their techniques isn't easy for them. Unpredictable factors influence decisions. Clinical judgement allows experts to decide how to deal with subtle variations in each new case.

B felt very strongly that a machine should not attempt to interpret abnormal ECGs, because 'a machine can't talk to the patient and get a history, and the machine can't examine the patient' (24 April 1989).

It is clear that interpreting ECGs requires skill and experience-based 'know-how', the details of which are not always describable by the experts involved. Learning the skill is a matter of practice, and is best achieved through a period of 'apprenticeship' learning. How does this knowledge affect human experts' attitude towards the machine? What do they perceive as its role in practical settings? The next section addresses this issue by examining how the machine is used in clinical environments.

EVERYDAY USE

In everyday use practitioners are accustomed to machine failures and misinterpretations. G recounted an instance that had occurred a few days previously, which involved a patient with third-degree heart block. The machine had analysed the ECG and made an interpretation of 'normal sinus rhythm'. This mistake was serious, since most patients with complete heart block are immediately assessed with a view to pacemaker implantation. G summed up her reaction to the mistake:

> G: It's hard to believe that it could get something so basic wrong. I think it's because, in this instance, the rate was fast for third-degree block – it was about 60 – so instead of looking for the p waves it just assumed that it was normal sinus rhythm because it was so fast. I think it has real trouble sensing the p waves, and was only sensing the qrs.

Q: So what did you do about it?

G: I did another ECG with the interpretation switched off. You can't have them hanging around with false diagnoses on them.

(4 May 1989)

This dramatic example of a 'false normal' was the most severe that the technician could remember. However, an instance where the machine produced a 'false abnormal' soon occurred during this investigation. In the ECG in Figure 3.6, the machine has produced an interpretation that includes atrial flutter/fibrillation. It has 'detected' multiple p waves at a rate of 343 bpm, and a ventricular rate of 62 bpm. This interpretation is presumably based on the pattern evident in lead V1. In this situation a competent human analyst would view the ECG as a whole. This would provide a resource for finding the ECG to be of good quality except for lead V1, and they would subsequently be able to make an analysis based on the information in the other eleven leads. The result would be an interpretation along the lines of:

- loose electrode or interference in V1,
- normal sinus rhythm at 62 bpm,
- anterior ST elevation.

Instead of this the machine has detected a pattern in lead V1 which is classified as atrial flutter, a pattern which it has been programmed to define as abnormal. It has thus declared the whole ECG abnormal. However, it is not possible for atrial flutter or fibrillation to manifest itself in just one of the 12 leads of the ECG.

This example shows the mistakes the machine makes when screening ECGs for abnormal traces and how human operators are used to, and attend to, the possibility of mistakes. A consultant (D) suggested that the problem of over-diagnosis – the interpretation of normal ECGs as 'abnormal' – arises because:

The philosophy of the machine is to diagnose normality with certainty. The corollary of that is that it must also diagnose some normality as abnormality in order to be certain.

(H: 25 May 1989)

Another doctor (I), at hospital Z, supported this assertion when he said:

I think sometimes, an ECG that I would consider to be normal, the machine would come up with a list of possible abnormalities.

(I: 24 May 1989)

This possibility produces a split amongst practitioners. Some see the machines' propensity to diagnose normal traces as abnormal as acceptable, whilst others do not. For instance, F remarked that:

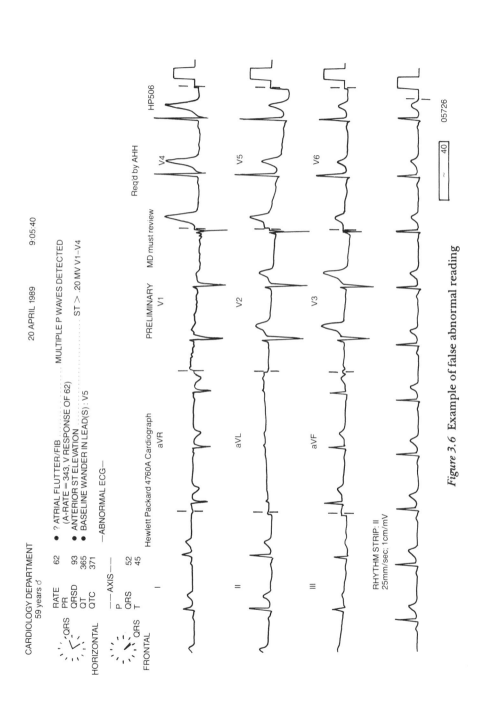

CARDIOLOGY DEPARTMENT
59 years ♂

20 APRIL 1989   9:05:40

	RATE	62
QRS	PR	93
	QRSD	93
	QT	365
	QTC	371

HORIZONTAL

——AXIS——
P   52
QRS 45
QRS T

FRONTAL

● ? ATRIAL FLUTTER/FIB .... MULTIPLE P WAVES DETECTED
  (A-RATE = 343, V RESPONSE OF 62)
● ANTERIOR ST ELEVATION .... ST > .20 MV V1–V4
● BASELINE WANDER IN LEAD(S) : V5

——ABNORMAL ECG——

Hewlett Packard 4760A Cardiograph

I

II

III

RHYTHM STRIP: II
25mm/sec; 1cm/mV

aVR

aVL

aVF

PRELIMINARY   MD must review   Req'd by AHH
V1

V2

V3

V4   HP506

V5

V6

[∼ 40]   05726

Figure 3.6 Example of false abnormal reading

It may give out abnormals when they are not. That is a step in the right direction. It is better for it to say 'query abnormal' when it is normal, than it saying it's normal when it's distinctly not normal . . . so that someone has the chance to over-read it.

(F: 25 April 1989)

He saw the production of false abnormals as a small price to pay for a machine that can carry out the screening process. However, other practitioners were opposed to the idea of over-diagnosis of this sort and offered an equally credible argument: 'When normal ECGs are diagnosed as abnormal, inexperienced staff become alarmed' (C: 24 April 1989) 'Time and money is wasted on unnecessary referrals to hospitals, and patients become anxious' (D: 17 April 1989).

B pointed out that the idea of 'normal' changes as more information becomes available to the analyst, and they become more confident. As this confidence grows, they become able to say:

This, although it is a bit odd, is normal in the absence of any other problem, whereas a machine does not have the confidence because it's not built in to have confidence to say – 'Well, on balance this is probably just nothing, and is just a q wave in V2, maybe the heart is just a bit rotated – forget it'.

(B: 24 April 1989)

C, who is a cardiac consultant, also admitted that problems may arise if the machine is asked to interpret subtle variations on normal and determine what these mean clinically in each individual case. He voiced concern at the machine's tendency to produce ' worrying reports . . . on what are actually normal variants' (C: 24 April 1989). The practitioners are thus aware of the possibility of machine failure with respect to 'normal' interpretations.

What about the machine's abilities in the area of interpretation of abnormal ECGs? We can explore this by looking at a classic example of the machine's incompetence. An ECG at hospital X was recorded on a 69-year-old man. The machine produced an interpretation of sinus rhythm with first-degree AV block – which it categorised as abnormal – at 15.01 on 25 May (Figure 3.7). However, this interpretation is inaccurate, as is the suggestion that the patient presented right-axis deviation. After some discussion with the technician in charge, a second ECG was recorded, with no adjustments to the recording leads. The trace in Figure 3.8 was produced at 15.06, and this time the machine suggested that the ECG was borderline, showing a non-specific conduction delay. No mention now of right-axis deviation. This interpretation is also inaccurate. Finally, the trace in Figure 3.9 was produced at 15.13, and this time the machine gave a more accurate interpretation – atrial flutter with a 4:1 block. For the first time, the possibility of right bundle branch block was suggested in the analysis.

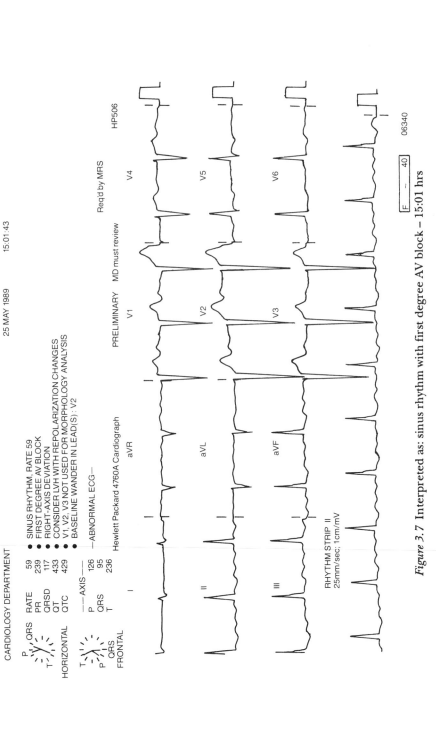

Figure 3.7 Interpreted as: sinus rhythm with first degree AV block – 15:01 hrs

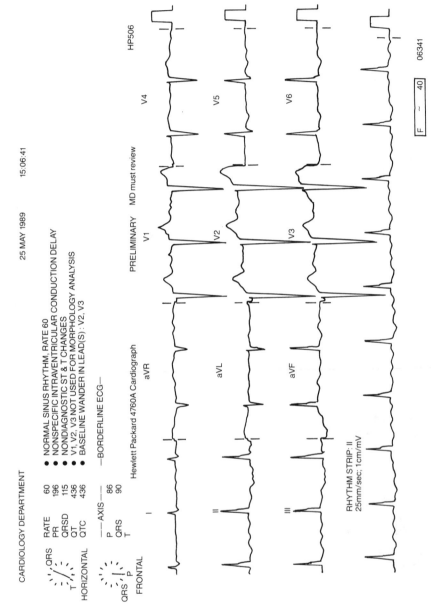

CARDIOLOGY DEPARTMENT

25 MAY 1989   15:06:41

QRS

HORIZONTAL	RATE	60
	PR	196
	QRSD	115
	QT	436
	QTC	436

—— AXIS ——

	P	86
	QRS	90
	T	

FRONTAL

- NORMAL SINUS RHYTHM, RATE 60
- NONSPECIFIC INTRAVENTRICULAR CONDUCTION DELAY
- NONDIAGNOSTIC ST & T CHANGES
- V1, V2, V3 NOT USED FOR MORPHOLOGY ANALYSIS
- BASELINE WANDER IN LEAD(S): V2, V3

—BORDERLINE ECG—

Hewlett Packard 4760A Cardiograph

PRELIMINARY   MD must review

HP506

aVR   V1   V4

aVL   V2   V5

aVF   V3   V6

I

II

III

RHYTHM STRIP: II
25mm/sec; 1cm/mV

F — 40   06341

Figure 3.8 Interpreted as: sinus rhythm with non-specific intraventricular conduction delay – 15:06 hrs

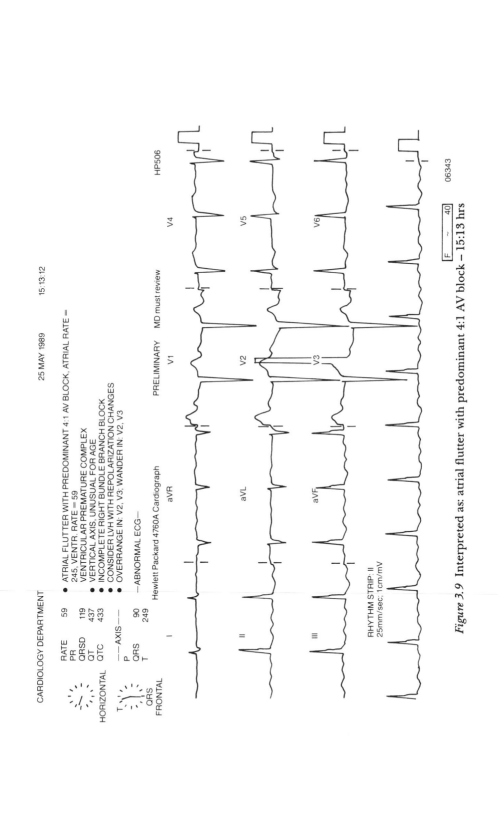

CARDIOLOGY DEPARTMENT

25 MAY 1989   15:13:12

	RATE	59
PR		119
QRSD		437
QT		433
QTC		

—AXIS—
P		90
QRS		249
T		

HORIZONTAL

QRS
FRONTAL

• ATRIAL FLUTTER WITH PREDOMINANT 4:1 AV BLOCK, ATRIAL RATE =
  245, VENTR. RATE = 59
• VENTRICULAR PREMATURE COMPLEX
• VERTICAL AXIS, UNUSUAL FOR AGE
• INCOMPLETE RIGHT BUNDLE BRANCH BLOCK
• CONSIDER LVH WITH REPOLARIZATION CHANGES
• OVERRANGE IN: V2, V3; WANDER IN: V2, V3

—ABNORMAL ECG—

PRELIMINARY   MD must review   HP506

Hewlett Packard 4760A Cardiograph

RHYTHM STRIP: II
25mm/sec; 1cm/mV

F   ~   40   06343

I   aVR   V1   V4

II   aVL   V2   V5

III   aVF   V3   V6

Figure 3.9 Interpreted as: atrial flutter with predominant 4:1 AV block – 15:13 hrs

For trained operators, recognising something as the same as, or different to, something else seems to be a straightforward matter. From a cardiological point of view the ECGs in Figures 3.7, 3.8, and 3.9 are the same in terms of rhythm, rate, and morphology. When technicians and physicians were asked to comment on these ECGs, the responses were as follows:

Ha! Identical. The rhythm is the same, the qrs morphology is the same. It is identical. These three are identical ECGs.

(H: 26 July 1989)

They are the same ECG basically.

(K: 27 July 1989)

Yes, same, yes.

(L: 27 July 1989)

I would say that they are probably all the same. I haven't measured the things, but they look all the same to me.

(B: 27 July 1989)

Yes, I can't really see any difference.

(I: 27 July 1989)

All the experts that were approached considered the ECGs to be the same. Yet finding them 'the same' is an achievement on the part of the practitioners, since the traces are in fact slightly different: the ventricular rate varies, the voltage of the complexes varies, and there is artifact on Figure 3.9 in lead V3. Yet to experienced practitioners these ECGs are sufficiently 'the same' in terms of the important criteria to be classified as the same – they ignore the differences. Thus, concepts of similarity and difference do not come 'ready packaged' so to speak, but are organised in the context of their situated application. What people see as 'the same' or 'different' is a product of their expertise and experience. Cardiologists are able to respond to these three ECGs in the same way, in the knowledge that other cardiologists will also respond to them in that same way, because of their cardiological socialisation and training. The machine, though, is programmed to recognise specific differences. So, differences that the experienced human ignores cause the machine to come to, what is in practice, a wrong conclusion.

Another example of the mistakes that can occur arose when the machine encountered a trace exhibiting a ventricular ectopic (Figure 3.10).

The interpretative ECG machine has suggested that the aberrant beat is an atrial ectopic rather than a ventricular ectopic. This is not a life-threatening mistake – neither variety of ectopic is dangerous if it occurs singularly and infrequently. However, this mistake is interesting because it

70

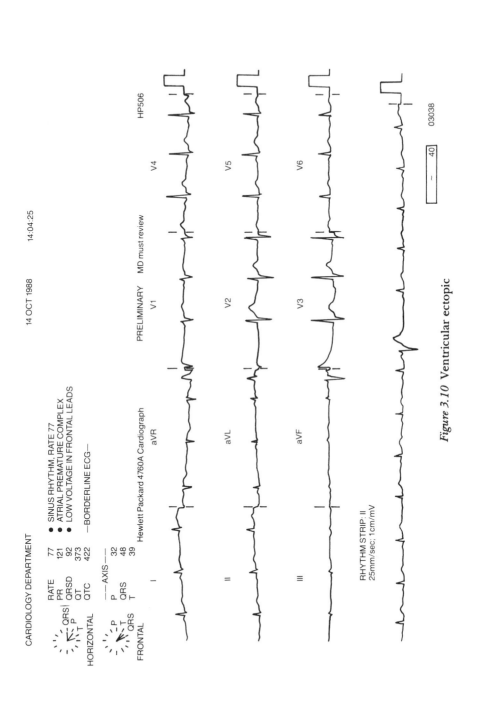

Figure 3.10 Ventricular ectopic

is so basic. The characteristics of an atrial ectopic are quite different from those of a ventricular ectopic. The machine has failed to interpret the ECG correctly and has failed to recognise the distinct characteristics of the most common abnormal beat – the ventricular ectopic.

It is clear that in practice the interpretative ECG machine can make quite drastic mistakes. Just as the classification of an ECG as 'normal' or 'abnormal' is a situated achievement, so too is the classification of a series of traces as 'the same as' or 'different from' each other. During interpretation the machine applies criteria in a pre-specified manner which does not match the way that human experts interpret ECGs. Machine mistakes arise as a result. The operators of the machine are aware of this, and adapt their working practices to accommodate the interpretative machines. We can see this in the following section which examines the importance of the human role in this 'automated' process.

THE HUMAN ROLE

Occasionally technicians make mistakes when applying the electrodes to the patient. If the arm leads are reversed, or a leg and an arm lead are swapped, the ECG will display unusual characteristics. These are normally noticed by the technician when the ECG is printed and the mistake is corrected so that another ECG can be recorded. However, the interpretative machine does not always detect human error in limb lead application, as is shown in the following experimental case.

Two ECGs were recorded – the first with normal limb lead application (Figure 3.11) and the second with the arm leads reversed (Figure 3.12). The trace in Figure 3.11. which was recorded correctly, has been interpreted as abnormal by the machine. Figure 3.12 also has a list of abnormalities printed on it and an interpretation of abnormal. The machine has not noticed that the trace in Figure 3.12 has been recorded with the arm leads reversed. (The machine has requested a repeat ECG because of the artifact present in some of the leads, not because of the incorrect limb lead application.)

More of these experiments were performed on several patients. The machine did occasionally suggest that the limb lead application was incorrect, but far more often it attempted an interpretation on a trace that was recorded from wrongly positioned electrodes. The details of these examples are not of prime importance here. The major point that I am making is that the machine is unreliable in its ability to distinguish acceptable input from unacceptable. Users of the machine are aware of this and take corrective action when confronted with machine inaccuracy.

Users respond in a similar way when the machine produces unacceptable outputs. An example is the ECG described earlier in Figure

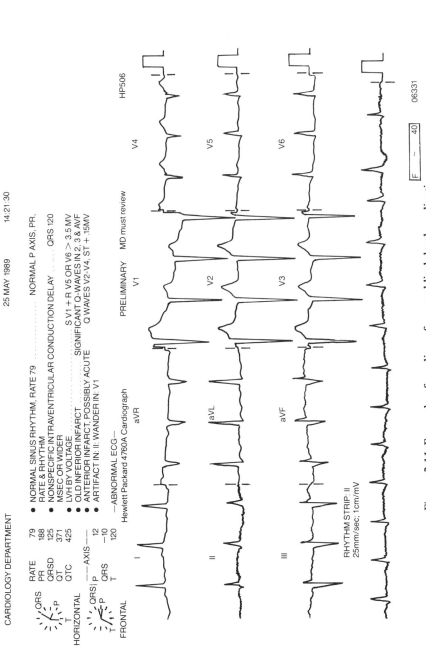

Figures 3.11 Example of reading of normal limb lead application

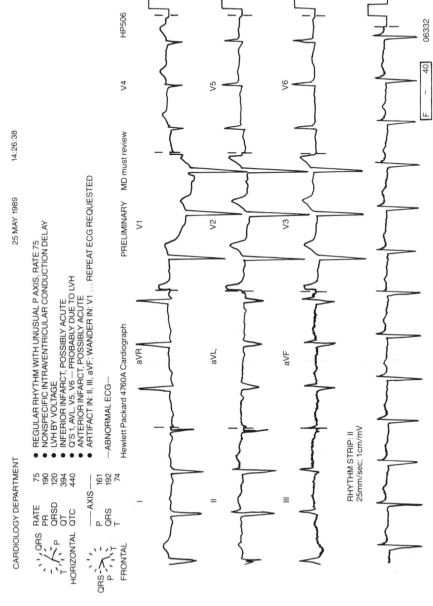

Figures 3.12 Example of reading with arm leads reversed

3.6 which shows normal sinus rhythm and which the machine described as atrial flutter/fibrillation. In that instance, the technician immediately 'repaired' the machine's faulty output. She realised that the interpretation was wrong and she adjusted the V1 electrode so as to receive an improved signal and recorded another trace – this time with the interpretation mode switched off. Similarly with the trace described above, where the machine suggested that third-degree block was sinus rhythm. G ignored the machine's 'normal' decision, over-read the ECG herself, and decided that the machine had made a serious error. G then produced another recording without an interpretation.

This illustrates an important point with respect to the way in which the machines are used in practice: the machine's normal decisions are not relied on in practice by experienced operators in hospital X. All the ECG traces are routinely and automatically checked. Experienced human experts do not accept the normal/abnormal distinction made by the machine, but instead rely on their own interpretations. Comments made by the technician, K, who was in charge of the pacemaker clinic in the same department, reinforce this idea. Patients for the pacemaker clinic are routinely given an ECG. K said:

> When I get the ECG, I may read what it says on the top [the machine's analysis], but I don't take it in. I always interpret the ECG myself, because that's what we've always been taught here.
>
> (K: 19 April 1989)

As well as showing that the machine's decisions are not relied on, the mistakes illustrate how charitable users are towards these machines. Rather than making a complaint to the manufacturers, or demanding an explanation, the mistakes are noticed and rectified by the operator. Business as usual is then resumed. It seems that such mistakes are expected of machines and accepted by their users. Humans acknowledge that part of their role when using these machines is to ensure that such mistakes are recognised. Evidently the machine's performance is dependent on the charity of the humans who operate it.

More examples of this charitable clean-up procedure came to light. Figure 3.13 has been interpreted as abnormal by the machine, and a pacemaker rhythm identified. In fact, no pacemaker activity is present. To an experienced eye, the mistake can be explained because the qrs complexes are regular and of high voltage – similar to pacemaker spikes. The operator in this case cleaned up the output by ignoring the misinterpretation and the extraneous suggestion that a pacemaker rhythm was evident.

Figure 3.14 has been interpreted as abnormal, but the essential abnormality – that of a malfunctioning pacemaker – has not been listed. This omission is serious, the patient is liable to collapse at any moment. The lack of ventricular activity on the rhythm strip shows that spontaneous

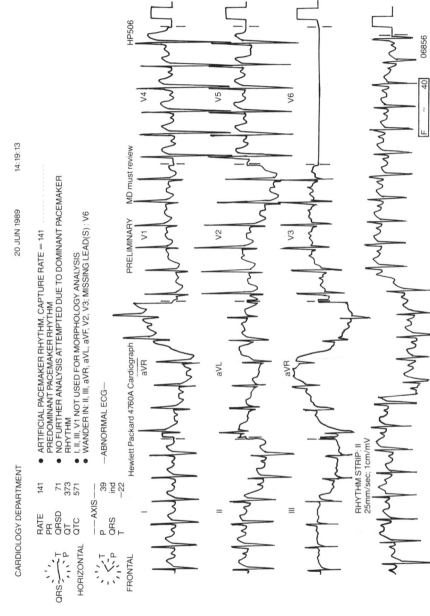

Figure 3.13 Example of machine misreading rhythm strip (a)

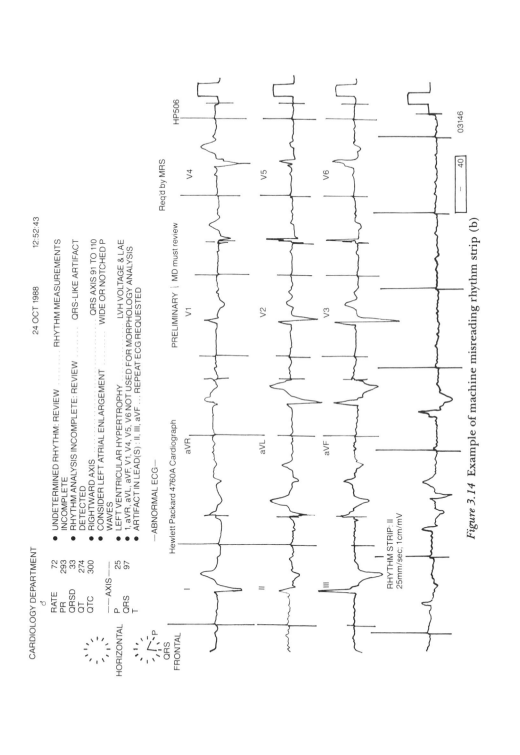

Figure 3.14 Example of machine misreading rhythm strip (b)

ventricular contraction cannot be relied on. The pacemaker spikes on this trace are not followed by ventricular contractions, and the machine has mistakenly identified these redundant electrical pacemaker impulses as high voltage qrs complexes which are suggestive of left ventricular hypertrophy. All in all, this interpretation misses the vital characteristics that humans would notice and use to categorise this ECG as dangerously abnormal. The operator cleaned up this output by recognising the mistake, mentally inserting the missing portion of the interpretation, and ensuring that it was brought to the attention of a physician.

At this point it became clear that at hospital X most of the technicians never used the interpretation mode, because checking the interpretation and recording another trace when necessary was a waste of time. Furthermore, using the interpretation facility was in itself time consuming, because it involved asking the patient detailed questions, typing this data into the machine and waiting for the machine to produce an analysis at the end of the recording. Invariably, the technicians either extracted the ECG from the machine before it was given a chance to print an interpretation or else they requested a measurement-only report and ignored the interpretation facility. Their justifications for this policy were wide ranging:

It is much too time consuming to punch in all the data that it asks for.

Sometimes patients don't know how tall they are, let alone the drugs they are taking.

It takes so long to decide on its diagnosis after it's printed the ECG.

It takes too long, and then it's sometimes wrong!

If you are busy you just can't wait – it takes ages. You could have done a whole ECG while you were waiting for it.

Doctors here shouldn't need it – this is cardiology!

I'm not confident to give it to them [doctors], in case I don't check it, and it turns out to be wrong, and they may take it at face value. Who would be at fault then?

(These comments were collected from the technicians at hospital X
between 18 April and 25 April 1989)

At hospital X, the technicians felt that their own interpretations were quicker and more accurate than those produced by the machine. Few of the technicians delegated the interpretation task to the machine. In the light of these arguments we could ask whether or not it matters that the machine's interpretations are so unreliable? In a large hospital such as X, no, it does not matter. Human cardiological expertise is available literally 'on tap', and the machine's ECG analyses are over-read and often overruled. But this is not the case everywhere. In the smaller hospital – Y –

involved in the study, there were no resident cardiac staff. There the machine was often relied on to give a definitive ECG interpretation. A sales representative for one of the machines admitted that:

> You will find that cardiology departments will use it as a definitive machine, to give them an interpretation. . . . I would say that of the market, one out of twenty buy it for that reason.
>
> (A: 29 November 1988)

A doctor at hospital Y reported that:

> Most of the SHOs [senior house officers] here are specialising in ophthalmology, and I'm sure they'd be the first to admit they are not crack ECG interpreters.
>
> (I: 22 May 1989)

When an ECG interpretation is required, the machine's analysis is referred to. The technician in charge remembered that 'We have had one or two people who have actually looked at the diagnosis and taken it as fact' (M: 22 May 1989).

Bearing in mind the machine's mistakes described above, such reliance is alarming. The consequences of using an interpretative ECG machine are obviously different in this environment where human ECG interpretation skills are in short supply than in the large teaching hospital (X). A visiting consultant to hospital Y set out a vivid example of the problems associated with the use of the interpretative machine there.

> When an abnormal ECG [according to the machine] comes up, the switch is flicked, and the patient is discharged, and if you put yourself in that patient's position, they've come to hospital, apprehensive, psychologically prepared to undergo an unpleasant experience. They get to the last stage and somebody flicks a switch, the trap door opens and out they go again.
>
> (H: 25 May 1989)

The machine was used as an exclusion device to decide who was and who was not fit to undergo anaesthetic and surgery.

CONCLUSION

The examples of the machines' mistakes described here took many working hours to collect. These examples were carefully selected from many cases where the machine did give what was counted as accurate screening and interpretation decisions. In practice, the machine coped well with many straightforward traces. Beyond this, the amplitude and voltage measurements produced were believed to be extremely useful in clinical settings, during drug trials, and most importantly for

79

measurements on heart-transplant patients' traces. The machine is very useful in these areas. However, the cases described above show that fully successful automatic ECG interpretation has *not* been achieved. Programs often fail to produce interpretations that equate with human interpretations. Despite the practical problems highlighted here, interpretative ECG machines are becoming increasingly common in practice and continue to stimulate great interest. In establishments where human cardiac expertise is in short supply, staff look favourably on potential solutions to the skill shortage. Large and advanced medical units recognise other attractions of the machines – high quality presentation, glossy traces with no evidence of messy human intervention, and a series of useful amplitude and axis measurements. In both environments, manufacturers' 'special deals', which frequently offer interpretative machines at the price of non-interpretative models, are the final persuasion. One chief technician summed up the situation when he said: 'Who wants to be the only cardiology department without an interpretative machine?' (D: 17 April 1989).

The spread of these machines seems inevitable. Under these circumstances it is vital that the disadvantages and the advantages of the systems are made clear to all users, because the tendency is that:

People will believe anything that bloody machine writes, because it looks so formal, it looks so impressive. Their attitude is, this can't be wrong.

(H: 25 May 1989)

The danger is that physicians and technicians who are not themselves expert ECG interpreters are impressed by the nature of the trace and the mechanical interpretation and sometimes accept that interpretation without considering the value of its content. It must be recognised that the presence of an expert human interpreter is always necessary. The machine needs supervision. Only an experienced human can clear up ambiguities, explain anomalies to novices, check the validity of unusual measurement decisions, and decisively over-rule an interpretation. The role of the charitable, knowledgeable human is essential. In essence, these machines can be employed as tools, under experienced supervision. They are never suitable as replacements for experts, unless an informed decision has been made that the machine, with all the faults that have been highlighted here, is more acceptable than the available alternative. This decision may be made in situations where the available alternative is no interpretation at all.

4

THE POLICE AND INFORMATION TECHNOLOGY

Douglas Benson

The uses to which computers can be put in commercial and industrial environments fall into the two broad categories of numerical computation and data processing. The former, involving the analysis and provision of solutions to mathematical equations, is used, in the main, in engineering and science. The latter use, involving the assemblage of data into files and records and the manipulation of such data into a format suitable for printing, has application in commercial and managerial areas.[1] This paper is addressed to this latter type of computer application and will attempt to indicate, through an examination of embodied practices of police work, how situated, locally organised actions subvert the attempt to use data processing as a tool for measuring organisational performance and enhancing managerial control. The ambit of the argument is not amenable to clear-cut demarcation but has its locus in 'people work', that is, in organisations, or sections of organisations, whose operating tools, materials and products are 'people'. A sense of this is available in the following:

> The contrast with the business world, where increasingly the office clerk or supermarket check-out assistant routinely communicate via sophisticated computers, is quite stark. There are, moreover, important parallels between policing and most types of business activity. Both are crucially dependent on the collection and transmission of information, and both have to recognise that computers can often perform . . . many of the functions hitherto performed by people . . . . There are of course vital differences. One is that, unlike sales or manufacturing data, the subtleties of human behaviour – the prime concern of policing – are not easily reduced to computing language.
> (Burrows and Dumbell 1990: 471)

As will be argued, the 'subtleties' of human behaviour are not the analytic point. It is that the events, actions, and personages of social life do not come precoded for data processing. The local aegis of description, re-description, and the re-working of the settings and events in the social world preclude definitive objective categorisation, and it is *this* which prevents the gloss 'information' being transferable wholesale from binary bits to phenomenal pieces.[2]

The interest that the police have in the use of information technology stretches back to the 1950s, when it became increasingly clear that the new computer technology would enable the storage and retrieval of the large amounts of information contained in the various criminal records and files.[3] As a result of consultation between the Home Office and the Metropolitan Police it was recommended that the future storage of, and access to criminal records, fingerprint data, and the like be investigated and developed. From the start, then, there was an impetus to develop large databases with a view to using these databases as a means of enabling better police work.

In terms of command and control it is hoped that information technology will produce an improved utilisation of resources, and in certain areas this appears to have happened, as can be found with the Police National Computer. For the patrol officer the Police National Computer provides a tool which, through the rapid provision of information concerning motor vehicles and people, can greatly enhance the performance of certain aspects of the work. If a vehicle is spotted in a particular place or if a vehicle is seen to be out of place for its surroundings – an expensive car in a 'poor' area – then through radio contact the officer can obtain information from the PNC as to whether the car has been stolen or the like. Similarly, with the name and date of birth of a person, an officer can quickly obtain information from the criminal records index on the status of that person. This kind of utilisation of information technology appears to have been quickly accepted by patrol officers and the police more generally. Once that sort of information is on the system it can be accessed speedily, saving time both at an incident and in terms of the hours involved in obtaining such information if a computerised system was not in place. However, when the use of the computerised systems is looked at in terms of command and control activities, a different picture emerges.

The expectation of the introduction of the new technology in command and control was that, through the centralising of information of all kinds, from monitoring the activities of known criminals, suspected criminals, 'subversives', to the logging of incident reports or the counting of offences and their distribution, greater efficiency could be achieved. This expectation has not been fulfilled. Part of the difficulties encountered might be regarded as revolving around practical problems encountered in the installation and varied type of systems used. Many of the forces throughout the country have put in place different computer hardware and different software systems so that computer cannot talk unto computer. This type of matter is, with financial aid, resolvable. Other types of problem appear when the HOLMES (Home Office Large Major Enquiry System) is considered. This system, which was set up in the aftermath of the 'Yorkshire Ripper' case, aimed to provide a standard system for information and retrieval. It too is beset by the problem of different systems but also by the fact of its limited use. Most crimes are not solved by detective work for which this system could be used as a tool; also the type of major crime it was set up to solve is extremely rare: a large expenditure for little return. Given the fact that technology can often 'drive' activity, it may well, however, find other uses.

The introduction of information technology into the police has not proceeded as smoothly as had been hoped. In part, the blame for this is attributed to two main factors: the organisation of the police into forty-three separate forces, which has inhibited collaboration across the forces and at a national level, and police culture, 'which is not so readily attuned to the potentialities of the computer' (Burrows and Dumbell 1990: 471). With regard to the issue of there being forty-three separate forces, one problem stems from the purchase of differing hardware so that computer cannot talk unto computer, but there is also the more central problem of different forces having different ideas concerning police work and hence different priorities. As Burrows and Dumbell note in regard to the patrol officer:

> The task of providing facilities that will assist the officer on foot, bicycle or patrol car is not an easy one. *The primary difficulty is not technical*, it is simply that patrolling fulfils a variety of functions, which are perceived differently even within the service.
>
> (Burrows and Dumbell 1990: 471, emphasis added)

Importantly, the different perceptions of patrolling and the nature of decision making are not simply an issue of different policies between the forces at a managerial level but in terms of different policies as they are enacted by individual police officers. In order to examine these matters we now need an examination of police organisation and operating practices.

THE POLICE AND POLICE ORGANISATION

The police force is not an homogeneous organisation, being organised into a number of separate departments which deal with specific areas such as drugs, juvenile offenders, road traffic, serious crime, and fraud. In addition there is the distinction between the uniform branch and the plain-clothed CID. Information technology plays a part in many aspects of the police as an organisation, from producing payrolls through to the logging of incidents. What is going to be focused on here is the use of information technology in two areas: assisting the patrol officer in the work he carries out, and in command and control systems which are used by management in their efforts to control the use of manpower and obtain efficient use of resources.This paper is not especially concerned with the specifics of police organisation but some understanding of the way in which the force operates is required. This will help to illuminate comments which will be subsequently made regarding the use of information technology in the effort senior ranks make to gain better managerial control over day-to-day police work.

The police force in England and Wales today is comprised of forty-three regional forces. This number is the result of a series of amalgamations which took place in the 1960s and 1970s which effected a reduction from an initial 158 local forces. The reduction in the number of forces was introduced with the intention of making the police force as a whole more effective and efficient. Some observers of the police scene have noted that, whilst some gains in efficiency and effectiveness might have been achieved, there were also some losses. One of the perceived losses to the police was the availability and use of local knowledge that had been built up over the years. This is of particular relevance to the argument to be pursued here, namely that there is an incompatibility between much of the current utilisation of information technology and the actual working practices of the operational officer. Prior to the amalgamation of forces it was not uncommon for officers to come from and remain within the communities which they were policing, enabling them to establish and maintain close contact with the people and places in their area. As Bittner (1968) has shown, there are many aspects of police work which require the use of local knowledge and police operations can be impaired when such knowledge is unavailable. With this diminishment in local knowledge there arose a more centralised and 'bureaucratic' style of management which attempts to control the larger number of officers in a wider, geographically spread force.

In addition to these changes in the scale of the police forces and the consequent relocation of officers within the force, there were also changes in the pattern of policing. Many commentators have discussed these changes and it is a matter of public discussion and concern: the police moved from a pattern of foot patrol of areas to one in which the use of motor vehicles became predominant. The way in which this came about relates in part to the speed of response which becomes available to the police equipped with a motor car and radio-telephone. The officer on foot patrol simply arrived too late on the scene. The use of centralised incident report room and radio communication to officers with cars greatly increased the speed of response to calls from the public.

These two areas of development, amalgamation of forces and greater reliance on radio communication with a mobile force, facilitated the move to greater centralisation. Studies of the police have suggested that this move to centralisation has combined with an emerging ethos of managerial control to produce a situation in which the use of information technology seems ideally suited, particularly in two main areas: the production of a system for the command and control of the officers within the force and the enhancement of the capacity of the police to fight crime. Before moving to a consideration of these two areas a few further comments on aspects of the organisation of the police will be made.

While these moves to greater centralisation were emerging, other factors were also in play. In terms of organisation, there was the introduction of more specialised policing, creating sub-divisions within the force. Drug squads, for example, were developed partly to deal with what was seen as a growing problem and also to create a branch of the force whose specific job was to cope with an area of illegal activity which had tended to be neglected because it was not 'crimed'. Specialisations such as drug squads and fraud squads have been described as having a counter-effect to that of centralisation. The argument that has been advanced in this regard is that centralisation and bureaucratic managerial control have tended to reduce the scope for autonomous action by the individual officers. The increased specialised branches however have provided an area within which such autonomy of action can be regained because of the greater power of decision making which can be related to the 'knowledge' which attaches to specialisation. On this account there is a tension between increasing sub-division into specialisations and the increasing tendency towards centralisation and central control.

Alongside these organisational factors which might inhibit the managerial control function there is also the matter of police culture. Many aspects of what is taken to be a specifically police or 'canteen' culture have been described and one aspect which might be considered relevant here is the way in which the more junior ranks perceive their superiors. One aspect of this is evidenced by common remarks like 'with each promotion they remove a bit more of the brain'. The higher the rank the more 'forgetful' is the officer of what doing the job actually entails. Combined with this is the concern not to be 'found out' by superiors in the transgression of the rules, whether legal, procedural, or rules of deportment. Together with the desire to retain autonomous areas for action a mix is produced which can run counter to the managerial goals of greater central control and increased efficiency. The culture is one which distrusts and views with suspicion any attempt to reduce the independent actions of officers. The lower ranks will actively 'hide' activities from managerial view. Given that management needs to collect accurate information upon the activities of its active officers in order to be able to control their efficient use of manpower, such an oppositional culture amongst the lower-ranking officers will vitiate such attempts, whether the information-gathering system is computerised or not.

The picture drawn so far suggests that increasing centralisation, with commensurate tendencies to bureaucratise police work in order to give the higher ranks in the force sufficient information on, and control over, its manpower, runs into problems because of the countervailing factors of specialisation and oppositional tendencies within the culture of the lower ranks. There are other aspects of police work to consider before commenting upon this view.

In the public mind, police work is about the fight against crime. The reality is somewhat different. Whilst the control of crime is the top priority for the police service, in terms of the day-to-day activities of the police, the fight against crime is only one aspect of the work that the police undertake. A number of studies have indicated that large amounts of time are spent by the police on non-crime matters. One such study in 1975 showed that, for uniform patrol officers, the time spent responding to crime incidents involved only some 3 per cent of their total hours worked.[4] A further 15 per cent to 20 per cent was taken up by follow-up work, but not necessarily follow-up work to crime incidents. The vast majority of a patrol officer's time, about half, is simply spent on patrol. The rest of the time is spent on a wide variety of non-crime incidents with their attendant follow-up, paperwork and administration, court attendance, briefings, and the like. Perhaps this is in some ways unsurprising, in that inspection of many occupations reveals that large amounts of time are spent in activities other than some central activity: surgeons spend only a certain amount of their time in slicing, cutting, sawing, and stitching human tissue. For the police the issue is not so simple, the reason being that it is not simply in the public mind that crime fighting is central to their consideration of police work, it is also a consideration which the police themselves use in coming to an understanding of how poorly or how well they are operating as a police force.

Put simply, crime fighting and detection are important to the police not only because they are part of the set of tasks for which they have been empowered, but also because crime is countable.[5] The police are of course aware of all the methodological problems attendant upon the use of crime statistics, more so perhaps than most sociologists, even though they do not discuss the problems in quite the same language. From the standpoint of the organisation though, these methodological problems are tangential to their use. The police do not use the statistics as a basis for, say, generating theories about the aetiology of crime. They do, however, use them as a measure of organisational efficiency and as part of their armoury in the fight to gain increased resources from central government. An awareness of the problematic nature of the statistics related to crime does not preclude their use in political and rhetorical arguments of persuasion, although from time to time some senior officers do express doubts about the public's perception of the reality of crime being influenced by criminal statistics which indicate a relentless escalation of criminal offences.[6] This has become pertinent as 'after a decade of rising police expenditure and rising crime the act [of using the crime rates when bidding for resources] does look extremely wobbly'.[7] The practical difficulty here is that public debate about the police is almost invariably in terms of crime and clear-up rates. They are the currency of discussion, whilst at the same time there are no other 'measures' which are seen as acceptably 'objective'. Crimes are counted, again because they are countable. Crime is also one of the two major areas of concern for which information technology was introduced, the other being its use in the control of personnel. The utility of computerised databases as a tool in the fight against crime and as a means for measuring organisational efficiency is undermined if day-to-day work practices or processes bear unknown relationship to the 'outcome' upon which managerial decisions are based. Measurements of efficiency in the public service sector are notoriously difficult to devise in the absence of the relatively simple cash measures of profit and loss. [8]

The use of measuring crime, or counting the number of offences committed, is seen then as: i) a deficient way of coming to a better understanding of the way in which the police work; and ii) a deficient means of assessing police efficiency. This is so because crime and police response to it is only, for the patrol officer at least, a relatively small part of the work actually undertaken and also because the 'reality' of crime in society today appears to have little relationship to the picture which the crime figures present. An area of police work which relates these two matters together turns upon an understanding of police discretion.

The police are officers of the law. One of their functions is to uphold and enforce the law. As with many statements of principle, such formulations are not very informative when it comes to an examination of how situations are viewed and actions undertaken in practice. Police officers do not simply enact the law of the land as though they were pre-programmed automata wandering the streets of cities and towns arresting anybody and everybody who could be seen as having broken the law. To do so might be counterproductive, not only in that courts would become clogged with cases for trial but also that effective long-term policing of an area can become disrupted by such 'indiscriminate' arrests. Field-work notes that formed part of the research upon which this chapter is based reveal that in the research area there was a night club in which drugs were commonly available and used, often in full view of members of the local drug squad who used to visit the club to 'keep an eye on it'. Arrests were not made when it was obvious that illegal activities were taking place. The reasons for this were illuminated by an interesting encounter which took place after the night club changed ownership. The new management in the club wanted to change the type of customer the club serviced and decided to take the club 'up-market'. In order to do so it was felt necessary to remove permanently the drug users from the club. During a discussion with the management at the time of this transition it was reported that members of the drug squad had talked to the club owner with a view to maintaining the status quo. The club was useful to the squad as a place where they could see what drugs were around, which persons were involved, who was spending money, who was 'new' to the area, and the like. Such information was necessary for the practical purposes of controlling local drug use and for gaining access to drug suppliers rather than drug users. The police were using 'discretion'. Now much of the discretionary work of the police is permitted by statute but from a sociological standpoint the more interesting aspects of 'discretion' reside in the way in which this aspect of police work is an essential feature of practical policing. For the police not only have a duty to enforce the law, they are also mandated to maintain order, and these two principles can come into conflict. It could be considered, for example, that part of maintaining public order is to retain the respect that the public have for the police. With this in mind, would it make for effective policing to charge every citizen who violated traffic laws? Bearing in mind the paperwork involved and any subsequent follow-up procedures to enact, it may well be in the judgement of the officer involved, and with due consideration to other circumstances and the deportment of the offender, that a verbal warning is considered sufficient. No official recording of the incident may be made.

It was noted above that one view of the police as an organisation sees the move to centralisation as coming into conflict with the autonomy of the specialised branches of the force. Whatever the merits of such an abstracted version of police activities, it can be seen from this example that it is in relation to the local character of police actions that the rationality and sense of those actions derive their warrant. Abstracted, free-floating structures do not account for the situated actions of officers going about their work any more than, as will be argued, computerised categorisations of police work capture the actualities of such work.

That the police use discretion in their daily work has an important consequence in the way that their work and managerial control of their work can be understood. Being in an hierarchic organisation, it might appear that an officer's work is controlled by orders or commands coming down the chain of command; the officer's work being the enactment of the relevant law and local commands and procedures, etc. The role of discretion in police work shows this as an inappropriate picture of the actual nature of the wide variety of activities undertaken and the various contingencies which officers take into consideration in carrying out their work. In some ways it might be better to picture decisions as moving up the chain of command rather than orders flowing down. A consequence of this is that the 'information' received by the organisation, the 'official' reports that are logged can bear unknown relationship to the actual work that has been undertaken. The tenuous relationship between the official figures on crime and the putative 'real' crime rate is witness to this. Under the common-sense perspective, not only are all crimes not reported to the police but also not all crimes reported are so recorded. One officer interviewed gave the example of a person reporting that their lawn-mower had been stolen. The officer said that, he took the view that since the last time the person could remember having seen his lawn-mower was the end of the previous summer and that it was conceivable that it been lent to a neighbour and been forgotten, he would not record the 'offence'. He had, however, covered the possibility that the owner might make further inquiries about police progress in the case by asking the owner whether the lawn-mower was insured. It was not. If it had been, it would have been recorded.[9] In a similar vein the police might receive a call from a householder's neighbour that the house is being broken into. Upon investigation by an officer no evidence of a burglary is found. Does one decide to record the incident officially or not given the differential contingencies that could arise from either decision? If one records it, then what follow-up investigative work might be entailed, at what cost and to what benefit? If the incident is not officially recorded, then might there be any 'come-back' resulting from further enquiry from the person who phoned or the alerted householder? These are just some of the situated decision-making activities which reveal the 'local' character of the organisation of police work.[10]

Discretion, then, is an essential feature of police work. It is not some eradicable nuisance that can be removed by imposing stricter guidelines or statutory control. It is part of the very work involved in bringing some action to be seen as being in accord with some rule. The social world that the police deal with does not come pre-coded or neatly packaged and self-assigned as coming under the transgression of one particular law or type of incident.They are not alone in this and the issues involved here relate to other occupations and activities. However, many of the discussions of the role of discretion in the police service have often sought its origins in terms of historical factors affecting the development of the police, of police culture, or particular aspects of the organisation of the police.[11] Assessing character, events and circumstance and the making of judgements and decisions are part of 'doing the job' of policing. Discretion is irremediably involved in doing the work, in getting the job done: 'police work routinely involves choices: whether to institute proceedings; whether to ignore or focus upon specific offences, suspects or populations; whether to invoke formal rules and procedures or to resolve the matter informally without reference to the criminal justice system' (Kinsey, Lea, and Young 1986: 162).

The 'choices' outlined are themselves contingent upon circumstantial features of the incident. Again, field-notes record a road traffic accident witnessed where a pedestrian was knocked down by a car and suffered minor injury, the driver was positively breathalysed but effectively let off with a warning with no proceedings taken. The reason for this lenience was related to the fact that the pedestrian was clearly heavily intoxicated and that the patrol car which attended the accident had been called from patrolling part of the city in which some 2,000 recently landed US naval personnel were intent on having a good time. The officers' priority was to get back to assist in keeping the peace rather than processing yet another driver over the limit. The outcome was the result of an *ad hoc* decision, and since *ad hocing* is involved in rule usage, bringing actions under the auspices of a rule and so on, then to control the activities of persons in an organisation by tighter specification of the rules under which they operate does not necessarily produce the changes desired.

COMMAND AND CONTROL

At the juncture at which there is a call for the greater control of the police, whether in terms of economic constraints, civil liberties and the like, or in regard to the current language over the question of efficiency versus effectiveness, this is the point at which a theory of the development of organisations is required. Whilst many such theories are on offer, in actual practice social scientists in the guise of either sociologists or management consultants have had little success in producing efficient ways to control institutions. One aspect of this lack of success can be understood by considering the phenomenological view that society is *pre-constituted* by the subjects that comprise it. People's self-understandings are part and parcel of the very institutional arrangements that are required to be brought under control. So what can happen is that the action of advancing a particular view of management, say management by objectives or by controlling financial limits, can change the self-understanding of people within the organisation and thus alter the nature of the activities control of which is being attempted.

What is being discussed here is the widespread view, the social engineering stance, that it is possible to improve the effectiveness or efficiency of the police or, to take another example, the educational standards of the country by improving and controlling police and educational institutions. It has been argued that at root this social engineering approach is premised on the idea that in science we have an institution that is able to control and ensure its own development.[12] It is only a short step from this to the assertion that institutions, be they military, social services, welfare and the like, can be improved upon by the introduction and use of 'scientific methods'. And by 'scientific methods' it is now often the case that this is understood as scientific technology, that is, computerisation and information technology.

The role of science in the rationalisation and bureaucratisation of institutions and of society more generally has been debated at great length by sociologists, but instead of entering into that particular argument it will be more fruitful to pose the question as to whether the social-engineering approach actually engages with the day-to-day practical and locally under-stood activities which comprise social institutions. For this approach almost immediately confronts one particular set of problems, and these problems involve the debates, arguments, controversies, and political confrontations that are involved in societies social affairs. Is there to be a limit on the funding of the police, health service, or education? Should certain crimes be targeted? Should the targeted crimes be those that concern the public or are they to be defined by the police or central government through the Home Office? Should crime prevention have greater emphasis or should greater effort be made to increase the level of response the police can make to calls from the public? Efficiency or effectiveness?

Whatever might be said about these questions, they are not questions that can be *solved* in the way that certain questions in science can be said to be solved. Criticisms that can be made about policy do not have the same nature as criticisms that can be made in science.[13] One way in which an argument about policy can be made would be to reference the moral grounds of the policy but it happens that what would provide grounds for justification for one person would be the very reason why another would reject it. To reduce the number of motorised patrols in Liverpool 8, Toxteth,the scene of riots in the early 1980s, could be seen as justified by reference to the 'provocation' such patrols can produce. For others it meant that 'no-go' areas were being produced in which crime and drug use would flourish and that the 'ordinary people' in such areas were not obtaining sufficient police protection. Still others maintain that 'no-go' areas can make racial ghettos. The area is ring-fenced in such a way that a black face outside the area can now be seen as suspicious and more likely to be subject to police questioning or 'harassment'.

The attempt to control institutions via formulating policy and instituting policy changes runs into the buffers of the day-to-day actions of individuals in an organisation attempting to 'get the job done' with all the swarms of contextual features which surround the particular case being attended. To attempt to change the purpose and activities of the police by the adoption of particular policies is also constrained by the fact that the police, as is the case with other institutions, have many and diverse purposes which come into conflict, crime control or the maintenance of public order being one such commonly mentioned area of dispute. The simple introduction of policy changes does not necessarily mean that such conflict over purpose is resolved or that the conflicting purposes simply disappear. In the way that a rule does not specify the grounds for its interpretation, the formulation of a policy does not have as a corollary that everyday actions by personnel in an institution will be determined by the policies and principles which have been adopted. The policies enacted are the policies involved in getting the job done.

Bearing in mind the fact that studies have shown that a patrol officer spends roughly half of his time walking the streets, crime – which is regarded as the real police work – is rarely encountered on such patrols.[14] Much of the work that is undertaken is 'fire brigade' response to calls from the public. A call will be made to the incident report room which will log the call, with a classification of the nature of the incident – burglary or public order, for example – and officers are dispatched to the incident. Even at this point in the sequence of events 'discretionary activities' take place. Earlier, when referring to discretion in the context of the police, what was intended was the way in which an officer, when encountering an incident, has to use judgement, in the light of his statutory responsibility for the disposition of the incident. The use of discretionary activity now is intended in a wider sense in that the use of *ad hoc* judgement in attending to the local circumstances is involved in many other activities from cooking to coding. An incident may be reported but what the nature of the incident is to turn out to be has yet to be discovered, and what the nature of consequent decisions and actions to be taken might be are, as yet, to be decided. For example, some people are known both by the police and by the civilians who work in the incident report room as often making complaints which turn out to be 'nothing' and to respond to such calls immediately may be considered a waste of resources. Local knowledge is required for the 'sensible' disposition of such calls. This can even be the case when an officer, rather than a 'civilian', is calling in with an incident. If the incident is extremely serious, then a special code can be given in the call which will alert the police to respond in numbers and with extreme speed. The use of such a code is, of course, restricted, not least by officers not wishing to cry wolf too often. The seriousness of an incident can be gathered however by the perceived agitation of the officer making the call. Some officers can get more agitated than others and, again, judgement of proper response takes this into account. [15]

Interwoven with this type of issue is the question as to what exactly the call is about. So far it has been taken for granted that, with exceptions of known 'troublemakers', it is unproblematic as to what the nature of a call to the incident room is about and that questions as to the disposition of the incident are resolved through the situated interpretations made by the officer attending the incident. This glosses over the kind of interpretative work that has to take place in the incident room. Reports to the police themselves stand in need of interpretation. Such reports themselves do not arrive pre-coded. A brief examination of a tape-recorded conversation will reveal some of the matters involved.[16]

1 P: Newton Police
2 C: Hello:::
3 P: Yes,

4 C: I ha:ve a complaint um my neighbour is (0.5) le–subl– well renting her garage out, and ah there are young boys, now they seem awfully nice an' everything but I don't know they're missing an awful lot of school, they're fifteen year old types (0.5) an' they've got, apparently they've got seven old cars, I guess they buy these old cars, but about a month ago they went to town sma:shing one of them with a pick-axe just absolutely annoying you know pounding all day,=

5 P: (Mm)

6 C: =and I: have a dog that ba:rks a lot an' I guess he's not taking too kindly to these kids.

7 P: (Mm)

8 C: But anyway there is two more cars in the garage now: and –ah, the neighbour works in fact she's away all day 'n' she doesn't know what's going on but these kids are just spending their ( ) one particular is spending most of the day there, and I know::? that he's taking parts like driveshaft I–I just saw the muffler going with him just now?, (0.5) They take them an' we live close by, it's in {section of Newton} Willow Heights an it's by Gull Park; an' they take these (1.0) you know big enough parts to ca:rry and I: think they're dumping them in the gully; (1.0) and I'm just getting a little annoyed about it because –ah you know I–I think they've got about seven cars, I talked to one of the boys and I didn't let on that I was you know, and I wasn't at the time.

For the police, what is being reported? Just what exactly is the nature of the complaint that the caller is phoning in about? In utterance 8 towards the end we have 'and I'm just getting a little annoyed about it because –ah you know I think they've got about seven cars', so is the caller simply envious or is it something to do with the fact that the '15 year old types' are dumping bits of car in the gully or is it, as is mentioned in utterance 4, that the people involved are annoying because of the noise they make. Which, if any, of these is the problem and which if any of these are a problem to be dealt with by the police? The police recipient of the call would appear to have difficulty in coming to see what the call is about, and the next utterance is

9 P: Do these cars all got license on them lady?

Here there is an orientation as to what might constitute an issue for the police. Because of the way that the caller is presenting the complaint in the form of a story, then the point of the complaint has to be taken from the story by the hearer, it being transparent that not everything that is in the story is the complainable item. In terms of utterances 4 and 8 made by the caller there are a number of things which could stand as candidate complainables: that the neighbour had rented out the garage; that the boys were missing school; that the boys possessed seven cars; that the cars were being broken into pieces; that the smashing of the cars upset the caller's dog and that parts which have been removed from the cars were being dumped in the gully. All of these items under some relationship between the caller and the called could constitute a complainable matter, but, given the projected design of the business, that the call is to a police station, then 'Have all these cars got license on them lady?' is seeable as selected from a collection of business having to do with police work.

Also involved is the attendant possibility of the provision of an alternative account being constructed from the materials offered by the caller. Somewhat later in the call is the following interchange:

16   C: . . . they're sorta taking over the area with this business of eh
          you know,
          smashing up these thing
17   P: (repairing)

'Repairing' overlaps with 'smashing up' and stands in strong contrast to it in that, if that was provided as a description of the boys' activities, then a different rendering of other parts of the account may become relevant. This in turn may involve alternative police action. One looks out of the window and sees some youngsters doing – what? Smashing up old cars or taking the parts of old cars in order to repair other cars. Which of these is the case, given that what is seen is only a slice or segment of a course of action which could be assembled up to be acts of wanton vandalism, opportunist capitalism, or neo-conservative ecological conservationism?

The conversation continues for many more turns in which further descriptive work is done and the officer brings the talk to closure by interrupting the caller with

79   P: No well – I'll fill in a report Miss's Thompson and eh–thank you
          so much
          for phoning.
80   C: O?kay, thanks
81   P: Bye now
82   C: Bye-bye

The call ends with the officer saying that he will file a report but what that report will be about and what category of offence remains for the officer to determine; whatever categorisation is made will involve obliterating the contextual specifics of the call, assigning it to a class of other cases each of which in themselves bear unknown relationship to the specifics of the circumstances which gave rise to them as instances of that class or category. This means that the utility of the information for those auditing police work, be it contained as 'hard-copy' in the paperwork or on computer disk, is subject to the same kind of interpretative dilemma indicated by Kitsuse and Cicourel (1963) in their discussion of the utility of criminal statistics for developing sociological theories of crime causation. To recall briefly their argument, they suggested that, since the criminal statistics were the outcome of a whole range of police organisational practices and procedures, there were no good grounds to regard such statistics as a valid indicator of incidences of crime; criminal statistics are more a measure of police activity than of criminal activity. What we are suggesting here is that the closer one moves to examining the practices that make up police work then the 'statistics' which are generated to audit that work are still an abstraction from the actual local and situated actions in which police officers engage in the course of their daily work. The computerisation of such information and the speed with which such 'data' can be collated and in the hands of senior ranks for use in deployment decisions and the like does not alter one whit the fact that police work entails the use of independent judgement by officers on the street, as it were, the audit of which remains essentially in an as yet to be determined relationship to that work. Put more prosaically, because the information glosses over the actual activities, paperwork, and time involved in various police tasks, from giving directions to strangers to dealing with serious and violent crime, what the information means, what the 'data' signify, remains essentially open.

CONCLUSION

Nothing which has been said above is intended to imply that the introduction of information technology into the police force has been a fruitless exercise. Clearly this is not the case. What is intended is that in relation to command and control and the auditing of police work a phenomenon is encountered which has features in common with the phenomenon located by Garfinkel (1967) – the irremediably local and situated production of sense, objectivity, fact, and social order in human action. Because of the necessarily constructionist approach to human action embodied in information technology this phenomenon is not locatable and, not being locatable, is encountered as a nuisance to be otherwise glossed and otherwise made accountable. In the way that in the social sciences statistical results are not determinative of sociological 'findings', then the audits of police work are not determinative of policy nor policy of police work.[17]

What this chapter has attempted to show is that the difficulties encountered in introducing information technology into the police and the problems that have been encountered utilising the large databases of files and records which the organisation produces do not stem from the intransigence of officers or from the problems of coordinating disparate forces which have different objectives. Even if a unified national force were to be produced under a unified set of objectives and priorities, the matters detailed here would still remain. The formal logic required of large databases – e.g. the categorical distinctions between type/sub-type, object /property – collides with the informal logic of situated decision making and actions necessitated by the local relevancies of day-to-day activities. This, clearly, is an area of wider import than the police. Whilst this analysis is somewhat negative in its implications, it needs to be squarely faced so that scarce resources can be allocated to more tractable problems.

NOTES

1 There are uses which combine both numerical analysis and data processing such as simulation.

2 Researchers working in the area of the theory and practice of database design are aware of these matters but are prejudiced in favour of attempting to produce clearer semantic demarcation. As Garfinkel (1967) has shown, this elected procedure runs into the sands of indefinite iteration. Typical of the type of thinking evinced in this area are the following comments on an initial paper by Bo Sundgren, 'Data base design in theory and practice'. The comments are by John Miles Smith. 'Another difficulty caused by his merged infological model is the "object/property" dilemma . . . . One argument suggests that this distinction is inappropriate . . . since one man's "property" is another man's object' and further 'A "father" is not normally considered as a relationship between two persons. A "father" is a person who is male and has an offspring. "Father" is therefore a category (or subtype) of "person"'. And again, 'I want to emphasise the importance of including "invariants" for each semantic construct . . . . The invariants express the semantics of such constructs as "object", "relationship" and "category". A typical invariant is that a relationship instance must reference existing object instances . . . . For example, an employee cannot be hired before a company is formed, and a company cannot be formed until an owner is created.' The paper by Sundgren and the comments by Smith are to be found in Weber and Wasserman (1979).

3 Newing (1988).

4 Comrie and Kings (1975): the statistical breakdown of data from this study is referred to in Val King's MA thesis 'Managing police work', University of Lancaster, 1990. The data presented there show that, for patrol officers, the amount of time spent attending incidents ranged from 9–14 per cent. Of this, 36 per cent was for crime incidents and of these crime incidents roughly one in three were false alarms, such as there being no evidence of anything of a criminal nature having occurred.

5 Other tasks which devolve on the police include the maintenance of law and order, control of traffic, and being available to help those in need of assistance. The actual range of activities which these descriptions gloss is, of course, extensive.

6 The most recent example of this was a speech given at the Chief Police Officers' Conference by the Chief Constable of Gloucestershire. He was reported as saying: 'We should cut out the minor "crimes", consider introducing other categories more relevant to current requirements, stop publishing overall figures and detection rates and purge ourselves of our obsession with them . . . . Even the media and some members of the public are beginning to realise that the crime statistics, as recorded by the police, bear little resemblance to what actually is happening within our society' (reported in the *Guardian* 6 June 1991: 4).

7 Ibid.

8 The 'relatively simple' can become extremely complex once one moves away from a notion of accounting based upon the debits and credits of personal finance. The notion of 'creative accountancy' glosses over the myriad ways in which corporations and large firms can manipulate capital values, capital depreciation, transaction values, and the like in order to present themselves as efficient and healthy economic organisations. The general point, that organisations such as the police have particular difficulty in obtaining and having publicly accepted measures of organisational operation and efficiency, remains.

9 Data from ESRC project 'Community reactions to deviance' directed by J.M. Atkinson.

10 The use of the word 'local' is intended to resonate with the sense in which ethnomethodologists write about the sense of social structure as being 'locally organised'. That, and how a sense of social structure is constructed and displayed for participants, is considered to derive solely from the local activities of the parties to the situation. It is not considered as deriving in some neo-Durkheimian fashion from trans-situational rules deemed to govern the setting. In a similar way, the activities of police officers are, at this point, being considered as part of the constituents of making sense of 'what happened' (Garfinkel 1967).

11 See, for example, essays in Fine *et al.* (1979). Also, for discussions of the various 'political' positions that have been taken on police discretion, see Kinsey and Young (1986: Chapter 8).

12 Rush Rhees discusses the work of Karl Popper in this light (Rhees 1969). See also Benson (1990).

13 Over recent years there has been some interest in debunking science through an analysis of scientific controversies such as whether nuclear power is safe or whether fluoride ought to be put into municipal water supplies. Typically such studies show that scientists line up on opposite sides in the debate and reveal themselves as human by engaging in political invective and *ad hominem* disputes. The conclusion often drawn is that natural science is no better than social science because natural scientists engage in such debates in the same way as ordinary mortals. This misses the point. Political argument will use the findings of natural science in rhetorical attempts at persuasion. It would perhaps be best to see these 'controversy studies of science' as social controversies in which 'scientific findings' are bandied about as part of the armaments of the opposing contestants.

14 Whilst the foot patrol officer will encounter incidents on his beat, it has been estimated that encountering 'real police work' on such patrols is extremely rare. A London patrol officer could wait eight years before coming across a burglary (see Clarke and Hough 1984).

15 When interviewing one of the civilians who works in an incident report room it was said that an over-agitated message typically came from female officers. When pressed as to whether there were other types of officer who became this way he replied that there were 'the Jocks'.

16 The data here are from a collection of phone calls made to a police station in North America. The conversations were transcribed by Rudiger Krause.

17 On the way in which statistical results do not lead to unequivocal sociological findings and the wide import this has for the human sciences generally, see Benson and Hughes (1991).

5

TAKING THE ORGANISATION INTO ACCOUNTS

Graham Button and R.H.R. Harper

The preceding chapters in this section have examined working environments into which technology has been introduced in order to facilitate aspects of the work that occurs within them. They have variously reported how, within the particular settings they have been concerned with, the introduction of new technology far from facilitating that work actually creates difficulties that then have to be worked around. Thus the technology can cut across existing 'good working practices' by creating interactional difficulties that had not previously existed or it can create working difficulties because it is insensitive to the contextual reasons for the existence of those practices in the first place. The reactions to these problems can be extreme, for instance, as reported by Hartland in Chapter 3, actually to switch the technology off.

Part of the reasons for these difficulties in working with technology is occasioned by the fact that the design of the technology does not support what Suchman (1983) and Suchman and Wynn (1984), drawing from an ethnomethodological understanding of action (Garfinkel 1967), describe as the 'situatedness of activity'. These papers attempted to introduce to the design community the importance of understanding the specific contexts of work and the local, contingent skills workers use as part and parcel of 'achieving' practical ends. Yet, the full implications of bringing the social into design have not been realised (Bannon and Schmidt 1991: 3–17). At best, lip service is paid to the notion, at worst, sociological ideas are badly distorted when used as part of the design process.

This can be explained, in part, as due to the failure to appreciate what on the face of it might seem a deceptively simple point: that, when technology is sited in the work-place in order to computerise some existing processes (such as the computerisation of the accountancy system, an example that will be a major focus for this enquiry), it is placed into an already existing social organisation. In this chapter we wish to underscore the fact that work practices are situated within the context of an *organisation* and examine the interplay of these practices, the organisation, and the introduction of a new technological process. In so doing we want to explore the possibility that sociologists may be able to make *design recommendations.* This is a risky business, especially since the recommendations that we do offer with respect to this study are very coarse for we will restrict ourselves to reflecting upon the type of technology that would suit the organisation we examine. Yet, if it is possible for sociologists to make even this order of contribution to the design process, it might also have been possible to resist the introduction of the type of system that figures in our examination.

THE STUDY

The organisation in question was a multi-division foam manufacturer in the north of England which had purchased a tailor-made system for sales and order processing (SOP). The particular division that is the object of this study was located some ten miles from the head office and manufactured foam composites for the furniture industry. Members of the division felt considerable dissatisfaction with a system that had been introduced a year prior to our investigation. This dissatisfaction was summed up by their chief accountant who observed: 'the system has nothing to do with what we do down here', 'it's too damn slow', and 'it's totally impractical'. The thrust of his allegation was that the system was not sensitive to the daily work routines of the division, work routines that resulted in, as we shall shortly elaborate, effective *manufacturing to order.*

We want to argue that the reason for this sort of reaction by the division has to do with the local, organisational circumstances relating to ordering and manufacturing. Although the sales and ordering system that was introduced modelled the stages of ordering, manufacturing, and invoicing, it did not adequately reflect what ordering, manufacturing, and invoicing looked like *as a day's work within the organisational context of the division.*

The model implicit in the system necessarily stripped the work practices of ordering, manufacturing, and invoicing of their situated details and dislocated these processes from their organisational context. However, as we will soon see, it was these details and this context that gave the ordering and manufacturing activities the sense they had for the people involved. They gave, in part, the very accountancy process in the division its working rationale. Thus the system turned the process of ordering, manufacturing, and invoicing into a sequential process where i) an order resulted in an order form, which ii) initiated production which filled the stipulated order, which iii) resulted in an invoice. Although consulting the records of a transaction would suggest that the division had indeed conducted its work in these stages, both the records and the representation of the stages included in the accountancy system based upon those records omit the work practices of the people involved who constructed the record of the day's work. When these actual practices of ordering, manufacturing, and invoicing are examined *as they unfold as a working day in the context of the organisation of the division,* it soon became apparent that ordering, manufacturing, and invoicing are *not* done according to the record. The accountancy record was a *post hoc* assembling of the day.

For instance, according to the records of a transaction, the process, as we have mentioned, appeared to be sequential: orders precede manufacture, manufacture resulted in an invoice. As a transaction *unfolded,* however, as we will describe in more detail below, manufacture could begin before an order had been processed by the front office and before an order form, which according to the records initiated manufacture, had actually been issued. Since the system modelled the activities of ordering, manufacturing, and invoicing according to the record as opposed to according to the unfolding day's work in the division, it did not match the contingencies of the day's work. These contingencies, far from being aberrations, were in fact seen to be 'good working practice' within the organisation of the division. The system then had to, and indeed was found to, cut across good working practice.

In order to appreciate fully just what is involved here we can develop a comparison between the model of the ordering, manufacturing, and invoicing stages contained in the system and the actual working day as experienced by those party to it.

Stripped of the circumstantial details of the working day, the work of ordering and invoicing was represented in four stages. First, a document representing an order was made up; second, copies were moved through the offices and the factory; third, the order form became an invoice; and, lastly, once payment had been received, a single copy was filed for audit purposes. The four stages were thus described as:

Stage one. Most, although not all, orders are received over the telephone. These are given to clerks who enter them up and produce duplicate copies of them within about fifteen minutes. Four copies are sent to production, one for each phase of the production process, and a copy to dispatch. Another, making a total of five, is kept for reference.

Stage two. The four copies of the order are given to the men who cut the foam from the large blocks in the warehouse. These individuals select a template from the manual or make one up as the case demands, and decide which foam type and thickness is appropriate. They keep one copy of the order, take the remaining three, the slices, and the hardboard templates to another group of staff, who make a precise cut. These also keep a copy of the order, before passing the remaining two and the foam cuts to another part of the factory where the foam pieces are glued together. One copy of the order remains here, the last is sent to dispatch, along with the finished product.

Stage three. Once in dispatch the order form becomes an invoice and is attached to the goods and delivered with them.

Stage four. By this time, typically a day, the original copy of the telephone order will be filed as an invoice in the front office, and will remain pending until a 'receipt of delivery' note has been returned by dispatch.

In this model of the accounting and manufacturing stages it would seem at first glance that the work of ordering and invoicing was quite straightforward. A document representing an order is made up, copies of this are used in the production process, and a copy becomes an invoice. On the basis of this representation of the ordering and invoicing stages, computerising the system would seemingly and without too much difficulty enhance its operation, as, indeed, the system introduced was meant to do. Thus the system boasted amongst its features a relational database, enabling operators to search for the relevant information. Each template (or window) was devised so that the particular costing for a customer could be provided and even calculated automatically, so that the types of order particulars (i.e., the designs of the foam cuts) could be accessed in accordance with the past history of dealings with that customer, and so on. All of this could be done, almost instantly, from one terminal.

Such a system would appear to have merits. It rationalised and proceduralised the accountancy work of ordering and invoicing and provided an interface tailored for the particular business. The system could reproduce the stages of ordering and invoicing represented in the description of the four stages given above.

However, in the actual course of use certain problems arose for the division we examined. One problem was that orders which had unique particulars could not be accepted by the system, only standard ones could be. Orders with standard particulars but non-standard foam types would be rejected. Nor was it easy to remedy these problems. It was not possible to take 'pieces' of files to make up new ones; rather, each item had to be typed in individually; it was not possible to simply make a file for a new customer by copying all the foam sizes, costs, etc., common with other customers and just add the missing items. Instead, everything had to be typed in from scratch.

Further, small changes in particulars, costings, foam types, etc., necessitated what was called a 'composite file', which effectively meant starting a file for a customer all over again, digit by digit, line by line. Finally, although this is by no means a complete list, another problem was that every category on a file template had to have some entry or else the system would reject it. So it was not possible, for instance, to process a file without a cost on it.

The upshot of these problems was that the division *rejected the system and worked around it.* This caused administrative difficulties, tension arose between the division's accountancy department and the shop-floor; and between the division and the head office. In short, the computerisation of the accounts, a large and costly undertaking for the company, resulted in interdepartmental friction, loss of morale, and loss of productive efficiency.

On the face of it the fuss might have appeared to be undue because the problems we have pointed to above could, seemingly, have been designed out of the system in a re-evaluation of its operation. However, the accountants and the process workers in the division recognised that the particular problems they were having with the system could not be simply removed within the existing design framework. That is, they recognised that the problems they faced were merely indexes of an underlying problem with the system that would reproduce the same order of problem no matter how much the system was re-worked. For them, it was much simpler to carry on their work as near to 'normal' as possible and work around the system.

This underlying problem can be gleaned from the above quoted remarks of the chief accountant (p. 99): *the system did not integrate into their existing work practices*. Within the organisational context of the activity of producing foam cuts to order, the SOP system was viewed as irrelevant to the work of the division; it had 'nothing to do with what we do down here', and it was 'too damn slow', and 'totally impractical'.

The telling feature of this context related to the routines and expectations of the furniture industry. These placed an overwhelming injunction upon the division to produce the foam cuts for the *end of the day on which orders for those cuts were placed* (at worst the next day). This injunction caused many manufacturing problems in working to the time available for a job which workers in the division had devised many working practices to overcome. The apparent simplicity of the work of ordering and invoicing, as depicted in the representational description, the model, of the stages of ordering, manufacturing, and invoicing, disguised the fundamental problematic, of manufacturing to order in a day

The heart of the problem was summed up by the chief accountant for the division.

> Our ability to predict orders and thereby coordinate production and sales is the singular dilemma we have to face. On the office side the inability of customers to fix their orders over several week periods and their keenness to stick to short notice, telephone orders, means that the days are cluttered with efforts to get orders through to production as quick as possible. If the orders are made more in advance, the office could coordinate its ordering procedures more competently . . . . As it is, orders are often accepted without a price agreed, since the orders are made over the telephone for same day delivery. We do the pricing after the goods have been made.

The overwhelming pressure was to get the orders to the production floor and the finished product invoiced as quickly as possible, normally within the day the order was received. This is a feature of the organisation of furniture manufacture business. Customers did not place orders for the furniture foam in advance because they mainly produced to order themselves. Therefore they required the foam on an immediate basis to satisfy their own clients who would be pressing them for delivery.

These organisational production constraints had a number of consequences for the accounting practices of the division. Having such a quick turnover of order–delivery–invoice meant that minor clerical mishaps could cause serious delays. For instance, when an order was received and files consulted to produce the costing, those files could still be in use when required by another person who was taking another telephone order. Whilst that person was waiting to get the files, he or she sometimes received two or three other orders, and, despite the best intentions, orders sometimes got lost and were buried under other papers. They were typically found, but sometimes not for several hours. Given that the entire process from order to receipt was a day, this kind of delay was a major problem indeed.

These sorts of problems were compounded by there being seven people who could take orders, and only one file, for example, with costings. However, the problem could not be allayed by having several copies of the file. There were approximately 10,000 standard possible order particulars and 200-odd customer accounts. Costings varied between order particulars and the customers. Some customers received preferential treatment per item; others were dependent on the size of their orders. The costings file contained a page for nearly all possibilities which meant that it was huge – about 16 inches thick.

In order to operate under the constraint of the specific problematic of the furniture foam business concerning one-day ordering and production, if we can express it that way, *ad hoc practices of ordering and invoicing* had developed that the model of the accounting stages disguised. In particular, these practices involved the *interweaving of ordering and invoicing into the very production process*. The following remarks by the deputy foreman tell all in this respect:

> production is organised on a day to day basis . . . in fact telephone orders are mostly . . . . go straight to the works manager. These calls get treated rather like inter-shop floor messages where the question of accounting, process and all that, is a secondary issue.

Thus *in practice* not only were orders processed by the front office, they were also processed by production workers on the factory floor. The first line of production workers then did not wait for the four order forms to be sent down by the front office before beginning the work. This consequently meant that orders would start to be processed before the order forms that were supposed to initiate the production process were compiled. It was not unusual for an item to be in production before being priced and the price accepted. The order forms were then *post hoc* productions, done by the front office after the commencement of production, which in practice constructed an organisational rationale (that later appeared as the record for the transaction) for production, rather than being the first stage in ordering, processing, and invoicing. The production workers would inform the front office that production had started and the order form would then be produced and join the job in some part of the manufacturing process. This seeming 'jumping the gun' was recognised by all concerned as *good working practice* because it meant that production within the organisation of the furniture manufacturing business of getting the order in and the goods out in one day could be best satisfied.

Matching these practices to the accounting activities as constrained by the SOP system would inevitably lead to problems. There was an asymmetry between practices and the technology. Applying the system in the context of ordering, production, and invoicing, far from enhancing work activities, had the potential to hinder them. This was because the system required that orders be processed in accordance with the sequential model of the processing stages. Now, obviously, the system could speed up some matters, for example those that could be put into the relational database. Thus, it could be expected that, by placing the information in a readily accessible database, the tasks of fixing prices, using the files, and the rest mentioned above could, theoretically, aid the process of ordering and producing in one day. However, because the system generated an order form that then initiated production, the system resulted in a slowing down of production because it precluded the production workers from getting on with the job before they had received an order form. In working practice order forms were *post hoc* organisational rationalisations for the production process, and not, as demanded by the system, an initiating step in the production process.

The actual writing up of an order form exemplifies another asymmetry between the working practices as modelled in the system and the working practices as part of an organisational expediency. The order form, as rendered by the system, was a given fixed document that initiated the production processes. In working practice, however, the order form could be a *developing document* tied to and constituted by the production process. This feature of the document was made transparent in the handling of production troubles. As with any large enterprise, there were times when information on orders was confusing or incomplete. However, the fact that orders were taken by production personnel meant that the production floor was also involved directly with clients and they could quickly handle contingent production problems by directly approaching the client without having to go through the front office. The shop-floor manager could simply ring up the person who had called him, sort the problem out, and consequently the shop-floor workers would amend the order form accompanying the job.

In this respect, production was not done to order as the records portrayed and the system demanded. In practice what working to order could mean was the ongoing construction of the order in the process of manufacturing. The production of the order form was part of the production of the product; they simultaneously constituted aspects of each other, or, to put it another way, they were mutually elaborative. The system, however, conceived the relationship between an order form and production to be a *causal* relationship where the order form initiates production. Therefore, the system demanded that any changes to the order form had to be routed through the front office. If this was not done, then the system would not recognise the final copy of the order when it became the invoice. The system would be unable to match the invoice with the order. According to the system, any change in the order would have to go from the production floor to the front office and back to the production floor, via the client. The system in effect organised the production and ordering processes as separate from one another, and in so doing actually hindered the efficient process of ordering, producing, and invoicing, the very process it was designed to enhance.

IMPLICATIONS FOR DESIGN?

Increasingly, as we suggested in the introduction to this chapter, sociologists are offering helpful suggestions to systems designers based upon their sociological studies and some designers are turning to sociology for descriptions of the social world that they feel to be consequential for their design. A fair question that could consequently be asked of us is: having actually studied those work practices and having advocated the description of action as a situated and contextually located phenomenon, is there anything we can say about what the design of that technology could look like taking account of those practices? To put it another way, we have i) studied a situation into which a system was placed, ii) argued that, because its design did not take account of the organisational context of the work of the division and the work practices of manufacturing, it iii) resulted in production difficulties; thus, is it now possible to iv) translate this sort of sociological study into concrete design proposals and what order of proposal could they be? The following proposals that we make are coarse ones that concern the type of technology that might have better suited the organisation. Yet it was this very sort of coarse decision that was the first step in the design of the system the introduction of which we have examined. The coarse decision was to design a standard accountancy package much the same as other packages that had been sold to other companies. Based upon our observations it might have been possible to have conceived of a different type of technology from the one introduced.

First, we can note that the problem that the division experienced with the new technology was that it required drastic changes in their ways of working, but those changes were dysfunctional for the work of the organisation in manufacturing to order within the time constraints. Thus, whilst the division could countenance changes in the way in which its personnel did things, it could not countenance changes in *what* they did. Thus the concept of *change* is an important one in this context. It is also an important concept in design where the popular adage is that *design should bring about change*. On the basis of this study, we can argue that the idea of 'change' is perhaps not such a straightforward matter as some designers have it, for the nature of the change can seriously enhance or jeopardise the utility of a system. The division required a technology that brought about what we shall call *evolutionary change*, as opposed to *radical change*; that is, change that emerges from the existing process, and which enhances those processes, as opposed to change which sweeps away existing practices and replaces them with new ones. This order of change can preserve *what is done whilst possibly changing the way it is done*. This means that it is important that the technology supports what is done. That is, if the sort of change that is envisaged emerges out of and enhances existing practices, then the technology needs to be designed so as to *support existing work practices* and, consequently, *designers may require some knowledge of the work that the technology supports*.

A second issue is that the way in which the division's existing work practices could be supported was via a technology that could be interleaved into those practices. The practices of instantly manufacturing to order meant that the work of production and accountancy were entwined. The system fractured that relationship by being located in the front office and, in order to reinstate that entwined relationship between production and accountancy, a technology that embraced the whole organisation was required. A technology that was orientated to the organisation of the division as a whole, as opposed to fracturing the division into supposed discrete spheres of operation, was needed. That is to say the division required *technology that was distributed* in all the places it was needed. This effectively meant throughout the places that 'manufacturing to order activities' occurred: the accounts office, the foreman's office, the shop-floor, and so on. In short, the technology needed was *ubiquitous technology*.

A third issue is that the form this ubiquitous technology could take that would best satisfy the work of the division would be sets of individual technologies that could be linked together. For example, the works manager needed a device for inputting a phone order to his foreman on the shop floor who could then begin production and for simultaneously inputting the order into the accountancy system in the front office and alerting the front office to the fact that an order was going into production. The front office needed devices that could then enable them to cost and price the job and relay a flexible order form to the shop floor. The production workers on the shop floor needed a device that would allow them to register changes to the order as they worked and relay those changes to the front office. In short, the technology needed to take the form of multifarious *tools* that would support particular work tasks and that could be linked together into a system that covered the whole of the organisation.

In summary then, understanding the social organisation of the workplace allows us to make some coarse proposals about the type of technology that would have best fitted that context, the technology needed to: i) initiate evolutionary change, ii) be supportive of existing work practices, iii) be distributed in a way that reflected the distribution of work, which iv) also needed to be a tool-based technology. Now we stress that these are coarse proposals, but we also stress that it was just this order of proposal that was first made with respect to the design of the system.

CONCLUSION

What is our implicit conclusion here about the relationship between sociology and design? That designers should become sociologists? That design teams should have a mandatory sociologist in their midst? That sociologists have all the answers? This would be rather arrogant: after all, designers have been alert to the difficulties of design for a long time – indeed, one might say they have been all too conscious of design failures (albeit that failures make the headlines far less often than successes). They are aware, for instance, that interviewing users does not always provide sufficiently accurate descriptions of work activities. Sometimes an interviewee, say an accounting department manager, will give the impression that accounting procedures are much simpler than they really are. This may be motivated by a naive wish to make the designer's task easier and quicker and so minimise the cost of the system. They are aware, too, that one individual may have his or her own way of using procedures and that these do not reflect practices elsewhere. For a third possibility, there may be a degree of wish fulfilment, an individual defining a system that is ideal rather than realistic. These kinds of problems have now entered the folklore of design practice. To avoid them designers try to ensure that they get at least several views of what a system needs to provide, supplement interview data with observation, information flow charts, and so forth.

If sociology is to join other human science disciplines such as psychology and ergonomics in the design process, then what we have argued here is that the full import of that suggestion has not been realised. Our view is that any contribution sociology can make resides in the methodological recommendation that description of the details of the practices that make up work-in-an-organisation may, for certain design purposes, be preferable to viewing work as a de-contextualised phenomenon.

Part III

WORK PRACTICES IN THE USE OF TECHNOLOGY

INTRODUCTION

In the previous section a variety of work settings into which computer systems have been placed in order to computerise already existing work practices, activities, and routines, have been examined. It was seen that across the range of these settings a number of problems have arisen because the situated, local, improvised, contingent, and *ad hoc* nature of the interactional work within the exigencies of organisational life was poorly understood. Thus, the systems often failed to support the work of the participants in those settings. In this section of the book, work settings and work activities that are actually and specifically organised around technology are examined and the way in which the technology is used in the accomplishment of the work of settings' members is addressed. The settings are ones that Lucy Suchman in the first chapter of this section calls 'centres of coordination'.

In her influential book, *Plans and Situated Actions* (1987), Suchman first underscored the relevance of ethnomethodological studies of practical action and interaction for computer systems development. The idea that human action displays itself to be locally and situatedly organised and achieved through the work of parties to it was a serious challenge to the way in which human action was conceptualised by the cognitive models and formalisations of artificial intelligence. However, it not only contributed to debates in AI but it also paved the way for ethnomethodological studies of the use of technology in the actual circumstances of its deployment and the receptivity of those studies to those involved in computer systems development. Understanding how computer systems are used in the accomplishment of participants' work activities is not only a sociologically interesting topic in its own right, but may contribute to a better understanding of what those systems should look like. This is also the hope of the collaboration between computer scientists and sociologists at the Centre for CSCW at the University of Lancaster, and the second chapter in this section is authored by two sociologists who have been involved in that collaboration, Richard Harper and John Hughes.

In the first chapter in this section, Lucy Suchman examines the work that took place one afternoon in the operations room of a commuter airline at a metropolitan airport in the Western United States. She describes it as 'centre of coordination', the salient features of which are that is a setting in which: i) distributed activities have to be managed in such a way that the success of the operations depends upon the cooperation of the setting's members and their clients; ii) the work is open to indeterminable troubles; and iii) the work involves the deployment of people and equipment across time and space. Two contradictory forces operate in these work settings: first, the settings have to be fixed sites to which persons who are distributed across time and space can orientate, but, second, persons within those fixed sites need access to those who are temporally and spatially distributed. In centres of coordination it is technology that is used to organise that access.

Suchman describes how in the coordinated work of the participants the technology is used to produce and sustain an ordered state of affairs. That is, the technology is not just used as a means of tracking persons and objects, but as a structuring device in the activities of those things that are being tracked. Thus the work of coordination in the operations room she examines involves the 'artful use' of computer, communications, and display technologies to organise and produce the one-at-a-time order that is a viable feature of the processing of the aircraft.

A centre of coordination is also the setting for Richard Harper and John Hughes' investigation in the second chapter in this section. It is the London Air Traffic Control Centre, and, like Suchman in the preceding chapter, they are interested in the way in which the technology is used, in this case by Air Traffic Control Officers (ATCOs), to structure and order the objects of their attention, in this case the aircraft in the sky they have responsibility for. Harper and Hughes describe how the technology is used to apply the *Manual of Air Traffic Services* circumstantially and locally as a set of instructions for seeing. In this way the technology that is part of the control room 'becomes not so much a material object the performance of which is governed by the technical specifications which its design incorporates, but an integral part of the organisation of things which a controller needs to do in his or her work'.

6

TECHNOLOGIES OF ACCOUNTABILITY

Of lizards and aeroplanes

Lucy Suchman

This chapter is part of a larger inquiry into constitutive practices of designing and using technologies. I am concerned here with the following problem: how is it that the material practices of a possible class of work sites, and of one site specifically, constitute those sites as *centres* for the co-ordination of human activity, in two senses: first, as concerned with the production of a coherent *temporal* relation between prescribed and observable-reportable events; and, second, as constituting *spatial* centres within an extended system of distributed activity. I hope to show how persons, in their work's material practice, act as skilful mediators between temporal representations and among spatially distributed participants in the joint reproduction of a contingent social order.

In his study 'The externalized retina: selection and mathematization in the visual documentation of objects in the life sciences' (1988), Michael Lynch examines the technology of diagrammatic images in the work of biology. Among the examples that he cites is the scientist's work of tracking the movement of lizards within a given habitat. He describes how it is that an array of stakes is driven into a plot of ground to form a grid, against which the movements of the lizards can be plotted. To distinguish a lizard within the habitat from its fellows and to aid in the process of tracking its movements, each lizard is assigned a unique identification number. Grid and numbers then provide the basis for a diagrammatic representation of, and claims about, lizard behaviour.

In their paper 'Formulating planes: seeing as a situated activity' (forthcoming), Charles and Marjorie Goodwin consider various devices for perception in the work of airport ground operations. One of their instances involves the use of a particular form by airlines personnel to track the status of aeroplanes on the ground. They describe how it is that planes are parked in rows on a ramp. To distinguish a plane from its fellows and to aid in the process of tracking its movements, each aircraft is assigned a unique identification number. Aircraft numbers are marked on a schedule, which provides a grid used to map and control activities around the planes.

In such processes of representation, to borrow Lynch's phrase, 'the form provides a convenient basis for specific practical actions' (1988: 176). In the documentary practice of the life sciences, the diagram mathematises and makes claims about the 'nature' of objects. Through the impositions of the grid, as an 'exogenous' format applied to their 'endogenous' terrain (Lynch 1985b), lizards come to occupy territories with a graphically depictable shape, in much the same way that planes can be diagrammed as moving through time and across space within the orderly array of the schedule. In the case of the lizards, their movement is taken by their observers to be independent of the tracking process; that is, to be a 'natural' event of which the technology of the grid and its numbers simply provides a map. In airport operations, in contrast, the movement of planes is itself coordinated within a process of which the schedule and its numbers are a part. Like the lizard diagram, the schedule represents a course of events as 'coordinates' on a two-dimensional grid. However, the work of the grid and its mathematisations is not to explicate the aeroplane's properties, so much as to enjoin the plane and its personnel into a specific course of practical action.

CENTRES OF COORDINATION

Ethnomethodological studies of the discovering sciences take up phenomena such as lizard diagrams as organising devices for the *in situ* production and reproduction of a normal order, and in that and other ways provide signposts for the investigation of indefinitely many other settings of material practice. In this chapter I want to focus on one family of settings within which a new corpus of studies has emerged. For purposes of assembly, I'll gloss these settings as *centres of coordination,* and count among them (to name those with which I'm presently familiar) the work of Whalen (1991) and Whalen and Zimmerman (1990) on 9-1-1 emergency centres, of Harper *et al.* (forthcoming) on air traffic control centres, of Heath and Luff (1991) on line control centres in the London Underground, of Grosjean (1989) on the Paris Metro, of Hutchins (1990) on navigation, and of our own work on airport ground operations rooms. [1]

All of these settings share the following general concerns:

- Each site is dedicated to the ongoing management of distributed activities in which one set of participants is charged with the timely provision of services to another. The success of these operations requires the engagement and cooperation of both setting members and their clientele.

114

- The activities being managed are open and vulnerable to an indeterminable horizon of troublesome contingencies, some of which the work of the site is designed to address, some of which arise in the work's course.
- Each of the sites shows a preoccupation with pressing problems of space and time, specifically the deployment of people and equipment across substantial distances, according to a canonical timetable and/or the emergent requirements of rapid response to a time-critical situation.

Centres of coordination are designed to maintain two contradictory states of affairs. On the one hand, to function as centres requires that they occupy a stable site to which participants distributed in space can orientate, and which at any given moment they know how to find. At the same time, to coordinate a system of widely distributed activities, personnel within the site must somehow have access to the situation of others distant in space and time. A job of technologies in such settings is to resolve this contradiction through the reconfiguration of relevant spatial and temporal relations.

THE OPERATIONS ROOM

Within these centres, work is characterised by a strong mutual orientation among co-present members to each other and to developing situations. At the same time, co-workers' attention is differently structured through a division of labour that assigns to each particular responsibilities for communication, via various technologies, with other relevant locations. The case at hand is taken from an afternoon of work in the operations room of a commuter airline at a metropolitan airport in the Western United States.[2] I want to look at this work as the control* (with an asterisk, borrowing the convention proposed by Harold Garfinkel et al. 1989 to denote a placeholder for a series of topics yet to be explicated) of the movements of aeroplanes and the coordination of the activities of their operation.

I want to begin by proposing, building on the insights of Lynch (1988) and Goodwin and Goodwin (forthcoming), that the work of the operations room can be seen as the production of a coherent relation between a normal order of events, described by particular representational technologies, and an order of events observable by operations room personnel in the work of the local site. Like the grid of the lizard mappers, a central device for that work is the schedule – a technology which allows the plotting of aeroplanes into a two-dimensional coordinate of space and time. The schedule is produced at one site and distributed to others throughout the United States, where it is taken up both as an instruction for the work and as a form on which to inscribe its course. Note that the site of origin of the schedule is constituted as a 'centre' for the system as a whole by just this relation to other sites. The operations rooms at each local site, in turn, are constituted as centres in their relations with ramps, gates, and the like. And so forth. In this way the schedule travels throughout a network which, through those travels, it helps to produce.

SCHEDULES AND THE DISCIPLINE OF TIME AND SPACE

The schedule as instruction and record is both an immutable mobile in the Latourian sense (1990), and a dynamic participant in the work of the local site. Personnel at each site are orientated to achieving a normal order of on-time arrivals and departures, in the face of endless contingencies some subset of which, due to requirements of interdependency and accountability, must be recorded and/or conveyed to other sites throughout the network. For the operations room of the commuter airline, an enumeration of the work of maintaining that order should include, as a set of glosses, tracking the status of arriving flights, mapping flights to specific aircraft, assigning aircraft to parking spaces on the ramp, communicating those assignments to pilots and to ramp personnel, announcing the arrival of aircraft to the ramp, communicating parking directions to pilots, tracking the status of planes on the ground, and entering departure times into the computerised scheduling system.

The discipline of the schedule is implemented through the medium of the nationwide computer system, accessible at each local site. As mentioned, one task for the local site is to enter departure times for each aircraft into the system, both as a resource for colleagues at other airports and as an audit trail of the day's work. For example, on this particular afternoon we see Randy, one of two co-workers in the operations room, entering the time out for a flight 5321.

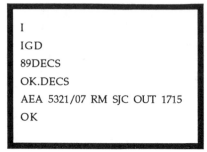

Figure 6.1 Randy's screen showing time out for flight 5321

We have here a simple bit of screen-based activity – an entry by Randy, received with an 'OK' from the system. 'Time out' here refers to the time at which an aircraft leaves the gate, the performance of ground crew being measured by the difference between the scheduled time and the time of actual departure (all other things being equal; that is, in the absence of delays attributable to circumstances beyond the local site's control).

Randy next enters the 'ETO' or 'estimated take-off' time; that is, the time at which the plane can be expected to leave the ground. On this occasion, his entry elicits a routine bit of machine-initiated repair.

```
I
IGD
89DECS
OK.DECS
AEA 5321/07 RM SJC OUT 1715
OK
AEA 5321/07 RM SJC ETO 1535
TIME OUT OF RANGE
```

```
I
IGD
89DECS
OK.DECS
AEA 5321/07 RM SJC OUT 1715
OK
AEA 5321/07 RM SJC ETO 1735
OK
```

Figure 6.2 Estimated time off entered as 15:35 with error message

Figure 6.3 Estimated time off corrected to 17:35

One aspect of the discipline of the schedule, then, appears as a logic of time with which operations workers must negotiate. In this case, the work of inspecting for logical inconsistencies in time entries has been delegated to the machine, in a way that becomes for Randy a bit of machine support for the detection and repair of a routine error made at the keyboard. Part of Randy's competence is his familiarity with this machine-based logic. In fact, it turns out that the work we have just watched is not a simple reporting on events at the gate at all, but a subtle round of negotiation with a machine-based system of temporal accountability, with Randy as mediator. Let us look at that more closely.

At the close of Randy's interaction with the computer system he turns to another machine, a video monitor placed just to his right, then glances out of the window in front of him before turning to a document beside his keyboard.

At this juncture we get an inquiry from the ethnographer who is running the camera, regarding the sense of the work he's just seen:

5:14:20 pm
Chuck: S'cuse me, Randy, what were you just doing there? You were– getting some stuff from the computer and then you were jus–

Figure 6.4 Room view at 5:14:05

Randy: Oh. Yea, this is our Tahoe trip, it's supposed to leave at 5:15
          and it('ll be) boarding abou- a couple of minutes late. It's–
          they're starting right no:w which, we like to have, actually the
          engines running a couple of minutes before departure time.
Chuck: Uh huh.
Randy: So I just (inaud) y'know and I check and just look at the
          screen and see, you know, (how they hold out and if they
          close the door) they're just starting the engines now:://so
Chuck: //Uh huh, uh huh.
Randy: Uh, I just want to make sure he stays on time.

I have suggested that Randy's job is to maintain a consistent relation
between an order of events prescribed via the computer network from the
national centre and events at the local site. Through his entries into the
computer system, Randy must represent the site's adherence to the prescribed order — in this case, that the Tahoe trip is supposed to leave at 5:15
— while ensuring that his entries also have a reasonable correspondence to
events observable by him through the video monitor and outside his
window.[3] In this instance his visual inspection of the Tahoe flight shows it
to be boarding a couple of minutes late: a situation he judges to be close

118

enough to be recorded as on time, but problematic enough to require continuous monitoring for signs of further delay. It is in that sense that Randy's work is, as he says, 'to make sure [the pilot] stays on time'; that is, to maintain an acceptable relation between the on-time departure he's just entered into the computer system and the inevitable contingencies of an actual on-time departure, findable by him through a routine round of situated inquiries to the ramp.

Randy's judgements regarding time, read off as a relation between the scheduled order and an observable order at hand, are among the routine competencies of his daily work. It turns out, however, that the basis for Randy's 'estimated take-off' time, which was 17:35 or twenty minutes from the 'time out', is not simply his observation of the work outside his window but his orientation to another discipline of time inscribed in the machine. Moreover, his estimate is orientated to that discipline not as a simple form of compliance, but as a skilfully managed routine. As Randy goes on to explain it, once he's entered the time out of the gate for a particular plane a clock starts ticking within the system which, if a time off is not forthcoming within a specified interval, triggers an alert message. To forestall the alert message Randy can enter an estimated take-off time, before which the system will not complain. He routinely enters that time as twenty minutes after the time out, giving him generally ample time to receive and enter the actual time off from the pilot.[4]

MAINTAINING THE ORDER OF ONE-AT-A-TIME

We noted in passing Randy's inspection of the video monitor to his right. Work in operations makes artful use not only of computer technologies, but of a range of other communications and display technologies as well. In the case of the airline's jet operations at this airport, responsibilities end when a plane has pushed back from the gate and moves onto the taxiway, at which point control is handed off immediately to the tower. In the case of the commuter airline, however, the arrangement of the parking ramp, the terminal building, and the taxiway requires extended participation by the operations room in the hand-off of planes to ground traffic control.

Specifically, the ramp is behind the terminal building, out of visual range of ground traffic control. To get to and from the parking area, the pilot must navigate a narrow passageway beside the terminal building, also out of the control tower's view. During the time that the plane is in this space, its progress is controlled by operations. It turns out, moreover, that at one interval along a plane's traversal of the passageway between the parking area and the front of the terminal, called 'the wall' by operations workers, it passes out of visual range of the operations room as well. To extend their vision, operations has installed a camera at the wall positioned to feed back into the room a visual image of the plane as it passes through

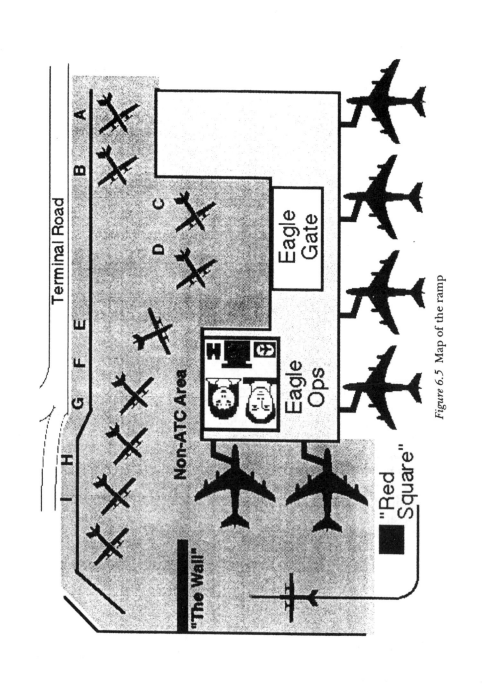

Figure 6.5 Map of the ramp

that blind spot. Moreover, as the hand-off from operations to ground control and vice versa must be precisely controlled, a specific place for that hand-off has been created in the form of a red square painted into the taxiway just outside the wall. On reaching that square the pilot stops and radios operations if he's arriving, the tower if he's departing. All of this is monitored by operations via the video image and the radio, as Randy explains.

Figure 6.6 Close-up of Randy's point to monitor

5:17:10 pm
Randy: This fifty one thirteen has left the gate, he's going around the corner to the wall here, and he'll come up to red square. (7.0) And there he goes. So what happens is he's contacting the tower, he gets up here, and then he says he's right here, (and I guess) yeah I just heard him on the radio talking to the tower, so he's (gonna tell him to) come on out to the taxiway. And the tower then directs him out to the end of the runway where, y'know, he queues up with the other planes, and they tell him uh, y'know, they give him his clearance to take off.

Along with audio and visual display technologies, this work site has introduced another device for managing their extended responsibility for control over planes passing into and out of the ramp area. This is a restructuring of the division of labour in the form of a second position which has been added to what was previously a one-person operation. The work of this position, filled on this particular afternoon by Nancy, is to coordinate the passage of planes into and out of the ramp area, including conveying their assigned parking spaces to the pilot.

To see that work in its detail, we can turn to a point just before the onset of what's called a complex or a series of commuter planes that arrive together in coordination with the scheduling of the airline's jet operations. Nancy has been out of the room and returns in time to overhear Kevin (who has taken over from Randy) announce to the gate the impending onset of the series, one member of which, Nancy knows, has in fact already landed.

Figure 6.7 Nancy returns to the operations room

5:51:04 pm

Kevin: (radio to ramp) Uh, just about everybody's called in, uh//sompin' should be landing here any second.

Nancy: (returning, touches K on shoulder) //(There's one) comin' up on the wall.// There's one comin' up on the wall.

Angie: (radio from ramp) Thank you.

122

(3.5)

Kevin: W'll boy, it's a good thing you got here then, huh?

Nancy: I was out there watchin.'

Kevin: heh heh

Nancy: (radio to pilot) Fifty one eighteen, uh, come in for hotel?

Kevin: (radio to ramp) One fifty eight at the wall for hotel.

Angie: (radio from ramp) Go ahead, bring em on in.

A central theme that has emerged in all of the control room studies cited above, developed by each in different ways, is that of mutual monitoring. In this case, Nancy's overhearing of Kevin's announcement as she enters the room indicates the immediate relevance of information she has gained while out of the room. She announces her return to Kevin with a touch on his shoulder – a device that exploits his skills of attending to the technology-mediated interaction in which he is engaged, while maintaining peripheral awareness of others within the room. Her first report of 'one coming up on the wall' is placed in what could be a transition point in Kevin's radio call, but turns out to overlap with his continuation 'sompin' should be landing here any second'. She recycles her news and there follows a joking reference by Kevin to their respective responsibilities in the room; more specifically, to her responsibility for conveying that news to the ramp. She then moves into her position and radios the pilot his assigned parking space, followed by a corresponding call from Kevin to the ramp.

The design of operations' informings is orientated to the respective relevancies of their intended recipients.[5] Specifically, Nancy identifies the plane by its flight number, 5118, in her call to the pilot, Kevin by its aircraft number, 158, in his call to the ramp.[6] The response from Angie, the crew chief on the ramp, in turn shows her orientation to Nancy's role in controlling the pilot's progress. It is precisely such interactions and orientations that constitute operations as the centre of this particular system of activity.

Nancy's work in these interactions is to convey the assignment of an arriving plane's parking space both to the ramp and to the pilot, as in the following bit of routine work.

6:19:55 pm

Nancy: Well, whatawe got.

Kevin: Three forty five.

Nancy   (radio to ramp) Three forty five here for bravo. (radio to pilot) Fifty two fo::rty two::: (3.0) (look to ramp, back to radio) Come in for bravo.

Pilot: Bravo.

Nancy: (radio to ramp) Angie you copy? Three forty five's comin' in for bravo.
          (2.0)

Angie: Yea, send em in.

Figure 6.8 Nancy conveys parking directions to the pilot

The assignment of planes to parking spaces is a device designed to coordinate activities in space and time. The success of that design, however, requires not only the orderly arrangement of planes on the ramp, but the orderly management of procedures by which each plane arrives. The practical accomplishment of the parking assignments must contend, among other things, with the topography of the physical site, in particular with the narrow passageway that planes must navigate in order to reach the parking ramp. The mediating role that Nancy plays between the passageway and the ramp is visible in her body, as she negotiates the limited perceptual access provided her by the two windows facing out from the corner in which she sits.

The passageway imposes a locally specific, temporal order onto the work of arranging planes on the ramp which calls up a classic topic in ethnomethodology; namely, the work of the queue.[7] That is to say, in entering the parking ramp, arriving planes must follow an order of 'one at a time'. But the placement of the passageway in relation to the ramp and the limits on the pilot's view require the displacement of the situated work of negotiating the queue from the pilots themselves to operations personnel; specifically, to the position that Nancy occupies. This queuing requirement

124

routinely gives rise to troubles in maintaining the order of one at a time through the passageway.

5:55:19 pm

Nancy: (To pilot) Fifty three eleven come in for Foxtrot. (To ramp) Six fourteen here for foxtrot.
          (3.0)
Angie: (Can you stop) foxtrot for a second.
Nancy: Ah, fifty three eleven you still on?
Radio: (I'm here.)
Nancy: Yeah, why don't you make it a slow taxi around the corner the ramp's quite- not quite ready for//you.
Angie: //'Kay, go ahead and bring foxtrot in.
          (Nancy watches out window, checks monitor, previous plane taxis by.)
          (32.0)
Nancy: Thank you fifty three eleven (you're) clear for foxtrot (whenever you're) ready.
Pilot: (Roger)

In this case we see Nancy monitoring not just one but two planes in the queue: one, ahead of 5311, which is currently in the passageway (and which she follows through the window on her left), the other, 5311, still out by the wall (which she tracks through the video display). Again, as the intermediary between the ramp and the incoming plane, we see her redesign Angie's directive according to her own access to the situation of its recipient. So she reframes Angie's request to 'stop foxtrot' to a call to 'flight 5311', to do a 'slow taxi', then monitors the progress of that taxi via the monitor. Similarly, she delays her delivery of Angie's 'go ahead' as she monitors the progress of the other plane, not visible to Angie but visible outside her window, which is taxiing in ahead of 5311. In this way Nancy herself becomes a skilful coordinating device in an order of socially organised, distributed work.

OF LIZARDS AND AEROPLANES

This account of an afternoon of operations work is intended to develop some current themes in the investigation of technologies of order production and the particular requirements on such technologies when they are designed not only to track the behaviour of indifferent 'natural' objects but to act as structuring devices in the activity of animals who are themselves interested in a regime of control.[8] As in the discovering sciences, representational devices and represented phenomena are mutually constituted through their production as an intelligible ordered pair (Garfinkel *et*

125

al., 1989). In the case of the schedule and the *in situ* accomplishment of airport operations, the pair involves not only tracking the movement of the animal, but active engagement of the animals tracked in the collaborative production of their own ongoing activities as an accountably rational, normal order.

Lynch has raised a question regarding the possible need to re-examine the classic distinction between natural and social science in light of Garfinkel's proposal that each comprises a distinctive science of practical action.[9] The intriguing relation of lizards to aeroplanes suggests, I think, that his question is a salient one. I hope that relation suggests as well how the expansion of the project of ethnomethodological studies of science into other work sites leads to a re-examination of the dichotomy of natural and social in ways that retain its truth (for example, as the order of distinctions proposed here between the interests of documented phenomena in the cases of lizards and aeroplanes, including their respective orientations to and participation in disciplines of order production and control), while pursuing Garfinkel's call to replace generalised pronouncements regarding difference with an ongoing course of investigation into specific sites of practical reasoning and practical action.

NOTES

1 For other analyses of the airline operations rooms, see, for example, Brun-Cottan (1991); Forbes (1991); Goodwin and Goodwin (forthcoming); Jordan (in preparation); Suchman (forthcoming).

2 I am grateful to my colleagues Charles and Marjorie Goodwin for recording this particular afternoon's work.

3 The monitor here is used to enhance his view through the window, making it possible for him to inspect a scene more closely, or from a particular angle.

4 This routine estimate is presumably custom designed for the local site; that is to say, we should expect a somewhat longer interval at Heathrow or O'Hare.

5 Recipient design is extensively explicated within conversation analysis (see, for example, Schegloff 1972; Jefferson 1974; Sacks 1974; Sacks and Schegloff 1979; Schegloff 1979).

6 The term 'hotel' here refers to a parking space, parking spaces' names being alphabetic, e.g. 'bravo', 'foxtrot', 'hotel', rather than numerical to differentiate them from flights, aircraft, gates, and so forth.

7 For a concise statement of ethnomethodology's interests in the queue, see Livingston (1987: Chapter 4).

8 A powerful history of such disciplinary technologies is of course to be found in Foucault (1979). The ways in which this present is elucidated by that past remain to be fully explicated.

9 Lynch's question came to my attention in a symposium at the University of Wisconsin, Madison, in March of 1990.

7

'WHAT A F-ING SYSTEM! SEND 'EM ALL TO THE SAME PLACE AND THEN EXPECT US TO STOP 'EM HITTING'

Making technology work in air traffic control

R.H.R. Harper and John A. Hughes

Air traffic control (ATC) belongs to that class of communication and control systems which typically depend on a multi-user database of relevant information which is capable of reporting on specific states of the system, either as a result of interrogation by human operators or by continuous automatic updating. The operators rely on this database for information pertinent to their particular tasks. In the case of ATC much of this information is provided by a computer which drives both the radar and the flight data information which the controller, along with other members of the controlling team around the suite, uses to coordinate air traffic. In the early days the movement of what few planes there were could be left to little more than the pilot's eyesight to ensure that one did not crash into another. The inexorable growth of air passenger travel, much accelerated in the last decades with the advent of jet aircraft, required traffic regulation by means of flightway procedures and a corpus of personnel to coordinate the flow of aircraft directly as planes travelled from point to point and flew from much the *same* points through much the *same* airspace towards much the *same* points. It is this which remains the responsibility of the ATC system, namely, to prevent aircraft flying through the same airspace from colliding: a task that has its absurd side as captured by the quotation that is the title of this chapter. It is a task which has over the years accumulated, and necessarily so, a considerable amount of technological support for the controller (see Hughes *et al.* 1988, for further details, and Harper *et al.* forthcoming).

Contemporary ATC is a complex of sub-systems, technological, procedural, human, bureaucratic, regulatory, legal, and more. As far as the technology is concerned, it is a highly sophisticated arrangement of computer-driven radars, drawing upon an elaborate nationwide network of radar and navigation beacons, computer-processed flight progress data, control suites for communicating with other facets of the system, and so on; all arranged to facilitate the work of controllers whose task it is to direct

127

aircraft into an orderly flow of traffic. The orderly flow of traffic is the outcome of the working practices that deploy the technology 'to hand': a weave of practices and skills that constitute the work of air traffic controllers. The system is also a regulatory one in that aircraft are expected to follow certain 'rules of the road', rules contained in the *Manual of Air Traffic Services* which specify in great detail the routes, procedures, and regulations to be followed by air traffic and by controllers in directing aircraft. Thus, there is an important sense in which the work of controlling consists in applying this immense corpus of rules to aircraft entering UK airspace using technology to achieve this.

RULES AS INSTRUCTIONS FOR SEEING

Sociological interest in work and its relationship to rules was provoked by Weber's (1947) reflections on bureaucratic organisation, a concern developed and extended by ethnomethodology, in particular in its resistance to the notion that rule use, as a feature of the social organisation of activities, is straightforwardly one of stable compliance with what the rule stipulates (Wilson 1974). The orthodox view, very briefly put, is to regard rules, be they the cultural norms and institutions of Parsons (1958), or the proprieties of interpersonal conduct (Goffman 1959), or the formal rules of rationally conceived organisation (Weber 1947), as 'external' factors governing, even determining, the behaviour of those subject to the rules. Such a view fails to acknowledge that rules have to be applied within a setting such that what a rule or a procedure means, what actions fall under it, is a matter that has to be decided, judged, determined on occasions of its application. Social actors, that is, have to make judgements as to whether *this* rule applies *here* and *now* in respect of *these* circumstances. Action in accord with a rule is situatedly accomplished by actors and done 'in light of' the particularities of the setting (Coulter 1983). Rules do not stand as disembodied regulations 'mindlessly' applied, but are constitutive of the situation itself and can, across the endless variety of work settings for example, exhibit a variety of relationships to the 'things' and the practices of the work.

Baccus, for example, describes the regulatory rules that provide virtually no guidance and little relationship to the work of truck wheel maintenance mechanics because work-place personnel 'know better' than 'any standard provisions what safe work conditions consist of as in fact they know their job as a reasonable account' (Baccus 1986: 20–56). Wieder (1974), by contrast, describes how an informal 'convict code' of the kind regularly identified in studies of organisations of all types regulated in fine detail staff–inmate interaction in halfway house. The 'code' was never written down as a set of regulations, though it could have been, but was attended to, cited, mentioned, discussed, and generally manifested through the particularities of talk and action. Nonetheless, it was made intelligible and itself furnished

128

intelligibility to the actions and activities within the community of the halfway house. Harper (1988: 297–306) describes how the predictable features of routine accounts are used as rules to determine accounting errors. The point is that rules, procedures, regulations, endemic to work of all kinds, do not, cannot, stand independently of the activities of work but furnish those who do the work with ways of seeing and recognising things and activities as relevantly features of the work. And it is this interweaving of rules and activities that is also characteristic of ATC (Shapiro *et al.* 1991). The *Manual of Air Traffic Services* does not stand in some disembodied relation to the work of controlling but is integral to its activities and work as socially organised. The rules of controlling have to be imbibed *as activities* that constitute controlling as a situated and artful skill. They constitute a plan, to use Suchman's (1987) phrase, an enablement of the work of organising air traffic and, as such, furnish controllers with 'instructions' for seeing the information to hand, much of it technologically furnished, as proxy for the current state of air traffic. But, and to stress, the plan in its actualities is a continually evolving one in that, though, in general, a controller knows what he/she will be doing, it is not known in advance in detail. It is, we might say, in dealing with the unfolding details of air traffic that the work of controlling consists: in a word, it is a discretionary system (Shapiro *et al.* 1991).

The interest in the relationship of rules and action also raises the matter of skills and competencies incorporated in working activities, the skills and the knowledge involved in 'doing the work' (Lynch 1985a; 1982: 499–533; see also Garfinkel *et al.* 1981: 131–58; Livingston 1986, for example). Controlling air traffic is managing events in real time rather than following the kind of plan which determines in advance what it is the controller should do next. There are always inevitable and contingent factors, including technical troubles of various kinds, which have to be dealt with. The rules, along with technically provided information 'to hand', are resources reflexively deployed such that 'competent use' is founded on the controller's practised grasp of what particular actions are necessary on a given occasion to provide adequate aircraft separation *according to the rules and procedures*. Controllers' culture is saturated with the recognition of the artfulness of the craft – an artful and skilful use of rules and procedures, the anticipation of 'likely problems', the smooth control of an aircraft's flight, the organisation of the pattern of traffic to ease the work of controllers on adjacent sectors, and more – that is exercised within a 'working division of labour' around a controlling suite.

FLIGHT STRIPS AND THE PICTURE

What we particularly want to focus on in this chapter is one crucial element of controllers' working practices, namely, how they make Flight Progress

Strips, or 'strips', *usable* within the flow of work.[1] 'Strips' represent the movement of an aircraft through an airspace which is configured into sectors; that is, blocks of sky which are distinct areas of control responsibility. As an aircraft flies through controlled airspace it is passed from sector to sector under the direction of Air Traffic Control Officers (ATCOs) whose main task is to ensure the effective separation of aircraft one from another as well as the expeditious flow of the traffic. Not surprisingly, the means of achieving both of these goals requires accurate information about planned routes, flight levels, and directional headings. Coordination between sectors is one of the core tasks of controlling and one that can, potentially and in actuality, take up a great deal of a controller's time and attention. Configured airspace is the 'stage' upon which the patterns of air traffic are 'drawn' using the information and the rules and procedures of ATC. Air traffic flows into and out of controlled airspace in a variable stream which is the task of ATCOs to produce. The passage of an aircraft into, through, and out of airspace is, initially, indicated through a Flight Data Processing (FDP) application filed prior to departure. Updating these is done through limited radar links with the database through Radar Data Processing (RDP) and by inputting flight data. The information from the database is distributed throughout the operations room according to sectors.[2]

At its simplest and most general, the controller's problem is a scheduling one. For any controller the traffic has to be taken as and when it arrives in the segment of airspace for which he/she is responsible and threaded together into an orderly pattern before aircraft are handed over to the next sector. The scheduling has to be achieved in and through making the traffic flow. Aircraft cannot be parked for a couple of minutes nor can 'jams' be allowed. Even in holding patterns aircraft are still on the move, part of the flow of traffic, and must, therefore, be taken into account. It is the 'strips', a formatted strip of paper containing boxes of information relating to individual flights, next reporting point on route, time due to pass that point, call sign of the aircraft, its 'squawk code', aircraft type, planned flight path, requested cruising height, departure and destination airports, and more, which are crucial elements in the melding of the information available to the controller, which also includes radar and R/T, which constitute the mutually elaborating processes by which 'order in the skies' is assured.

The local culture describes a controller's orientation to the configuration of traffic in a sector and the likely problems it poses as 'getting the picture'. This is not a detached description but one used and understood within the controllers' culture to refer to various practices in controlling work, not least the regular habit of an incoming controller spending anything up to 10 minutes watching over the shoulder of his or her predecessor to 'build up the picture' before taking over the position.[3] An important part of this is 'looking about 5 to 10 minutes ahead all the time . . . sometimes a little further than that', in order to get an idea of the actions needed to be taken 'now'. As one controller described the process at some length:

the kinds of check you do is check your information which is your strips which will show you whether an aircraft is in there or not, and that means then that you don't have to look all over the radar . . . it would be an impossible job to sit down and look at the radar and look at all the different blips and try to avoid them by putting the aircraft into blank spaces on the radar, so you have got to have this information to tell you what traffic is coming into and out of the sector. From your strips you can find out whether or not there is a possible confliction . . . and what you can do about it, then you go to your radar and look for that particular aircraft and see where it is in reference to the, outbound from Heathrow, for example, and you want to climb it, to see where it is in relation to that. Then you decide what you are going to do with it, whether you are going to go underneath it, whether you are going to wait until it's gone past it, whether it's on on your frequency, whether you can put them on parallel headings and then you can climb it up to the other aircraft levels. Same as inbounds, it's the same sort of thing.

The controller's 'picture' has been of interest to ATC researchers for some time (Whitfield 1979: 19–28). Its potential significance was first appreciated during trials on Interactive Conflict Resolution, a computer assistant which extrapolated aircraft movements to detect potential conflictions (Whitfield, Ball, and Ord 1980: 569–80). This led to the development of various techniques to illuminate aspects of the 'picture' as a 'mental model' or 'internal representation' and its relation to measures of work-load (Jackson and Onslow undated). The analytic idea of the picture, best summarily characterised in Whitfield and Jackson's words as the 'overall appreciation of the traffic situation for which they are responsible', recognises that controlling work has a subjective dimension to it in the sense that the controller has to think and make decisions about the situation before him or her and, it is argued, that this process is characterisable as the matching of the 'picture' or 'mental model' with the information provided by screen, R/T, and strips. What is also important is that the idea recognises, albeit tentatively, that controlling is not simply a matter of unreflectively applying rules and procedures but a matter of applying rules with respect to an ongoing configuration of traffic; in short, a matter of using the rules and procedures along with the provided information for interpreting, *or making sense of,* what is going on 'now'.[4]

The importance of the 'picture' was emphasised by the growing possibilities for providing the controller with more automated assistance and the possibilities inherent in this of reducing the ATCO to supervisory control: an issue which raises the difficult question of deciding the appropriate mix of decision capacity between human operators and automated assistance given that the ultimate responsibility resides with the human operator. A major problem for designers, given that human beings are notably bad monitors, is to devise ways in which any automated facility could be elegantly overriden by the human operator; a matter also of keeping the operator 'warm', or engaged, throughout the period of duty so that if required to over-ride the automated system time is not wasted finding out what needs to be done.[5] Thus, the examination of the components of the controller's 'picture' seemed to offer a useful route to a fuller understanding of controlling skills which could inform the design of automated systems more adequately adapted to human capacities (Whitfield and Jackson 1982; Hopkin 1979).

Interviews with controllers suggested that, although they often found it difficult to describe the picture verbally, certain themes did emerge as important ingredients, such as 'getting the picture' before taking over, the value of experience in handling information, the division of traffic into foreground and background, planning and prediction, and, of course, the frightening possibility of 'losing the picture' (Whitfield and Jackson 1982). Further studies using the verbal protocol technique (Bainbridge 1974; Rasmussen and Jensen 1974: 293–308) where an operator is asked to give a running commentary describing his or her sequence of thought and action prior to taking over a position, which is recorded and analysed, provided the following counts of protocol elements:

- strips were predominant elements establishing the picture. Expected aircraft were not yet on radar and strips alone contain the detailed information about each flight;
- radar was mentioned less frequently, and then often in conjunction with information provided by strips;
- mental activities inferred, such as time check, memory reference, predictions, calculation, decisions, were small in frequency; search activities prior to the reference to the strip or to radar were relatively infrequent.

Further analysis of the strip category suggested that controllers appeared to use route information frequently when thinking about aircraft and obtaining a general sense of the traffic situation. The next most important one was flight level, then beacon time. However, it was noted that there are variations between protocols, even though the most frequent procedure when taking over a sector is to examine the flight strips in time order. Departures from this included exploring potential conflicts first, inserting a new flight strip and considering that first, overhearing RT, among others. Also, some controllers apparently organise their picture in terms of inbound and outbound flows for various airports, relying on their knowledge of typical routes and procedures, while yet others organise it in terms of flight levels. Some also focused on the picture on unusual and non-routine flights.

Yet, it seems to us that this approach does not treat as particularly problematical what it is controllers are doing when they perform their working tasks. That is, the reference to the 'picture' as the *analytic object* of inquiry, independent of its contexts-of-use, detracts from specification of the skills that are in use when the 'picture' is referred to, talked about, or even, and here we think use of the term is being pushed to its limits, when it is being depended upon.[6] From our point of view, these inquiries over-simplify situations of choice as they are encountered by those who make choices, in this case the controllers themselves. It also underrates the knowledge available to controllers as decision-making agents and ignores the socially organised, and thereby situated, features of the environment within which the choice is being made. While such an approach to the examination of controlling may lead to a generalised picture – if the pun is excused – of the activity in question, what is not clear is how that picture relates to particular cases, particular instances and competences as used and understood by those doing the specific job in hand: in short, its quiddity (Garfinkel *et al.* 1981: 131–58). What is lost is the realistic char-acter of the situation in which the practical decision making takes place. It is to avoid this that we propose one needs to look at controlling in detail, as it takes place.

From this perspective the first thing to note is that controlling is not an individualised cognitive activity, but a social one in that it involves team-work.[7] Controllers are part of a formal division of labour around the controlling suite normally consisting of the controllers for each of the two sectors, the chief and 'wingmen'.[8] Although the distribution of positions is work specific and directed towards serving the activities of the radar con-troller, the actualities of the 'working division of labour' (Anderson, Hughes, and Sharrock 1989) are such that all members of the team attend to the information and the tasks and activities it supports in distinctive but closely related ways. All explicate and interrelate their respective activities as aspects of a working division of labour which they trust and rely upon. To effect this, activities and the information that serves them are publicly available as 'accountable and witnessable' features of the work for those who 'need to know' and have the 'know-how'.

From the ethnomethodological point of view, the visibility of actions, and therefore their 'witnessability', is a key feature of social action. Within the operations room at LATCC for example, among those familiar with it, what a controller is doing is visible by looking at the strips, the screen, listening to the talk and so on, because of its familiarity to those doing the work involved. The incoming controller, in getting the picture, does not routinely have to interrogate the outgoing controller to determine what is happening but simply sits and observes the strips, the radar and the talk, and, from these resources, is able to determine what the active controller is doing and why.[9] From this point of view, ATCO work becomes not so much the accumulation and construction of an 'internal representation' as the production of an observable state of affairs at the console – that array of radar screens, VDUs, radio and telephone equipment controllers work with – this being done not by a sequence of inferred cognitive operations but by a succession of witnessable social actions done so that their recognisability is evident to those 'in the know'.

As said earlier, 'strips' are pieces of paper about one inch wide and eight inches long that are formatted into 'boxes' containing information about individual flights. The information is derived from the original filed flight plans for each aircraft contained in the computer database and is, in this sense, historical rather than a real-time record of flight progress. Although some updating may have taken place this is not a continuous process. Each sector will have three or four key navigation points, strips being printed for each point for each aircraft from the FDP computer up to 40 minutes prior to its arrival at the navigation point, though the time can be much shorter than this. These strips represent the aircraft at each stage of its journey through the sector. As each point is crossed so the respective strip is discarded by the controller.[10] The strips are placed in racks or bays, just above and behind the flat radar screens, and this is another way of making the strip informative. That is, information *on* the strip is not the only way in which it is made relevant for the controlling activities of the team. On the 'wing' positions are 'pending racks' containing the strips of traffic due in the sector which provide an early indication of incoming traffic, its routes and likely problems. They also help some anticipatory planning of flight levels at which aircraft can enter the sector.[11] When an aircraft enters the sector the strips become 'live' and placed in a separate rack in front of the radar controller.

The strips provide the template for what is happening and will happen in the sector. They are the material instruments that the controllers attend to and use in their work. They are also institutionally organised objects representing whole sets of institutional processes such as the filing of flight plans, the application of control regulations and procedures, prior control actions, and more. Yet the strips do not determine the sequence of actions of controllers in the sense that what comes along a production line determines what a production line worker has to do next. Rather, the controller has to organise the strips so that they can become an instrument that helps organise, and so make possible, controlling work. Strips are manipulated, glanced at, taken heed of, ignored, revised, written on, and so on. And not just when they are first placed on the racks but continuously all the time they are in use. The end result of these activities is that at any moment in time what the strips indicate and create is the sequence of controller actions that results in order in the skies. Thus, management of the strips constitutes a large part of the work that underscores controlling competence.

WORKING THE STRIPS

As pointed out earlier, the controller's problem is scheduling aircraft within a sector, taking each aircraft as it arrives and threading it into an orderly pattern of traffic before handing it on to the next sector.[12] The scheduling is achieved in and through making the traffic flow using the information resources of radar, strip, telephone, and R/T, together with specific information about weather patterns, for example. In addition, there is the accumulated 'know-how', much of it tacitly held and understood, relating to the system itself, its affordances and its problems, which is brought to bear on the information resources provided by the system's technology, to determine what, in respect of any configuration of aircraft, should be done.

Strips are not some detached record but a vital instrument of the work. (See Harper *et al.* 1989, 1991 for further details.) 'Working the strips' is a means of achieving a solution to the scheduling problem. As noted, strips are activitated up to 40 minutes before an aircraft is due at a navigation point. They are placed in the racks in front of the controllers. As already suggested, the controller does not treat these as determinants of his or her behaviour, but rather as a resource, among others, that can be used to organise the controller's activity. The next step is to order the strips in ways that reflect the work that needs to be done. Planes fly through a sector in a sequence which is reflected in the estimation of successive times at which aircraft will pass various navigation points. The controller uses these estimates and the navigation point to order the strips on the racks so that the next plane due at any point is at, say, the top of the rack, the last to arrive at the bottom.[13] Strips are not related to the real-time events in the sky as represented on the radar screens, since, at this stage, the aircraft the strips refer to are not yet the business of this sector controller. The actions described are very much preparatory. Though subsequently the strips may come to be seen, in as yet unforeseen and unpredictable ways, as in need of revision, supplementation, or may, indeed, turn out to be correct, the business of the controller at this stage is ordering this resource in such a way that what he or she may require from them is available in useful ways. To use a phrase made much of by Heidegger, it is an activity of making the strips '*come to be at hand*'. In fact the bulk of time estimates are fairly accurate and so ordering the strips in time sequence usually turns out correct and, hence, a useful way of ordering them. The controller will know immediately where a needed strip is, whether he or she should take account of any special features in relation to it (i.e., in respect of those circumstances that the controller thought worthy of being marked out), and so on.

This ordering enables the controller to get a clear idea of what decisions he or she is likely to have to make in the near future. Ordering the strips shapes the controller's attention in terms of what is likely to happen in the sector, for example with respect to standard traffic patterns but also towards any special problems that need to be anticipated. Special problems that need to be taken into account include such things as two aircraft estimated to reach the same point simultaneously and at the same height (the kinds of problems that the air traffic routing system can be thought of as causing itself). Although this may well be of no immediate concern, controllers mark out such problem strips by slightly lifting them, or 'cocking them', out of the rack. In this manner, when the strips become live, the controller will have already prepared them so that they indicate to the controller and others around the suite how they need to be read, specifically, and 'at a glance', in relation to that potential problem. The way in which the controller organises the strips, for instance according to arrival time over a reporting point, or flight level, or possible confliction points, organises information about the state of the sector. To move the strips is to organise the 'picture' by organising the information in terms of work activities and, through this, organising the traffic.

'Working the strips', or making them 'at hand', continues once they become live. Typically a strip becomes live on the receipt of a radio message from the respective plane when it enters the sector or nears the navigation point. The controller selects the appropriate strip and moves it down the rack to the live strip section: live and pending strips being separated by a strip designating the navigation point being used. The live strip is not placed in just any position among the already live strips. As with pending ones, it is placed in sequential order: for example, the latest at the top, old and finished strips exiting from the bottom. This order reflects, and helps organise, the fact that the controlling decision making is a sequential matter. So the latest addition to the sequential order will not be finished with ordinarily until ones beneath, hence before it, have been finished with.

The strip is also used to display information not configured as part of the computer output. Once outputted by the computer the information on the strip is 'frozen' unless altered by the suite team. Updating is provided through other members of the team around the suite, such as chiefs, assistants as well as controllers themselves, using the strip as a notepad. As a controller remarked, the strips are 'like your memory, everything is there' and, as a chief sector controller put it, 'Get used to writing it down as you say it. Every time you tell the airplane what to do, write it on the strip.' For example, as controllers instruct pilots to climb or descend, follow particular headings, and so on, these instructions are written on the relevant strip, as

136

are the pilot's acknowledgement and their attainment. Attention-getting information may also be written on the strip, such as arrows to indicate unusual routes, symbols designating 'crossovers, joiners, and leavers', circles around unusual destinations, and so on. Such 'notes' can include information indicating coordination, changes to ETA or to route, changes in call sign, and so on. The strip, that is, conveys to members of the team what actions have been done with respect to a particular aircraft. It embodies its control history.

The strip provides a facility for rapidly updating information by members of the suite team as they record their actions in ways relevant to them, and in ways mutually visible to them. This is formally recognised in the colour protocol used to make notes on the strips to show whether or not it is the chief, radar controller, or assistant who has written on the strip and using, but not exclusively, conventional signs to denote actions taken or about to be taken. This preserves not only *what* changes or decisions have been made but by *whom*, so adding to 'history' responsibility and accountability. Chiefs will normally write coordination agreements on the strips and the 'wings', or assistants, updates of ETA's. Any of the team may 'cock out', or slightly lift out from the racks, strips in order to draw attention to them. In other words, management of the strips is very much a collaborative activity exhibited in and through using it as an integral feature of the work.

Finally, when a plane crosses the navigation point represented by a strip the controller does not just throw it away but puts a cross through it. This is especially important on those strips which represent the last point through which an aircraft passes in a sector. The controller puts the mark through the strip when he or she directs that plane to contact the next sector controller. In other words, it is a physical mark to demonstrate that the controller's work has been properly completed and indicates that the strip has not 'just' been thrown away.

Thus strips play a key role in enabling controllers to use the radar quickly and effectively and achieve 'good technique'. As one controller put it, 'You've got to have a complete picture of what should be in your sector and what should be in your sector should be on those strips.' He went on to describe their use:

> It's a question of how you read those strips . . . an aircraft has called and wants to descend, now what the hell has he got in his way, and you've got ping, ping, ping, these three, where are those three, there they are on the radar. Rather than looking at the radar, one of the aircraft in there has called, now what has he got in his way? Well, there's aircraft going all over the place, now some of them may not be anything to do with you, it could be above or below them, your strips will show you whether the aircraft are above or below, or what the

aircraft are below you if you want to descend an aircraft and which will become a confliction . . . you go to those strips and pick out the ones that are going to be in conflict if you descend an aircraft, and you look for those on the radar and those, what those two are . . . which conflict with your third one, it might be all sorts of conflicts all over the place on that radar, but only two of them are going to be a problem, and they should show up on my strips.

The strips and their organisation are a proxy orderliness for the configuration of the traffic flow. While the radar is a computer-generated two-dimensional picture of the sky, the strips are the means whereby the patterns on the screen, and thus the sky, can be seen as the patterns that they are. Strips are not just placed anywhere but are organised so as to give a sequence to them which provides a sequentiality to the traffic flow through the airspace.

STRIPS, RADAR, AND R/T

Though we have concentrated on strips, and referred to other information sources only briefly, in particular R/T and radar, we suggested at the outset that all these resources come to be usable in being *mutually determinative.* That is, these sources of information are not distinctly separate items of information which are, as it were additive, but they mutually explicate the sense of each other. What each source of information means is reflexively determined by the sense made of the others: a mutuality that is premised upon 'learnt through experience' knowledge of controlling and the trust in the teamwork of others. These interpretative practices, the common-sense reasoning they embody to make sense of these resources, are not only not described in the manuals, but could not be; they are, in short, tacit features of controlling activities.

Whereas much of controlling is routine, problems can also arise which are regularly treated as 'routine problems'. The mutual determinacy of strips, radar, and radio is reflected in the ways in which discrepancies in the information are dealt with. Strips, as mentioned earlier, state when a plane is due to arrive in a sector. Failure of an aircraft to appear on the radar screen at the time stated or failure of the pilot to contact the controller at the appointed time is not normally treated as a reason for the controller to think that the strip is spurious, that the aircraft never existed, or that there is a technical malfunction in the equipment. Routinely, a controller in a situation such as this will assume that the radio and radar are functioning normally and that the strip should be set aside until further information clarifies its status. Controllers know, in other words, that there are many 'good reasons' why an aircraft does not arrive at the time indicated on the strip. Mutually checking and rechecking available information is a function of the 'working division of labour' and the 'working knowledge' of how information is relevant to work activities.

The mutual determinacy of strips, radio, and radar means that each is 'made sense of' by what the others indicate; a process of sense making that, for most of the time, is 'at a glance', and reflects what Garfinkel identified as the salient feature of common-sense practical reasoning, namely, its documentary character (Garfinkel 1967). It is this which makes 'what is happening' transparent. That is, on the basis of the information the resources provide and through the experience of aircraft doing-these-sorts-of-things-in-these-typical-ways, a controller can recognise or know where a plane will be in the future – in controlling terms a matter of a few minutes away – and hence, where it will be *vis-à-vis* all other aircraft in the sector. It is this ability to make transparent what is happening in a sector which is the quiddity of the controlling work. Team members make practical assumptions about what each datum represents or indicates and, on the basis of, among other things, the predictable ways aircraft fly, can judge whether the absence of one or other of these resources represents a serious problem or not.

The functionality of the strips resides in their status as one of the embodiments of the working division of labour around the controlling suite. As we have said, the printed strips quickly amass a great deal of written information, information that constitutes an evolving history and unfolding plan of the controller's intentions and decisions, recorded as they are made. The negotatiation of the information on the strips by members of the team 'trustably' incorporates them into work activities. Controllers are only too aware of the fact that mistakes are made, errors that can be alarming to the inexperienced outsider. But the trustability of the strips does not lie in any technical failsafe but in their accessibility to members of the team and the mutual checking that goes on. A routine part of the work is checking information and this begins as soon as the strip is printed. It involves talk about routes and destinations, questions to each other about procedure and the coordination between sectors, confessions about the need to do it this way rather than that, and so on. Thus, although coordinating rules and procedures are laid down in the *Manuals*, what is striking are the richly varied ways in which they are applied in the activities of controlling.

THE PICTURE AS A SEQUENCE OF WORKING TASKS

Newcomers to an ATC console cannot see there what the experienced controller can, though they can, very quickly, be given sufficient guidances to how to see on the screen what the experienced ATCO is seeing. They can see this in at least the sense in which they are shown where the outlines of the coast are,[14] the flight lanes, the major airports, the blips which represent the aircraft, how the data blocks identify the flight number and its height. Similarly with the strips: their left to right (navigation marker separation) and up to down (temporal) arrangement can be shown, what the letters and the figures in the cells refer to, what the coloured marks mean, and so on. However, none of these things can be apprehended in the fluent way in which the controller does. The ATCO, of course, does not just see a series of identifiable units and patterns of movement, but also the history and the likely future of these units and patterns and, furthermore, can see that these are not only a coherent and coordinated series of movements, but how they came to be coherent and coordinated.

It is this quality which we suggest is sought by the notion of the 'picture'. In vernacular terms, the picture refers among other things, to the controller's capacity to 'keep it all together'; to see and give coherence and organisation to the patterns of aircraft movements under varying conditions. As we discussed earlier, to date the marked tendency has been to treat the picture as an 'internal representation', the controller taking time to sit observing his or her predecessor's work, observe what is going on, and, through this, build up a sense of 'where things are' and, both generally and specifically, what is happening in the sector. At a certain point the incoming controller takes over and, presumably, begins to work in terms of the synthetic appreciation of the information available, putatively matching his or her internal picture with the developing information from screen, strips, and radio.

However, our case here is directed at viewing the 'picture' from a different angle. Our interest in the ATCO is not so much as an information-processing device, so to speak, but as a worker and, hence, it is an interest in the ATCO not so much as 'cognitive information-processing machine' but as someone working out the organisation of a set of tasks. To repeat an earlier comparison: ATCO work is not like an assembly line in which a recurrent sequence of steps has to be followed through, but one in which the work consists of putting the tasks to be done into a sequence of steps that can be followed through. Any current transaction between an ATCO and a pilot, or any other member of the team on and around the console, is not an isolated one but part of a developing sequence whereby current steps are built upon previous ones and shaping subsequent ones. The activities, that is, are treated as 'entrained' sequences (McGrath 1990) and their meaning derived from their location in stream of action. From this view, rather than thinking of the air traffic control situation as one which involves a pictorial representation of the state of affairs up in the sky, it is better to think of it as *a display of a set of task requirements*. This is how the ATCO is looking at the information presented in the strips, the radar, and the R/T: to see what needs doing 'now', 'in a moment', 'sometime later on', and so on. Accordingly the working picture is a term for the 'stuff' which is already dealt with, or which will take care of itself, 'stuff' which now or soon requires ATCO intervention, things that are coming along and will or not need dealing with, and so on.

CONCLUSION: THE SOCIALITY OF WORK AND TECHNOLOGY

In the context of ATC, the technology embedded in the suite becomes not so much a material object the performance of which is governed precisely by the technical specifications which its design incorporates, but an integral part of the organisation of things which a controller needs to do in his or her work. This includes such things as 'serving up the information when needed', 'giving information that is not needed just at the moment', 'providing facilities that are useless', 'telling me what needs to be done', all of which we have illustrated with strip use: meeting, in short, to a greater or lesser extent the practical needs of the ATCOs as experienced in doing the work of controlling. In this respect, conceptions of problems, ways of dealing with them, of likely exigencies, of efficiencies, and so on, are part of the technology as experienced by those doing the work. Controllers respond to technology and its operation in sensible and rational ways predicated on the motivations induced by the need to know 'what the technology can do as part of my work'. In this sense, the workings of the system as known yield determinate causes for occurrences.[15] A key element of this is working with the information that is available, reading and evaluating it. This is the kind of activity that anyone familiar with the work will be able to know without saying or describing. Working with the strips, with R/T, the radar is the routine stuff of controlling and the 'bottom line' feature of the ATCO's task is the continuing consultation of these resources.

Of course there is more to controlling than we have reviewed here. Our focus on how the strips are interwoven with the work activities around the suite has largely precluded other than passing reference to other important aspects of controlling work done by 'wingmen' and chiefs. Nevertheless what we hope to have shown is the situated character of the work in which, routinely and mundanely, the meaning of the technology and the information it provides, the rules of controlling, the activities of others around the suite are all interwoven and organised as a system-in-use.

What we have been trying to illustrate here is a way of approaching the study of the sociality of technology which abandons the classical, one could say 'natural', distinction between the technological system and the user. Describing the system-as-seen-from-within means declining to accept the analytic omni-relevance of the strict separation of the technical system and the user. From an ethnomethodological point of view the constructs around which the system is organised are treated as resources for the construction of the working system as an ongoing achievement. Far from

141

the technology and the user being set against each other, they are multi-layered and interwoven into a motile configuration (Anderson *et al.* 1990; Shapiro *et al.* 1991) The system-in-use is treated as a changing constellation of objects, activities, procedures, and actors within which the user is immersed in and through the specifics of the work. Controlling actions are not then to be looked at simply as the following of procedurally defined rules but as the contingent outcome of processes of interpretation as to how the rules fit the case to hand. Thus, solving the sequencing problem is a matter of moment-to-moment using the information, the technology, the rules to achieve, in and through the specifics of the flow of air traffic, an orderliness to that flow. The user, in this case the controller, is a manager of the technology and involved in getting specific things done through that technology using the procedures 'here and now'.

But, and this is an important point, the focus is not the individual but the individual-in-a-team. As we have pointed out and elaborated, the controller at the screen is part of a division of labour around the suite and thus part of an embodied collection of courses of action achieved by the working team. It is the team which circulates knowledge, which reproduces the production processes, checks 'how things are going', doing their respective jobs, and so on. It is in the work of the team that the invisible but vital skills, and other resources furnished by the system-in-use, are 'made to hand' for controlling. It is in the practical, accountable, visibly rational working of the team in the local circumstances wherein lies the sociality of work and its technology.

By way of final comment: there is an increasing movement in computer system design that argues for a greater recognition of the sociality of work and technology. Ethnomethodological studies, too, are being examined with this end in mind: a move which occasions no little controversy within ethnomethodology itself.[16] But whatever the outcome of this interest, there is no doubt that ethnomethodological analyses of work do, on the face of it, make the task of the designer much harder – the 'grit in the designer's vision' – not least because the user ceases to be some 'static entity' specifiable in terms of a list of cognitive capacities. Examining work, and technology, in terms of the situatedly specific activities as seen 'from within' raises the awesome spectre of a variety that is inimical to a design process which is increasingly becoming industrialised. Moreover, ethnomethodological analyses emphasise the skilful knowledge and resources which saturate the skill of the work but which are largely 'invisible', because routinely familiar, even to the parties to the work. It is these relied-upon skills which, in this case controllers but the point is generalisable, workers find hard to articulate. Nevertheless, in being vital to the work they cannot be substituted for by abstracted, decontextualised versions of knowledge and skill. But this is to simply restate the challenge for designers in trying to meet what has always been their ambition if not always their achievement, namely, a better 'goodness of fit' between the technology and the working environment in which it is located. Designers are increasingly seeking to make their technologies more flexible and adaptive. What the approach here at least offers is one way of throwing light on what kinds of flexibility are needed, what kind of technological support is appropriate, in what kinds of work: in a word, reappraising the distinction between the system and the user. Needless to say, whether such efforts will lead to better design has yet to be shown.

NOTES

1 The first stage of this research, completed in 1989, funded by the ESRC/SERC Joint Initiative, involved ethnographic observation and interviews at London Air Traffic Control Centre, or LATCC. The second phase, currently under way and funded by the HCI Initiative, involves additional ethnographic research directed towards building a prototype design tool for computerising flight progress strip interfaces. Fellow researchers on these projects included D. Shapiro, D. Randall, and S. Gibbons, all of Lancaster University; W.W. Sharrock of Manchester University, and R. Anderson of Rank Xerox, Cambridge EuroPARC. The computer scientists at Lancaster are I. Sommerville, T. Rodden, and R. Bently.

2 There are typically eight suites, each dealing with two sectors, in the operations room at LATCC. However, under certain traffic conditions sectors can either be merged or split further.

3 This time is not mandatory but depends on how busy the sector is. Occasionally on very busy sectors the time can be much longer. Normally, controllers work two hours on the 'tube' followed by two hours' rest.

4 What is going on 'now' is also a matter of 'scrolling forward' to see where things might be some minutes ahead.

5 A US National Transportation Board report on an accident in February 1984, when a DC10 ran off the end of the Kennedy Airport runway, cited the crew's 'habitual reliance on the proper functioning of the airplane's automatic system' as a probable cause (*The Independent on Sunday*, 23 June 1991, 'Who is really flying the plane?'). Trusting automated assistance very often means that operators, in the case of failure, have to make inquiries to determine what needs doing: a 'warming up' which can be fatal.

6 One of the problems of studying social action is the relationship between the ways actions as described by those doing them and the actions themselves. As Wittgenstein noted, it is all too easy to be confused by the use of the same word in different contexts. Here we suggest may be a case in point: the word picture is used by controllers to mean a certain kind of thing specific to their work; the same word is used in other contexts to mean things like a graphical representation. One needs to be careful, therefore, not to get muddled up or conceptually confused when one uses the word in analysis, or treats the word as descriptive of an analytic object. See Wittgenstein (1958).

7 We are not, of course, denying that cognitive operations are involved.

8 There are variations to this depending on the density of the traffic. If the sector is subdivided because traffic loads are heavy this complement will be increased.

9 Of course, not everything the ATCO does is intelligible in this way. There are occasions when the activities of a controller are puzzling even to the most

acculturated of observers. At such times interrogation might be necessary. But these are exceptions rather than routine.

10 The strips are in fact collected and used to calculate the cost of the ATC services. The agencies responsible for each aircraft are charged accordingly.

11 They can also be used *in lieu* of live strips when, for whatever reason, the latter are not output in time. They can also give advance warning of any input errors, such as incorrect flight plans and, in the event of computer failure, serve as a basis for manual calculation.

12 Controllers try to minimise the amount of communication between sectors, since it can take up valuable time, by using 'silent handovers', that is, using procedurally agreed flight levels for the transition between sectors.

13 Some controllers put the latest at the bottom. It depends entirely what is preferred by the individual controller. Nonetheless, assistants, who provide the new strips, need to be aware of this preference so that they can orientate their activities to ensure that they sustain the preferred order when placing new strips in the racks.

14 Though, as it happens, most controllers elect for the system not to display such data as it complicates the image presented on the radar screen.

15 Of course, and especially in complex discretionary systems such as ATC, what are diagnosed as 'routine' faults may, in the end, turn out to be so. This, if one likes, is the price paid for systems of such flexibility.

16 One of the more arguable efforts in this regard is the use of conversation analysis as informative for HCI design. See Luff, Gilbert, and Frohlich (1990).

Part IV

DESIGN AND IMPLEMENTATION

INTRODUCTION

The last two sections have been concerned with various aspects of the relationship between work activities, interactions and practices, and technology. In the second section the focus was upon how computer systems fit into the organisational and interactional contingencies of established work settings and in the third section upon work practices involved in the use of technology. However, the design, construction, and implementation of technology can also be thought of as the product of courses of practical action and interaction. That is, the actual development of technology can itself be viewed as, for example, in part the product of the 'work of design'. The two studies that make up this part of the book are both concerned with the activities and interactions that make up the work of developing technology.

In the first chapter in the section Wes Sharrock and Bob Anderson explicitly address aspects of the work of designers in an analysis of part of a meeting of software engineers who were attempting to solve a problem in the interfacing of two software components in a new photocopier. They show how, in part, the problem is one of a discrepancy in understanding between the two groups who have been responsible for the different parts of the software, and how work on the problem consists of the management of mutual understanding. Further, part of the solution to the problem consists of the parties to the meeting coming to an 'agreement' over a common problem. Thus part of the work of designing resides in the interactional work through which this agreement is organised.

This chapter also hits head-on the problem discussed in the first chapter of the book, which is how to preserve an understanding of technical work whilst also acknowledging the point that technology is a social production. It gives a particular concrete substance to some of the arguments made in the first chapter by considering how, for the people engaged in that work, matters such as reaching agreement, looking for and pursuing agreement are seen and understood to be, routine, ordinary features of designing technology within the exigencies of working in an organisation.

An interest in the practical activities and interactions involved in the actual development of technology is pursued by Kathleen Jordan and Michael Lynch in their study of the construction and implementation of a new molecular biology technique. Although the technology addressed in this chapter is biotechnology, nevertheless the problems faced in exporting the technology off 'the drawing board' and out of the laboratory or workshop and into production are problems common to computer systems development, and the processes of implementation that Jordan and Lynch discuss are processes that are equally involved in the implementation of computer systems.

Jordan and Lynch are concerned with how an 'experimental tool changes into a commercial means of production'. They suggest that what is involved is what they call 'mainstreaming' the technology. They use this term in preference to a more common term 'diffusion of technology' that has been previously used to gloss processes of implementation. They do so in order to draw attention to the situated work through which an application is organised as, and made to be relevant for, a project, or an industry. Thus, mainstreaming 'is meant to draw attention more closely to the activities through which a new technology is promoted and shaped for adoption in different domains of activity, while the activities themselves undergo systematic transformations in the process'. Part of the implementation process can then be seen as the creation of organisational milieux in which the application is then promoted as relevant. Further implementation also involves the spinning off and dispersion of the technological techniques involved. Just a cursory speculation about the way in which personal computers have become dispersed throughout whole ranges of work, through the promotion and organisation of their local relevance for work previously not associated with computer systems, will testify to the general applicability of 'mainstreaming' as a way of capturing processes of implementation.

148

8

WORKING TOWARDS AGREEMENT

Wes Sharrock and Bob Anderson

In Chapter 1 some of the issues of basic sociological principle which differentiate the studies collected in it were examined. The general direction from which this chapter approaches its topic (and without much preliminary discussion of issues of strategy or otherwise necessary disclaimers about the modesty of its aims) is that of 'ethnomethodology'. As such, it does not see itself as contributing to a putative 'sociology of software' which derives its inspiration from recent 'strong programme'-influenced traditions in the 'sociology of knowledge'[1] but follows in a line of 'studies of work' carried out by Harold Garfinkel and his colleagues.[2] Measured against the intensely demanding standards which Garfinkel has recently been setting for those studies, particularly that of becoming proficient in the work being studied, the modesty of our current investigations – into the design and development of photocopying and printing equipment – should again be stated: there is no prospect that we might acquire skills relevant to designing and building the software or hardware that goes into such equipment. This means that four studies provide for ethnographically informed conjectures about the work activities of those under study. Those studies so far are of design and development work on three projects being carried out at a UK site of the development and manufacturing division of a multinational corporation, and they have been routine observational inquiries, involving us in frequenting scenes of work activity and attending to (and recording) what goes on.

Though there will be no *extensive* theoretical/methodological preliminaries there will be some brief consideration of them, intendedly sufficient to orientate readers unfamiliar with the sociological meaning of our approach to the substantive materials discussed in some detail below. Those materials are intended to display the activities of a small group of software engineers in the midst of a meeting during which they are trying to work out why two interfacing software systems do not appear to be interacting properly. The examination of these materials represents very

149

much an initial and small part of the larger job of displaying and analysing the work that is involved in carrying through an engineering project. These preparatory remarks are needed to indicate that what follows is not intended to embody a (sociologically) theorised version of the nature of technological artifacts (be they hardware or software). Ethnomethodology has persistently been interested in the study of social phenomena as they can be found *prior* to the point at which they are subjected to reconceptualisation in terms of the (postulated) requirements of one or other of sociology's theoretical and methodological constructions. It has been interested, in a way that other sociologies have not been, in seeking to determine just what are, in the way of phenomena that, so to speak, 'anyone can find', the very phenomena that the other sociological strategies are (intendedly and indispensably) talking about. For example, amongst the proposed routes for a 'sociology of software' is one which aims to provide a 'labour process' analysis of it.[3] Our comments here are not critical of nor do they state any principled objections to the 'labour process' approach, but enable only the expression of a problem which 'the labour process' approach (or any of its direct rivals) present for us. The suitability of talking about a 'labour process' is dependent upon the invocation of a collection of pre-given *sociological* presuppositions *within which* it makes sense to talk of the work people are doing in such terms as the 'working of a labour process', with the claim being, of course, that the invocation of a vocabulary of 'labour process' provides the most correct and informative way to talk about the intended phenomena. We reiterate, the adoption, defence, and recommendation of those presuppositions is not at issue here, where the relevant question is: to talk about what? The phenomena which are to be written about in 'labour process' terms are ones which already possess a meaning, which are already assigned a definite sense within the world of daily life within which those activities are conducted. Talk about 'the labour process' is plainly intended to discuss in abstract ways whatever it is that employees are doing at work, those things which *make up their work*, the 'on the job' activities which are themselves observable and describable prior to and entirely independently of any invocation of the vocabulary of 'labour process' analysis or any competing sociological scheme. It is, therefore, *pre-theoretically* recognisable day-to-day work activities which a scheme like 'labour process analysis' proposes to discuss, it being the purpose of that (and cognate schemes) to reconstruct the character, and, most specifically and crucially, the meaning, of those activities.

The 'labour process' vocabulary (or any alternative to it) is designed to provide a re-description of activities which are pre-theoretically describable, but just what pre-theoretical identifiable activities are being re-described and just how the adoption of the vocabulary of re-description is intended methodically to transform whatever prior meaning they might have is something that ethnomethodology finds that standard sociological strategies fail to clarify. It is, of course, to the presentation of depictions of organised social activities *after* they have been transformed through theoretical/methodological re-description that the sociological literature devotes itself. It is to the identity that activities possess prior to and independently of sociological reconstrual that ethnomethodology by contrast devotes itself, taking the pre-theoretically identifiable day-to-day work activities as constituting the grounding phenomena of all sociological inquiry.

There is always some point in attempting to guard against gross, even crass, misinterpretation of arguments, especially when they are stated in the perfunctory way in which they have been here. What we have said perhaps runs a significant risk of being misunderstood, so as a precaution we should perhaps affirm in the strongest terms that we do not regard ethnomethodology as *an alternative* to 'labour process analysis' or any of the other potential sociological conceptions of software, as aspiring towards the production of an apparatus of theory and method which will enable the sociological re-conceiving of people's activities. Ethnomethodology's exercise is of an utterly different order to that conceived by 'labour process analysis' and its cognates.

Accordingly, therefore, we have no independently 'sociological' conception of hardware and software. The hardware and software are projected outcomes of the work in hand, and our actual investigative concern is, therefore, simply with whatever work is in hand – recognising, of course, that the work is hand is typically that which is directed towards the production of the projected outcome, that which comprises operations in the (elaborately concerted activity) of designing and developing (in the instance we shall be looking at) laser printing equipment. Most minimally, then, we will be simply reporting on some work – comprising an attempt to identify and resolve a problem in the software design which happens to get done on a particular engineering project. This particular episode from the work life under observation does not single itself out for any special reason, only for the reason that *any* episode might, that it provides an occasion to consider some of the multifarious circumstances with which those involved in software development have to contend and the ways in which these were practically 'managed'.[4] After all, this episode is one of those which any putative 'sociology of software' must inevitably claim to subsume. The fact that the episode involves a group working towards agreement does provide a modicum of thematic continuity between discussion of it and the debates which have been continuing for some years now within the 'sociology of knowledge' (which has in essential respects been equated, of late, with the sociology of science and technology).

Michael Lynch's adaptation of the notion of 'achieved agreement' from the work of Harvey Sacks[5] provides our guideline, as it replaces the more usual sociological concern with 'agreement' as something to be determined in abstraction from the overt concerns of society's members with that of examining occasions on which those members are engaged in explicitly attempting to bring about agreement. The software developers engaged in the exchange we present, describe, and discuss are quite overtly attempting to arrive at an agreement-in-so-many-words and we emphasise the situated character of such a quest, detailing (some of) the circumstances which provide them with the necessity for agreement and with the conditions under which agreement must be sought and brought about.

RECONSTRUCTING THE SOFTWARE

The following fragment of transcription provides a specific focus for our discussion, recording the exchange through which a small group of software engineers bring one phase of a protracted discussion to a close.

```
 1 Jay:    If we have 'out of paper' and 'duplex misfeed' is there
 2         any difference if the IOT or the ESS clears this
 3 Mick:   Before we do that although I agree that's the next
 4         logical step c'n we just test the understanding that
 5         what we have is a way of recovering from out of paper
 6         and a way of recovering from misfeed providing we do
 7         one or the other of these second columns.
 8 Jay:    Yeah's right. Is the conclusion then that in order to keep
 9         out of paper and misfeed operating in the same way
10         in re in recovery in the same way in the ESS we
11         only look at 'out of paper' when we attempt to
12         feed from an empty tray
13 Stan:   I don't know – I thought I heard from Sarah that the-
14         now she understood where our out of paper was coming from
15         you think that may be implementable
16 Sarah:  No no I could (0.1)
17 Stan:   because we would say we've got out of paper here
18 Jay:    Hold on that that's correct but that does not keep 'out of
19         paper' and 'misfeed' handled in the same way at all
20 Stan:   That's right, true true. I
21 Sarah:  (          )
22 Jay:    My preference for that was that if we make a statement that
23         we want to handle out of paper and misfeed in the same
24         way in recovery then we do not not take out of paper
25         when it goes empty only when we attempt to feed
26 Mick:   that's why I asked the question
27 Jay:    Yes
28 Mick:   I don't know what we have agreed
29 Jay:    I don't know if we're agreed, that was that was my
```

30   understanding.
31 Sarah: do you want to handle both in the same way if you want
32   this
33 Stan: I think it's totally up to the ESS to decide how they want to
34   handle it
35 Sarah: (   )
36 Max: but this happens very rarely it being
37 Sarah: I agree
38 Max: more an issue of very rarely it it's relatively unimportant
39 Jay: I think that's a very good point so Max consequently I would
40   think you'd like to recover in the same way so that the eh
41   image manager maybe doesn't have to do one thing in
42   one case and something else in another case eh
                             (0.5)
43   in any
44 Mick: Yep
45 Jay: in any event neither one of these two is the same as this
46 Sarah: Right
47 Mick: Agreed
48 Jay: Which everyone agrees to is so
49 Mick: So I think we can put a stake in the ground here and say
50   that because out of paper is the *rare* event we should make that
51   fall in line with the more common event which is misfeed
52   and the only recoveries available to us from misfeed are ones
53   which involve missed pitches. It really doesn't matter whether
54   it's one missed pitch or we cycle out and cycle back up again
55   as far as the communication is concerned. That's just an
56   efficiency factor.
57 Jay: Having said that very nicely can you capture that and pass
58   it on to Rick and Gordon so they'll understand why we're
59   arriving where we are.

These transcribed remarks occur after some ninety minutes of discussion in a meeting that lasted some six hours and involved five software developers, mandated to tackle a problem with the interfacing of two software systems.

The problem was (for those involved) a problem produced by the distributed production of the software. Two of the participants (Jay and Sarah) were from one of the corporation's sites on the West Coast of the USA, the other three (Mick, Stan, and Max) were from the local UK site in England's south-east. The software was for a laser printer which was designed to support networked workstations; the UK software engineers were building the software which would govern the operations of the output terminal (typically spoken of as the IOT) that transferred the image onto paper, whilst the US software operation was to develop an 'electronic sub-system' (typically called the ESS) that would generate the images and organise the printing jobs. Prototype machines had been built and a fleet of them were being put through tests at the UK site. At the time of this particular episode they were in a 'score test' phase. The machines were run under conditions intended to simulate routine use, with operators working their way through a series of prescribed 'jobs' and checking the machine's operations, recording all failures in considerable detail on a set of standardised forms. The testing involved the 'scoring' of identified problems against the various modules making up the machine (i.e. modules such as 'software', 'the stacker', 'the fuser', and so forth) and thus against the groups associated with the modules. The project itself was run on a 'management by problem solving' basis, which meant that all problems were catalogued on the computer and that project members were provided with 'problem lists' which effectively provided their work-load: they were required, that is, to work upon and solve the identified problems. Those problems were catalogued in terms of their seriousness and this identification provided, of course, a guide as to how tasks should be prioritised.

Whether or not the project was keeping to schedule was a persistent concern in all areas of its work and one of the ways in which the prospect of a schedule slip could be determined was through examination of the rates at which problems were being accumulated and cleared, i.e. whether they were continuing to accumulate new problems faster than they were clearing them. In the score testing phase, measures of machine performance relative to the standards which were set for exit from that phase also provided a basis for judging how the project was going. This, the 'Mersey' project, was failing to achieve the required standards and consequently suffering 'schedule slips'. The measures of performance were showing a substantial proportion of its current problems were attributable to the two software systems and it was at this point that the meeting which our transcript records was called; it was assumed that it was inadequate integration of the two software systems which was causing a significant proportion of the problems.

There were difficulties in the relations between project management in the two sites, with each (unsurprisingly) tending to blame the other. The test operations which were generating the fault reports were being conducted at the UK site and information about these was being routinely relayed to the US along with requests for corrective actions, but it was felt, at the UK end, that the US site was not recognising the seriousness and urgency of the situation and was failing to do necessary work. It was further felt that this was because the US team were not giving credence to the information from the UK and were discounting the problem reports they were receiving. It was against this background of reciprocal suspicion that it was agreed that two software engineers could be released from their work at the US site to visit the UK site specifically for the purpose of tackling problems of software integration.

Jay came over a week before the recorded meeting in order that he could obtain firsthand experience of the test operations and of the problems that were being identified there, as well as to talk directly and at length with those involved in developing the IOT software and managing its incorporation into the working machines – all this with a view to preparing a diagnosis of what the problem was. Sarah arrived in the UK the evening before the meeting and arrived on the premises a few minutes before the scheduled 9 a.m. start of the meeting. Sarah was the writer of the ESS software that involved the critical interfacing with the IOT software. The other participants in the meeting were Max, who was Sarah's UK counterpart, Stan, who was Max's software manager, and Mick, who was handling the 'systems problems', i.e. those that arose from assembling the machine's constituent modules into a working whole.

After his preparatory investigations Jay had provisionally identified a source of the integration problems, 'the clear stack command' and 'all its ramifications'. The printing operations involved the relaying from the ESS to the IOT of instructions for the formation of the image to be imprinted, and the system developed allowed the 'stacking' of a small number of commands prior to their execution. However, as everyone knows, the operations of printing equipment are hardly fault free and sheets of paper can fail to feed at the required moment: the machine can run out of paper or sheets can, in various ways, misfeed. Such failures require the abortion of the job in progress and the abandonment of instructions which have been stacked, and Jay's proposal was that it was the position in the sequence at which the command to clear the stack was given that was pivotal. The 'ramifications' of this had to do particularly with 'job recovery', with building software sequences which would enable the aborted printing operation to be resumed once the paper fault had been cleared. If a print job was to be aborted, how was this being done: was a 'hard shutdown' called with the machine's operations being immediately halted or would a 'soft' shutdown be used to allow the machine to continue operating long enough to eliminate sheets of paper that would be superflous to resuming the print job at the precise point at which it had been abandoned? And how was that resumption achieved? What complications did the fact that a print job involved 'duplex' printing (i.e. printing on both sides of the paper) have for recovery? In just what order were images transferred to paper to ensure that what was printed on both sides of the sheet was the correspondingly numbered pages?

These were matters which had been examined in the ninety minutes of talk which had preceded the point at which the transcript begins as its participants sought to determine whether Jay's diagnosis was correct. Their talk comprised, then, an attempt to reconstruct the operations of the software that had already been written and was implemented in the test machines, this operation taking place through their talking through the software operations, accompanied by the use of a flip chart to make a running record of the ongoing talk. Participants in the project typically manifest an intensely detailed knowledge of the features, operations, and ways of 'the machine', in the sense both that they are familiar with innumerable matters about 'the machine' as it figures in designs and specifications and that they are equivalently aware of the characteristics and performances of the prototypes in operation, down to the history of individual machines. This knowledge is one which they typically carry around 'in their heads', and against this background it is not, therefore, surprising that the parties set out to reconstruct the organisation of the software by talking it through rather than consulting records of its design.

The detailing of the sequences had revealed a discrepancy between the two groups with respect to the place in which 'out of paper' should be signalled from the IOT to the ESS. The IOT software had been written to call the fact that a paper tray had emptied at the point at which the fact that the last piece of paper had been taken from it was detected, but the ESS software was written on the assumption that this message would be sent not as the tray became empty, but at the moment at which there was an attempt to take paper from it, when there was an attempt to feed. The location of this divergence provided an opportunity for discussion of the possibility that symmetrical procedures could be followed in 'job recovery' for cases in which the paper tray had 'gone empty' and those in which the paper had, for some other reason, failed to feed, and it is towards the end of that discussion that the excerpt from our transcription begins.

Jay is advocating that a symmetrical procedure can be employed for recovery from both 'out of paper' and 'misfeed', and in the opening remark (lines 1–2) is canvassing a possible objection to his own proposal, that there might be a consequential difference as to which of the two software systems clears this.

Mick (lines 3–7) offers partial agreement with Jay, agreement that Jay has proposed a proper next step in working through the problem in hand, but provides an alternative proposal as to what the meeting's proper next step is, which is to ascertain what has already been agreed to, and Mick offers a characterisation of what that agreement is. Mick thereby initiates a sequence in which clarification of what has already been agreed to is sought.

Mick's characterisation of the agreed-to understanding is that there is a standard sequence of operations which can be carried out in 'job recovery' from the two different situations 'out of paper' and 'misfeed' which is portrayed on one of the flip charts (i.e. 'in one or other of these second columns'. Jay (lines 8–12) confirms this and elaborates the conclusion that he sees it to imply: that they should agree a standard policy for the point at

156

which 'out of paper' is signalled, which is when there is an attempt to feed from an empty tray.

This leads Stan (lines 13–15) to present a possible objection, though it is one which stands to be confirmed or rejected by Sarah, for it turns upon the understanding of what she had previously said. Stan has understood her as saying that now she has grasped the discrepancy between the ESS and IOT systems with respect to the place of the 'out of paper' signal in their respective sequences she could write software which would manage the discrepancy. Sarah's (line 16) response (which appears to disconfirm Stan's understanding of what she has previously said and to begin a restatement of what she could do) is overlapped by Stan's continuation (line 17) of his prior turn in which he begins to specify how 'we', i.e. the IOT software, call 'out of paper'.

Jay agrees (lines 18–19) with Stan's specification of how the IOT proceeds, but suggests that this is effectively missing the point at hand, which is to handle the 'out of paper' and 'misfeed' situations in the same way, and the point is conceded by Stan (line 20). Jay then (lines 22–5) reiterates in so many words the proposal that he is making which occasions Mick's tying back (in line 26) to his call for 'testing the understanding' (lines 3–7), and it seems as though Mick is saying that he had understood that this was what Jay was proposing but was uncertain as to how far others had agreed to this. Jay (lines 29–30) confirms that this is what he was advocating but does not know how far others have gone along with him.

Sarah (lines 31–2) attempts another intervention, one which begins as though it is going to spell out some of the practical consequences of any decision to adopt Jay's proposal, but it formulates this as a question to the others – 'do you want to handle both in the same way' – rather than as something for Sarah to decide herself. Stan's, reply (lines 33–4) disclaims responsibility for deciding this, returning this to Sarah and Jay – 'I think it's totally up to the ESS to decide how they want to handle it' – and Sarah's response is inaudible on the tape, but at this point Max, the software writer, intervenes (lines 36 and 38) in a way which intimates that argument may be unnecessary as the matter of the relative frequency of 'out of paper' and 'misfeed' events resolves the problem, a point which earns agreement from Sarah and from Jay who (lines 39–42) finds further support for his own position on the grounds that it provides the less complicated solution and therefore, perhaps, one which is 'easier to write'. Jay's contribution then draws expressions of agreement from Sarah and Mick and Mick then ventures (line 49) that the matter is settled and sets out (lines 50–6) in so many words what has been agreed to but also tying that back to what has been earlier determined, namely that there is no way of avoiding 'missed pitches'. 'Pitches' are the units in which the machine's belt moves and there is a recurrent concern with minimising the number of these which are unnecessarily made, and Mick is now drawing out that, having agreed to handle recovery in a symmetrical way and having agreed to handle it according to the procedures for recovery from misfeed, then they are also accepting that there will be 'missed pitches'.

THE RELATIONSHIP BETWEEN THE SOCIAL AND THE TECHNICAL

This sketch of the situation of the software problem within the engineering project together with some cursory observations on even a brief episode from a relatively protracted meeting may seem altogether too much (irrelevant) detail, though its presentation is not, in fact, without purpose. The provision of even a modest amount of detail shows how the work of engineering (in this instance, software engineering) is replete with social organisational considerations.

Against the background of recent work in the sociology of science and technology where the relation of 'the social' to 'the technical' is problematic, not to say controversial, the pervading of the detail of an episode of 'technical work' by social organisational consideration is hardly an irrelevant fact. The social organisational matters which we have identified are not, it should be emphasised, ones which we, as sociologists, have decided are relevant to an understanding of technical work, but are ones which the participants in that work pointed out to us or drew to each other's attention as relevant to the understanding and further conduct of their work activities. The connection between 'the social' and 'the technical' was *made for us* by those we studied in the course of and as part of the carrying out of their work activities, and it is, therefore, as phenomena of 'the day's work' that we consider these relationships.

The fact that there was a problem was, for those involved, one of the explicable and predictable troubles of their work. It was a product of the division of labour on the project, of work-load and work flow. With two groups independently writing software (which would, in operation, require detailed communication between and close coordination of the two systems) but without close reciprocal monitoring of the detailed designs, the likelihood was that somewhere along the line there would be unnoticed discrepancies between the two, which would manifest only when the two softwares were put into test. The division of labour was, further, the accountable source of the problem's character, which was not that there was a discrepancy between the two softwares, but that this discrepancy was persisting and producing a disproportionate and expanding share of the project's outstanding problems. The accountable source of this was divergent priorities between work sites. The major component of the UK site's current work was the running of the 'score test' and the solution of the problems that was generating, with part of that work being the recording and relaying of data on the problems scored against the US software.

Resolving the problems arising in testing was relatively low priority for the US operation but the UK designers were dependent on decisions about how the ESS was to be designed for the solution of some of their own problems, for in important respects the ESS was the dominant party, with the IOT group's own design decisions being dependent on those about how the ESS software was to be organised. This meant that, insofar as matters in the design of the ESS were unresolved, the IOT's problems could not be definitively worked out either. The integration problem was, further, in competition for attention: the work required for its solution would be additional to that scheduled for, and the recognition that the problem would not go away and would need to be addressed was accompanied by the recognition that it would not get addressed until it was 'worth' tackling and could be justified.

In this setting tasks are not entered into to see what it will take to do them. The carrying out of work is a matter of constant estimation: how much work is there to do, who is going to do it, how many people, for how long, doing what, needing what, with what assurance of success, and with what eventual product? It frequently turns out that the work does not go as estimated, very typically that it takes longer, is more uncertain of outcome, is more problematic, requires different personnel than have been estimated and resourced, but finding that the carrying out of the work is problematic is another of the 'normal, natural troubles' of this work. The carrying out of tasks is, then, typically a matter of trying to achieve them on the basis of estimated resourcing which may or may not prove adequate to their eventual completion. This *ad hoc* group assembled to tackle the software integration problem confronts the problem as one which they are confident they can solve; that there *will* be a solution is taken for granted, and the question is whether they will have 'long enough' to achieve it. There was the remainder of the working week at their disposal before the visitors returned to home base and to other work, and the target they had set themselves was that of finding ways of achieving 'a significant reduction' in the number of problems resulting from the interaction of the software systems. At the outset of their deliberations they could not say how long it was going to take them to work through the problem but they reminded themselves that they not only had to work out what the problem was/might be, but had to rewrite the software and try out the new version on some test machines to confirm that their diagnosis had indeed located the cause. They should bear in mind that there was some urgency to what they were doing, how much they needed to do in the time available, but should also recognise that the urgency was in the end to be subordinated to the need to ensure that they had an adequate solution: the risk of going for a solution just to get one was to be avoided.

That their deliberations were legitimately someone else's business was taken for granted by them. The *ad hoc* grouping involved collaborative work across two departments and the parties had their respective managers to satisfy, to show that assembling the group had been worthwhile and to convince that whatever solutions they might contrive were acceptable. Thus, Jay's remark which closes the excerpt from the transcript identifies Rick and Gordon, his managers, as ones who will need to be convinced of their proposals. However, not all interests in and demands on that work are necessarily legitimate. In Jay's view the design featured serious inadequacies, and there were pressures on the group to look for solutions which would compensate for those design deficiencies, but such requirements should be rejected. It was not this group's work to take on and solve problems built into the basic design, but to work for the best solution regardless of what others would like them to do.

The work on the problem in important respects consisted in the management of mutual understanding. The presumed source of the problem was in discrepant understandings between the two software writing operations, most specifically amongst those involved in writing the instructions that provided for the communication of their respective system with the other. The parties were all intensely, though variously, familiar with the design of the software and the performance of the machines, and the meeting proceeded – as already mentioned – through a round-the-table reconstruction of the organisation of the software, providing a collaborative specification of what they understood the software was doing or should be doing, with the result that uncertainties about each other's design were manifested and eventually (as discussed) a discrepancy in respect to the place of the 'out of paper' signal in the respective sequences was revealed. In respect of the solution of the problem the task then became that of defining a common policy, and the transcript records a part of that task, the formulation of an agreement to employ the symmetrical procedure in job recovery. The excerpt further shows the importance attached (as it was throughout the meeting) to ensuring that matters were explicitly agreed and that what was agreed to was understood in common ways.

CONCLUSION

The purpose of this sketchy exposition of a few moments in the life of an engineering project is to make the point that the claim that 'technical work' and the 'production of technology' are socially organised need not in itself be a contentious one, for its substantiation involves nothing more than drawing attention to things which are, for those engaged in such work, the most ordinary and natural features of carrying out their work, matters which they recognise as the routine (or not-all-quite-so-routine) exigencies of carrying through even a small, though currently critical, operation on the design and development of a piece of technology. In part, ethnomethodology's idea is to bring the abstractions of sociological thought 'back down to earth' and this we have here sought to do by offering a reminder that 'technical work' viewed from the point of getting it done involves the determination of such matters as how much work there is to do, specifically what things are required to do the work that is to be done, how long it will take, how many must be involved, how much time is available, how those involved are to combine their activities to carry the work through, and how they are to ensure that their activities will remain coordinated and synchronised over its course, what is to be done in various eventualities, who will make the judgement as to whether the work has been done satisfactorily and what it will take to satisfy them.

NOTES

1 For a review of such 'strong programme'-influenced initiatives toward a 'sociology of software', see Murray and Woolgar (1991).
2 See, for example, Garfinkel (1986).
3 The 'labour process' analysis derives from Marxian accounts of the organisation of work under capitalism, receiving recent impetus from Braverman's (1974) work. For the application of this approach to computing technology, see Friedman and Cornford (1989).
4 It may be important to add that we make no 'extrinsic' claims about the typicality of the doings we observed, are not concerned to advance our argument's cause on the grounds that it exemplifies things which are 'common', 'widespread', or 'typical' in software development. Our interest in these materials is not that they portray something which regularly happens but only in the fact that they did happen. Any concern with their putative generality is, for us, confined to that which is 'intrinsic' to the activities themselves, to the extent to which it matters, for those carrying out the activities, whether this situation is (say) a standard, familiar one or not.
5 Cf. the chapter 'Two notions of agreement' in Lynch (1985a: Chapter 6).

9

THE MAINSTREAMING OF A MOLECULAR BIOLOGICAL TOOL

A case study of a new technique

Kathleen Jordan and Michael Lynch

This study traces the construction and implementation of a new molecular biology technique as it changes from a highly specialised experimental tool to a commercial means of production. Like the computer technologies discussed in other chapters of this volume, biotechnology is sometimes described as a 'revolutionary' development with numerous social implications. Although digital computers are used by molecular biologists, the technique we describe in this chapter is largely a matter of manipulating an array of tools, biochemical extracts, and prepared ingredients. This technique, the polymerase chain reaction (PCR) has been developed within the past few years for quickly replicating specific target sequences of DNA. In theory, PCR provides an efficient way to create clonable reagents from single- or double-stranded DNA.

Like computer hardware and software a few years ago, PCR presently is being 'packaged' for use by scientists and non-scientists alike in an expanding array of fields. Biomedical researchers, archaeologists, forensics specialists, clinical diagnosticians, and others interested in analysing small or degraded samples of DNA can use PCR to 'amplify' the amount and upgrade the quality of the material. The technique is said to be much simpler and less time-consuming than alternative methods in molecular biology, and it is currently being promoted as an easy-to-use 'black box' for sale to medical facilities, forensics labs, and research labs in numerous basic and applied scientific fields. The corporate ownership and control of PCR is currently under negotiation. At the time of this writing, Perkin Elmer and Cetus are developing and marketing PCR kits and equipment, and their trade literature emphasises how it is virtually an error-free technique which can be used to increase the initial amount and quality of analysable DNA from minuscule and sometimes degraded samples of sperm, blood, skin, or hair. PCR figures prominently in AIDS research and in the nascent 'human genome project'.

When we speak of the 'mainstreaming' of PCR, we refer to a process

162

through which a technique with a specialised range of applications in an 'esoteric' activity is disseminated widely into a broad array of other institutionalised practices. Historians and sociologists are, of course, familiar with the fact that esoteric technologies can and often do develop into standardised production machineries and mass commodities. The theme of the 'diffusion of technology' is a common way for conceptualising this process,[1] but our use of the term 'mainstreaming' is meant to draw attention more closely to the activities through which a new technology is promoted and shaped for adoption in different domains of activity, while the activities themselves undergo systematic transformations in the process. In contrast to the picture of an entity gradually diffusing through the membranous boundaries between stable disciplines, the concept of 'mainstreaming' points intensively to the work, accomplished at any point of application, through which a new technology is made relevant to a project, industry, or practice. Moreover, it enables us more clearly to see how such projects, industries, and practices adjust to the technologies they incorporate, sometimes to the point of 'diffusing' disciplinary boundaries themselves.

Classical accounts of the 'rationalisation' of technique tend to describe a glacial movement through which a broad range of social institutions and practices become established. In contrast, the 'mainstreaming' of PCR has developed at an astonishing rate, and the rapid dissemination of PCR in diverse fields of activity has enabled us to perform a series of ethnographic 'spot checks' on some of the relevant points of distribution and transformation. This kind of study can supplement an historical overview of technological change, but it also opens up investigable topics that tend to be glossed over in the interest of a panoramic view.

The relevant time frame is so brief in this case that it has been possible for us to witness firsthand how a newly invented lab technique has been promoted and adopted in various fields and industries. PCR was invented just a few years ago, but the potential for applying it in diverse scientific, medical, and other settings was recognised almost immediately. It was intensely promoted, and efforts were made to develop and patent commercial PCR kits and accessory instruments which would enable easy, efficient, and error-free reproduction of the technique for a range of applications in science, medicine, criminal forensics, and the biotechnology industry. The technique is now a regular, and even an obligatory, part of the daily life and organisational routines in numerous disciplines, and great hopes have been invested in its potential for extending existing genetic knowledge and controlling an expanding array of individual and social pathologies. The brief history of PCR also indicates that there is significant technical and ethical controversy associated with its dissemination and use. Some of the controversy has to do with the apparent advantages of PCR when used as part of methods for 'genetic fingerprinting' (Dennis 1990) and 'mapping' the human genome (Rabinow

1990). Considered in the context of the massive development and deployment of electronic information technologies for encoding, monitoring, and managing human populations, PCR offers yet another enhancement of the ability to constitute, recognise, and control individual manifestations of 'deviance', and, less obviously, in conjunction with other molecular biological 'advances', it threatens to reinscribe the terms under which human subjects and their relevant identities are maintained in centralised files and made accessible to bureaucratic modes of intervention. As Rabinow points out, the encoding of genetic sequences with the aid of PCR is likely to boost the development of a neo-hygienics in which norms of health and behaviour are articulated in terms of a genetic code that becomes an increasingly public facet of personal identity. Although Rabinow recognises that efforts to enhance social control by investing in the development of one or another bio-informational register are by no means novel, he argues that the encoding of genetic standards of individual identity and normality promises to extend the degree to which bureaucratic authority can 'know' the individual and intervene in her life-world.

In this study, our focus will be a great deal more mundane and immediate than the futuristic scenarios painted by proponents and critics of the molecular biological 'revolution'. Both sides in debates about the human genome project and associated molecular biological developments tend to assume that, when sufficient time and money is allocated to the project, PCR and associated molecular biological techniques will enable an army of technicians successfully to map the sequence of a few billion base-pairs making up the human genome.[2] This assumption may be well founded, but it leaps ahead of a set of difficulties currently confronting efforts to routinise PCR. As we shall elaborate in this chapter, in many of the scientific fields and industries in which PCR is presently applied, it is far from a trouble-free routine. Practitioners in different fields give entirely different accounts of how the technique is accomplished, what it is good for, and how well it works. This is not particularly unusual in molecular biology, a field that is often said to involve an element of 'black magic' (Cambrosio and Keating 1988; Jordan and Lynch in press). Routine molecular biological techniques do not readily transfer from one lab to another, or even from one individual practitioner to another.[3] The number of steps, the degree of precaution exercised, and the specific ingredients used in the 'recipe' are subject to numerous local variations in research agendas and informal styles of work between particular research groups and individual researchers. Such variations can be viewed as inevitable, and for the most part trivial, slippages in the application of more or less standard routines, but as we shall elaborate in this chapter they occasionally become sources of confusion, contention, and frustration which can call into question the presumed uniformity and universality of the technique. The 'mainstreaming' of PCR has been a more contingent and complicated process than both the promoters and critics of biotechnology lead one to imagine. Our investigation is far from complete, but thus far we have been apprised of numerous complexities and contingencies in the application of PCR. Aside from informing us about the typical 'bugs' that need to be ironed out of a practice when it is adapted to a new setting, this investigation has opened up the issue of how the various producers and consumers of PCR technology struggle to maintain a stable and reliable complex of practices.

The research described in this paper covers some of the different sites and phases in the 'mainstreaming' of PCR. For the past two years we have followed the 'career' of PCR as it has been promoted in the trade literature and adopted in different fields of science, medicine, and industry. We interviewed lab directors, managers, post-doctoral researchers, and technicians in university and industrial laboratories covering different fields of science and medicine. The fields of study in these settings included population genetics, AIDS research, and diagnosis of prenatal genetic 'defects'. Some of our interviews were conducted whilst practitioners performed the steps of the PCR procedure, and we also were shown how to perform PCR ourselves. This enabled us to become better acquainted with the technical language and practices associated with the technique, so that we could more closely identify practical sources of error and contamination, as well as practical precautions against and remedies for those problems.[4] From the interviews and other materials, we were able to get a clearer idea of the way PCR has been 'packaged' for different scientific, medical, and forensic applications, and we gained an appreciation of the contingencies that come into play when the technique is performed by differently trained practitioners and technicians, and in different institutional circumstances.

In the sections below, we shall start by sketching the short history of PCR's development, and while doing so we shall outline the rudiments of how the technique is performed. Then we shall discuss how PCR has been promoted as a technique that unites the interests and practices of a broad range of disciplines. Following that, we shall journey into 'PCR Hell' to discuss some of the occasional and persistent problems associated with making the technique 'work' in actual practice. Many of these problems have to do with 'contamination,' and, as we shall argue, a concern with sources of contamination is a major impetus for transforming the 'cottage industry' of laboratory molecular biology to a more thoroughly disciplined manufacturing process.

BACKGROUND

The development of recombinant DNA technology (including cloning, gel electrophoresis, and southern blotting) fundamentally changed the focus and practice of biology, medicine, forensics, and numerous other fields.

The molecular biological 'revolution' is sometimes said to have resulted from the introduction of an array of diverse techniques rather than a central theory (Burian 1991; Kay 1991). A family of molecular biological techniques such as cloning, gel electrophoresis, southern blotting, and the like now form a common 'language' for uniting diverse disciplines (Fujimura in press).[5] As each new procedure adds to the repertory of molecular biological techniques, the rate, or at least the expected rate, of scientific production is accelerated, with consequent reductions in labour time. As an indication of the extent of these reductions, a panellist at the first Human Genome meeting in 1989 reminisced about a project that was performed in the early 1980s, in which '[a]bout 60 very bright young people worked for a year and a half. Six months ago, by new techniques, a single investigator generated the necessary information to clone a gene and execute the experiments in about 7 days. That's a remarkable difference in speed and ease, all driven by new technologic developments' (Caskey, quoted in Cantor et al. 1989: 8).

In a way, the 'world picture' promoted by molecular biology is a thoroughly technical one: *technique* is both the model of laboratory production *and* the substantive image of the intracellular 'work' through which genetic instructions are translated into flesh. Regardless of how one views the molecular biological revolution, it is clear that in many established disciplines entirely new sets of questions are being asked and new competencies are being demanded as molecular biological techniques are adopted. At the same time novel linkages between separate disciplines are being articulated. It is also the case that techniques like PCR, although they are relied upon increasingly in an ever widening set of fields, are presenting practitioners with many problems associated with getting even the more routine procedures to work consistently and reliably. As some of the practitioners we interviewed acknowledge, such problems can greatly reduce the efficiency and productivity promised by those technologies.

PCR is perhaps the most powerful molecular biological technique developed to date. Its invention is credited to Kary Mullis and the staff at Cetus Corporation, a major biotechnology firm. The procedure was first published in a methods report that appeared in a 1985 issue of *Science* (Saiki et al. 1985). From the outset, the technique was billed as a more direct, much more sensitive, quicker, and more effective means for the analysis and detection of genetic mutations.[6] Since 1985, the technique has become increasingly automated, less time-consuming, and less expensive.

PCR allows for quick replication of specific DNA sequences, thus enabling small (and sometimes degraded) samples of DNA to be 'amplified' (greatly increased in amount and analysability).[7] The larger amounts of uniform genetic material can be indispensable for experimentation, medical diagnosis, or forensics. The technique's effects are not especially glamorous, since they mainly have to do with duplicating genetic material more efficiently than was practicable with alternative methods. In essence, PCR accelerates the pace of production. This is no trivial matter, however, because in the domain of molecular biology this collapsing of time may have no less profound implications than did collapsing the scale of electronic components for the computer industry.

When a continuous sequence of DNA base-pairs has been characterised, PCR enables practitioners to multiply and purify an existing sample of such fragments. Before PCR was invented, the only way for researchers to purify a selected DNA fragment was through technically difficult, cumbersome, and labour-intensive recombinant DNA cloning procedures that usually required ample amounts of high quality starting material. One well-advertised advantage of PCR is that it circumvents such intricate labour-intensive procedures, thus making it possible to obtain sufficient quantities of targeted DNA fragments for analysis and cloning. PCR has become partially automated and easily packaged, much more so than perhaps all other molecular biological techniques. So, for example, assuming that appropriate chemical components are in hand, along with some knowledge of the DNA sequence of interest, all that is needed is a 'black box' in the form of a heating block termed a 'thermal cycler'. For many of the more common research or diagnostic tasks, PCR 'kits' are now commercially available. These contain pre-measured ingredients for a particular application (e.g., for amplifying an initial sample of a gene believed to cause sickle-cell anaemia), so that the lab practitioner no longer needs to prepare ingredients from scratch. The advantages are advertised much in the way a commercial cake mix is sold to a kitchen 'technician' as a neat way to avoid the time-consuming work of measuring out raw ingredients.

PCR is performed through a repetitive cycle of operations which is designed first to 'denature' or 'unzip' pairs of DNA strands from each other, and then, with the help of a polymerase enzyme, to build up a 'new' complementary strand of nucleotides along a selected portion of each 'old' strand. At the end of this cycle two new double-stranded DNA sequences have been produced from the initial strand, each being composed of one old and one new strand.[8] Each cycle consist of three phases: (1) denaturing at high temperature (94° centigrade) to unzip the DNA strands that will serve as templates; (2) annealing at a moderate temperature (50° C.) to bond the primers to their selected complementary region sequence on templates; (3) synthesising at moderate temperature (72° C.) to complete the replication of complementary strands. After the end of the first cycle, a double-stranded DNA molecule should be produced (i.e. a double helical sequence of complementary nucleotides). Repeating the cycle should then double the existing number of these pairs, and the process continues. Ideally, twenty-five cycles of denaturing, annealing, and synthesising should produce 33 million copies from a single double-stranded DNA segment. 'Workable' amounts of a DNA fragment can thus been obtained by repeating the cycles of the PCR technique.

An important aspect of PCR's development was the exploitation of an unusual bacterium 'thermus aquaticus' (Taq). This bacterium is found in hot springs, and its polymerase enzyme has the unusual property of being able to withstand high temperatures without breaking down (thus enabling the bacterium to reproduce in the hot spring milieu). When Taq polymerase is used as an ingredient in PCR, it enables a given sample to be heated repeatedly to 94° C. without degrading its ability to synthesise DNA. The thermostable property of Taq polymerase has allowed PCR technology to be partially automated, since it is no longer necessary to add a new batch of polymerase after each heating cycle. In the automated procedure, all PCR components – DNA samples, single nucleotide building blocks, Taq polymerase, primers and buffers – are placed in miniature plastic test tubes which are then inserted into a thermal cycler which is set automatically to raise and lower temperatures for a specified number of cycles. More recently, another enzyme known as 'vent polymerase' – extracted from a bacterium that lives at the edge of hot deep-sea vents – has come on to the market. It is supposed to have the advantage of a 'proofreading' capacity – a naturally built-in check on whether templates have been copied exactly – but some of the practitioners we interviewed described difficulties in realising these advantages in practice.

PROMOTING THE BLACK BOX

PCR is said to have several advantages: it is partially automated, only small quantities of sample material are needed, samples do not need to be of high biological quality (the DNA can be somewhat degraded), and the procedure takes only a few hours to perform. Most of the scientists and technicians we interviewed agreed about these advantages, and to an extent they echoed the upbeat trade literature and promotional campaigns sponsored by corporations that market PCR kits and thermal cyclers. PCR has been promoted as a 'black box' that eliminates much of the intricate and difficult craft of molecular biology. Two major components of this black box are the thermal cycler – which indeed *is* a box in which test tubes are placed and run through repetitive temperature cycles – and the commercial 'kits' that include pre-measured amounts of primers for specific genetic materials along with the polymerase enzyme. Further ingredients are available on the commercial market for enhancing the quality of performance and 'product' from PCR. With brand names like 'Perfect Match' and vernacular names like 'elf dust', these ingredients are promoted much in the way that products for enhancing health and technical performance are advertised for larger groups of consumers. Other items of

168

less specifically 'dedicated' equipment are used in association with PCR. These include plastic test tubes with snap-on caps, pipettes with disposable tips, and electrophoresis gels.

The metaphor of the 'black box' has become familiar in social studies of science; perhaps too familiar, because like many social science concepts its popularity has been accompanied by an increasingly diffuse set of meanings, and applications. In social studies of science a 'black box' can mean anything from a taken-for-granted practice, an established fact, or a device that is used without much understanding of its inner workings.[9] One of the more precise definitions is given by Latour (1987: 131) who says that a black box is a device (or a discourse) where 'many elements are made to act as one'. He gives the example of the Kodak automatic camera, in which the various components of previous camera models were fused into a fixed assembly. Where photography had previously been the province of professionals who continually assembled and reassembled the components of the camera, the automatic camera was sold to 'anybody' who could point the device and push the shutter release. An important point for Latour is that when Eastman introduced the automatic camera his firm assumed centralised control over the many elements that act 'as one', placing the numerous amateur photographers who purchased the device in a dependent relationship to the company's expanding array of products and services. Other examples of such fused and opaque assemblies include printed circuits, silicon chips, and 'user-friendly' software. At present, the various constituents of PCR are considerably more loosely coupled than the parts of an automatic camera. It is clear, however, that Perkin-Elmer, Cetus and other corporations that market thermal cyclers, kits, and other elements of PCR are working very hard to build a black box and control its distribution. Moreover, they are using patent legislation to assure a degree of control over the identity and distribution of the technique.[10] Aside from their efforts to objectify the technique, the proprietors aim to stamp it, along with various of its constituent materials and instruments, with a binding identity and trademark that controls its dispersion. Latour's general definition may serve to articulate the operative 'theory' of the corporate promoters and proprietors of PCR, as they attempt to extend and control the use of their product, and, if we were to attend to *their* accounts alone, we could rest assured that PCR (or at least some of its components) is a clear case of a black box that can be 'plugged in' and set to work, regardless of the local circumstances under which it is used or of the users' personal knowledge and depth of understanding.

PCR has been promoted through many of the established outlets for advertising in science and medicine. One of the more unique forms of promotion occurred not through advertising, but through commercial sponsorship of a theme conference in which scientists testified about the uses of PCR. In 1989 Cetus Corporation sponsored the UCLA Symposium

169

Series at Keystone ski resort in Colorado.[11] Along with Perkin-Elmer (the instruments company that produces the thermal cycler), Cetus promoted a five-day instruments workshop entitled 'The Polymerase Chain Reaction: Methodology and Applications'. The conference was organised at short notice, but Cetus later announced an attendance of over 400 scientists from a broad range of disciplines and applied settings, 125 of whom presented poster sessions on the technical uses of PCR in their disciplines. The topics covered included evolutionary biology, immunology, and the genetics of cancer, and numerous medical and forensic applications were discussed. The conference brought together scientists who otherwise would have seen little connection between their researches. With PCR as the organising theme and lingua franca, disciplinary boundaries were, at least for the duration of the conference, put aside in favour of a *technical* common ground. The gathering was not simply a promotional gimmick, since actual research was presented, discussions were joined, and lasting 'connections' between diverse specialists were facilitated. Of course, those in attendance were relied upon to spread the word about PCR's virtues and uses to potential subscribers. Although, for the most part, the conference was an interdisciplinary forum for biomedical researchers of various stripes, it was made clear that the technique was suitable for a range of applications in other fields.

The symposium was but one occasion in a complex set of efforts by scientific instrument and supply companies to proselytise applications for the new technique. Although it was a unique event, for us it provided significant evidence of a trend in the development of molecular biology where, as mentioned above, the basis is not a new conceptual framework that revolutionises a particular discipline. Instead, the 'revolution' manifests as a particular way of *disciplining* the organisation of work in an array of pre-existing scientific fields. Rather than manifesting through the emergence and resolution of controversy in a coherent disciplinary community, this 'scientific revolution' takes the form of a technical economy that infiltrates diverse disciplines. The 'battleground' on which this revolution is fought is not necessarily that of a theoretical controversy; rather, it assumes a dispersed and much quieter form of apparently disconnected struggles to adopt molecular biological techniques, and to 'make them work' under the local conditions of one or another practice.

A JOURNEY INTO 'PCR HELL'

I don't think you know how I hate talking about PCR. It has given me nothing but grief. I wish it never was invented. It just leads you down the rosy path to hell.

(A molecular biologist)

170

The lab directors, post-doctoral researchers, and technical staff we interviewed all acknowledged numerous problems with making PCR 'work'. The corporate promoters of PCR were well aware of these problems, although not unexpectedly they treated 'PCR Hell' as a problem to be remedied by one or another technological fix sold on the market. Many of the problems with PCR have to do with contamination. According to the practitioners we interviewed, the technique is very sensitive to small amounts of contamination. For example, when a fragment of DNA with a sequence similar to the target DNA sequence is transmitted through aerosol or other source of contact with sample materials used in the experiment, the results may be invalid. Although preventive measures are available, according to Dennis (1990: 11), under some conditions there are no reliable procedures to test for contamination. Prior research (Jordan and Lynch in press), indicates that questions of material contamination are bound up with sociological questions of ritualisation, rationalisation, and the social distribution of knowledge.

When laboratory practitioners conduct experiments and use laboratory equipment they operate with palpable materials and readable traces that are organised within the spatiality and temporality of the 'life-world'. While handling equipment, performing steps in a set order, keeping track of time, and dispensing measured amounts of ingredients, they articulate 'what they are doing' in terms of an invisible order of things. According to an account of PCR by a researcher in a biotech firm:

> you have to *believe* that there is a polymerase in there. Even though you never see the polymerase (you 'don't know his name') you know there's a polymerase there and that it's actually going to do what you want it to do. It's just amazing that you put it together, you put it through these 30 cycles or whatever and you get something out. I mean it's amazing the first time it works when you do it. To me it's amazing that it actually works.

This researcher went on to give us an analogy for thinking about this process of working with unseen agents and reactions that only become accountable through a display of the 'product':

> you can't see what's going on. It's like teaching a class over the phone and you don't know who's in your class. You don't know anything. The only thing you know is the average test grade that comes back. So you try a method of teaching and you get an average test grade and it's not what you would like, so you try something else and you know your teaching skills, you know all what *should* work, and you keep trying new things and eventually you get something . . . you never see what you're doing. You only see the results so you might even write a book and say: 'this is the way you should teach, because this will be the

result you will get.' But since every class might be different and people who are teaching might try different styles and what works for them, they might say, 'This is the way you should do it.' I think it's that way with PCR also.

(MM: 7–8)

It would be far too simple to say that the lab technique consists of two parallel tracks: a 'macroscopic' surface order of practices, described in a recipe and performed at the bench, and a 'molecular' deep structure of invisible events within the test tube (e.g., denaturing of DNA strands, annealing of primers, construction of a sequence of base-pairs between the primers, etc.). It would be too simple because the language of molecular events articulates what a practitioner is seen to be doing *at the bench.* To say that 'I just added 7ul of 10mM dATP to the 2x buffer' is a more precise description for many practical purposes than 'I am dropping a minuscule amount of this clear liquid from the end of this syringe-like pipette into this blue plastic test tube'.[12] Of course, the practitioner does not *see* the molecular order of things, even though that order is featured in any competent account of how the practice is organised and assessed. The success of the procedure is assessed by reference to the end product: an autoradiograph display of molecular 'product' (see, for instance, Amann and Knorr-Cetina 1990). When the graphic display shows a smaller amount of 'product' or a different molecular yield than expected, researchers are often baffled about what might have gone wrong: 'It's kind of funny because you can never see the stuff and you'd never know why it doesn't work' (MM: 3).

The mere fact of 'invisibility' does not by itself imply uncertainty, since invisible entities and forces are often implicated without question in the reliable operation of techniques and machines (Hacking 1983). The problem for many researchers is that they simply cannot get PCR to work with any regularity, and they are left with no account. Their situation is analogous to an imaginary one depicted by Wittgenstein 1958: §142): 'The procedure for putting a lump of cheese on a balance and fixing the price by the turn of the scale would lose its point if it frequently happened for such lumps to suddenly grow and shrink for no obvious reason'. In the case of PCR, the amount and quality of 'product' grows and shrinks, and practitioners are often left without 'a reason'. In molecular biology this problem has to do with the morass of possible sources of variability and contamination. For instance, a practitioner told us that when she attempted to replicate PCR after having gotten an acceptable product on a prior attempt, 'I did it again using the same conditions and it didn't work. Nothing worked' (VF: 5). Similar frustrations can attend a series of attempts to improve an initially 'poor' result by varying parameters of the procedures (temperature settings, timing, precautions, and amounts of sample DNA, primers, and buffers). A researcher can be led to ask, 'I'm an intelligent person, why can't I get this to work?' (VF: 4). Despite their belief that the procedure *should* work as described in publications and demonstrated by other practitioners, novices (and sometimes more experienced practitioners) can go through an agonising series of failed attempts to get acceptable data. *That* is what is known as 'PCR Hell'.

To a large extent, these problems with PCR resemble many of the troubles identified in previous laboratory ethnographies (Latour and Woolgar 1979; Garfinkel *et al.* 1981, Knorr-Cetina 1981; Gilbert and Mulkay 1984; Lynch 1985a; Garfinkel *et al.* 1989). However, the problems associated with contamination are particularly acute in the case of PCR and, by focusing upon them, we are able to grasp how the adoption of PCR in a laboratory has far-reaching implications for the practice and organisation of a discipline. Contamination is a bridging concept through which practitioners learn to 'see' the molecular implications of their equipment, embodied practices, purchasing decisions, and social interactions. It is a two-way street. On the one hand, researchers become attuned to the way their bodies, movements, equipment, and routine exchanges provide inadvertent practical pathways through which 'unwanted' DNA can travel and, on the other hand, the molecular 'product' is deciphered in terms of how a nexus of practices could have made it turn out that way.[13] Because PCR amplifies specific sequences of DNA in a sample, it can sometimes amplify genetic materials that were inadvertently introduced into the sample from a practitioner's hands or clothing, a pipette that was used in other experiments, water, mislabelled ingredients, and airborne viruses. An entire nexus of practical precautions, specialised equipment, purchases, segregations, and agreements are designed routinely to contend with these possibilities. In sum, these comprise a kind of organisational prophylaxis: disposable gloves and pipette tips are used; novices are instructed on how to draw materials into the pipette and to release them without introducing aerosol contamination; practitioners work out formal and informal arrangements for segregating stocks of equipment, bench space, and other laboratory territories that could conceivably introduce contamination; and primers and other ingredients are purchased in kits from a 'trusted' company that is alleged to have a good track record.

Problems with PCR nevertheless were said to persist despite the many precautions and remedies: 'The problems come and go. It's a *mystery*. Sometimes it works and sometimes it doesn't. Sometimes the DNA is very sequenceable and sometimes it isn't. I mean at the moment, it's pure *art*. And it's not even art, it's magic!' (PA: 4). The precautions and remedies were themselves said to be sources of further contingencies. Because results were uneven, and the sources of variation were never fully evident, each practitioner, and each group of practitioners, introduced further variations into the PCR technique as they sought to maximise their product and guard against contamination. They recognised that their 'own' variant of the procedure incorporated steps, recipes, methods of handling equipment, and so forth that were untested. They acknowledged that their procedure relied heavily on trusting colleagues from whom they adopted recipes and on a faith in the quality of a particular company's kits or ingredients.

> when you talk to people you kind of hear which technique seems to be working among the most people. . . . You know, some people make single-stranded, some people do double-stranded sequencing, you know, so you have the whole variation but you want to hear what method crops up the most. Which is the most reliable.
>
> (VF: 4)

Practitioners rarely have the time or inclination to perform controlled experimental tests of the many unique parameters incorporated in one or another variant of PCR. Given how difficult it is to get the procedure to work reliably, and to account for sources of variation, it is not at all clear that controlled runs would provide a stable enough background for conducting such tests. Consequently, researchers tinker with the recipes, try different variations in the heating cycle, and try out different commercial products until a 'good enough' yield of product results.[14]

FROM COTTAGE INDUSTRY TO A COMMUNITY OF LABORATORIES

Many 'contagions' and related difficulties with making PCR work are inherent in the informal routines, allocation of space, and equipment of a lab. One university facility stood out as the most informal of those we visited: it was outfitted with soft living-room chairs, as well as the shiny counter-tops, sinks, and other equipment usually associated with a lab. The lab director spoke of his field (evolutionary biology) as a 'relaxed cottage industry', and noted that his efforts to share information about the PCR technique using computer networks amounted to nothing. Participants in the field, he said, are neither competitive nor overly gregarious about such matters. The local research group was small, and it shared some of the more expensive instruments and specimens with other labs, and relied upon others to synthesise primers. A researcher in this lab was instructed in PCR by going to a colleague's lab: 'That's how we do it . . . . We all know each other, it's very informal . . . . If you got a problem and I can help you, well, call me up' (PA: 4–5). Despite this training, the researcher had an especially difficult time getting PCR to work, and it seems that much of her struggle had to do with developing singular applications of the technique for her lab's research. She relied upon word of mouth, customised primers produced at a university facility outside the lab, standard equipment, and formal recipes, and was largely left to wade through a morass of possibilities for adapting these resources to the task at hand. PCR was simply not a prominent, or even a highly valued, part of the intellectual or practical milieu.

The labs at a biotechnology firm we visited had a somewhat more standard appearance, but they were not remarkably different from many university facilities: the counters, shelves, and sinks that occupied the centre and lined the walls of each facility were filled with a jumble of equipment: beakers and vials, tangles of surgical tubing, stacks of paper and texts, small appliances, etc. Each lab was named after the researcher who headed the team that used it, although people moved freely about from one to another. Without marking their 'stalls' (Goffman 1971) with specific labels or barriers, practitioners laid claim to selected territories and equipment for their projects. They presumed common understandings about the distribution of communal supplies (materials, lab clothing, etc., supplied by the company), although these understandings were approximate, *ad hoc*, locally arranged, and unwritten. Although this was a corporate facility, it exhibited many of the 'organic' organisational properties of a university laboratory: collegial trust, flexible schedules orientated to tasks at hand, reliance on tacit knowledge and craft. Production of DNA products was done in small batches, custom fitted to the ever-changing demands of the experimental work.

PCR was used routinely in this lab for numerous experiments. The facility was outfitted with a thermal cycler, as well as a machine for sequencing genes and instruments for producing electrophoresis gels. Such equipment was not, however, set to work as though fused together in a 'black box'. A researcher who gave us a tour of that laboratory mentioned that he and his co-workers often mix their own buffers and 'make' their own primers, since their experiments often involve unusual segments of DNA for which commercial primers are unavailable. For convenience, he said, they sometimes purchase commercial kits with pre-mixed ingredients, but they maintain an intellectual understanding of the molecular biological mechanisms at work.

A different picture of how PCR was integrated with lab routines was given by the director of a commercial diagnostic laboratory. Unlike the more 'academic' labs, in this diagnostic lab, she said, 'you are performing the same amplification reaction over and over and over again routinely. You're not trying, you know, to make new products all the time on unknown regions of the genome' (LC: 5). Technicians were trained to do routine work, and to *expect* to do routine work. Overall, this firm had a generally more 'disciplined' production process.

> protection against contamination is something that has another order of magnitude of gravity in diagnostics. So for example, we don't do PCR in the same room that we do all the other analysis in

diagnostic labs. They happen to be actually at opposite ends of the building which is not that important but once a sample has been amplified, amplified products never go out of that lab and similarly native DNA samples that have been isolated from . . . patients don't go out of the other laboratory. And the equipment also never travels between laboratories. Only the people do. Technicians have to wear gloves when they're doing that work, which they have to actually for a variety of reasons.

(LC: 5)

Because of the serious consequences of misdiagnosis due to contamination of PCR, this research director noted that the field is likely to see more government regulations in the future. She also pointed out another trend in the control and distribution of PCR, which was the advent of patents on the technique and on certain of its applications. Cetus Corporation, as of this writing, still holds the patent for PCR,[15] and it negotiated with another company, Hoffmann-LaRoche, to give that firm exclusive rights to apply PCR technology for diagnostic purposes, and Hoffmann-LaRoche in turn can now sub-license other laboratories. For the 'community of laboratories' that began with academic research and adapted their research techniques to commercial purposes, 'PCR in diagnostics is sort of the first introduction to the discomfort and the realities of business, of the business world, which is characterised by proprietary information by proprietary methodologies by royalties and licensing fees left and right' (MM: 2).

CONCLUSION

The limited number of interviews we have completed thus far suggest a rough trend toward centralised licensing requirements, patent royalties, and stringent organisational controls against 'contamination'. However, we do not want to leave the impression that the 'cottage industry' of academic laboratory science is being transformed unilaterally and at every point of application by the introduction of PCR and related techniques. Reliance on word of mouth, informal controls against contagion, and the artisanal work of constructing primers and unique combinations of re-agents continue to persist whenever university and industrial labs investigate DNA sequences that are not yet part of a standard diagnostic or productive economy. A 'mainstream' demand for and dissemination of standardised primers, kits, and appliances presupposes a relatively uniform set of applications for that technology. To some extent that demand may be enhanced by the promotion of these kits and appliances, and by the construction of 'appropriate' organisational milieux for their use when biotech firms expand their ability to produce large batches of a particular genetic product. In brief, 'mainstreaming' seems to work not only by an historical transformation of a cottage industry into a factory system, but also through a series of collisions and mergings of relatively localised modes of routinisation. In some milieux, PCR is incorporated as another tool in a bricoleur's assemblage, while in others it becomes a machinery for producing an enterprise's product. The significance of 'product' (as data, diagnostic material, or legal evidence), the relevant standards and regulations, and the legal and practical concerns about contamination can vary accordingly. 'Mainstreaming' is therefore not a linear transformation, but a lateral 'spinning off' and dispersion of scientific techniques, some of which are appropriated and promoted as commercial tools and products.

NOTES

1 Latour (1987: 141ff.) criticises the 'diffusion model' of technological development for the way it implies that an innovation retains constant properties as it crosses the boundaries between different interest groups. To replace it he recommends a 'translation model' which identifies how a technological innovation is subjected to innumerable transformations as it is promoted, adopted, adapted, discarded, and hybridised by different collectivities in endless chains of association.

2 It is not entirely clear what the 'human genome' is, and in many respects 'it' is an ideal type. The idea that each human being is endowed with a genetic code – a unique sequence of complementary base-pairs making up the backbone of the DNA double helix – is not controversial. What is more problematic is the idea that it will be possible to define a species-specific genome that is not biased by assumptions about which variations in the 'endowments' of an individual or population are to be counted as normal or pathological. Relatedly, there is considerable doubt about what proportion of the DNA in any cell counts as part of the 'genome'. Much of the DNA in any cell seems not to be 'expressed' functionally in the traits and characters of the organism, so any effort to define the essential sequential elements of the genome will require an abstraction of genetically relevant DNA sequences from the matrix of 'junk DNA' in which it is embedded.

3 As Harry Collins (1985) demonstrates, the replication of experiments and the reproduction of technological devices from plans can be difficult in any case. These problems are, however, more explicitly acknowledged in biology, and especially in molecular biology, for reasons that have not been explicated in any detail in social studies of science. It is imaginable that molecular biologists have no more difficulty with the reproduction of their techniques than do particle physicists or radio astronomers, but, for some of the reasons we shall elaborate later in this paper, it seems likely that the quasi-serious association of molecular biology with 'black magic' is no accident.

4 Our interviews were tape recorded, because it was often crucial to get the exact words and phrases used by informants when they characterised their practices. The style of interview was open-ended, and conversational, using a consistent roster of questions designed to raise topics without constraining what the informants said about them. We aimed to elicit researchers' and technicians' accounts of how PCR works, how reliable it is, how it is adapted to different applications, and what can go wrong with it. Our interviews were informed by our having read technical and trade publications on PCR and related areas of

molecular biology (e.g., Maniatis 1982/1989; Erlich 1989; Innis *et al.* 1990; Young *et al.* 1990). These sources enabled us to gain an understanding of the range of applications, the methods of promotion, and the actual uses of the techniques.

5 Gel electrophoresis is a way of separating negatively charged DNA fragments by size or length of base-pairs through a gel medium. Southern blotting is a more specific targeting procedure for identifying DNA fragments of interest. The technique transfers DNA that has been separated by gel electrophoresis on to a mitrocellulose membrane.

6 In January 1988 a major advance in PCR technology was published once again in *Science* by the same Cetus research team (Saiki *et al.* 1988). At that time, a polymerase enzyme for thermus aquaticus bacteria (Taq), which remains stable at high temperatures, was incorporated into PCR.

7 Like all molecular biological techniques, PCR is based on the assumption that DNA is made up of complementary strands of four nucleotide bases, which are conventionally labelled by the letters A, T, C, and G (adenine, thymine, cytosine, and guanine). Strands of DNA are said to be made up of variable sequences of these nucleotides, and pairs of these strands are joined by relatively weak chemical bonds between complementary nucleotides, where each 'A' on one strand is always linked to a 'T' on the complementary strand, and each 'C' to a 'G', etc. In accordance with Watson and Crick's famous model, the arrangement of nucleotide bases is organised in a double helix; a spiral staircase with each base as a step.

8 The building of a new strand from the 'template' of an old one is made possible through the use of the DNA polymerase enzyme. In molecular biology, polymerases are said to be enzymes whose natural function is to replicate chromosomes and base pairs during cellular reproduction. In PCR, these enzymes are relied upon to generate complementary sequences of nucleotides for a strand that is 'bracketed' at each end by an agent called a 'primer'. DNA polymerase primers are two short single strands of nucleotides (usually 16–25 bases long) which are constructed in the laboratory or purchased commercially. Each primer sequence is designed to anneal onto single stranded templates at opposite ends of the DNA sequence to be amplified. Only when a primer has bracketed the ends of a single strand template can the polymerase replicating process begin to synthesise the complementary strand.

9 Various uses of the 'black box' metaphor in social studies of science and technology are discussed at greater length in another paper (Jordan and Lynch in press).

10 See Cambrosio *et al.* (1990) for a study on the relationship between a patent dispute and the arguable identity of a molecular biological technique.

11 Kathleen Jordan attended sessions at this conference and interviewed some of the participants.

12 See Livingston (1986) for an elaboration on the matter of 'precise description' in mathematics.

13 This theme of the reflexive incorporation of invisible agents within institutionalised human relationships is nicely elucidated by Guillaume (1987) and Latour (1988).

14 In Garfinkel's (1967: 21ff.) term, they develop 'ad hoc practices'. This does not necessarily mean that such practices cannot work effectively and reliably.

15 There are some indications that Hoffman-LaRoche will secure exclusive rights to the patent in the near future.

Part V

HUMAN–COMPUTER INTERACTION

INTRODUCTION

Despite the controversy and conceptual confusion that surrounds the idea that a computer could engage in 'meaningful social conduct' and thereby be said to be 'interacting' with the persons who use, operate, and work with it, human–computer interaction has become an increasingly significant field of research within the sciences of computer systems development. It has been primarily dominated by computer scientists and psychologists and has primarily focused upon research that can be applied to the design of computer interfaces.

Recently, some researchers in HCI have attempted to use sociological findings about the nature and order of human interaction as the basis for developing design guidelines and actual interface designs. This move in the direction of sociology has, in part, been the result of two issues faced by the HCI community. First, the increasing, for some, uncertainty about the plausibility and productiveness of the dominant 'cognitive' model that holds sway within the discipline and, second, the desire to build working natural language interfaces. In both cases, the area of sociology that researchers in HCI have turned to in an attempt to work through these matters has been that of ethnomethodology and conversation analysis.

The first two chapters in this section are authored by people who have been at the forefront of the exploration of the relationship between sociology and computer science. In this respect it is not an insignificant feature that in both cases the chapters are the outcome of the collaboration between sociologists and computer scientists, for, whilst Christian Heath and Robin Wooffitt are rooted in sociology, Paul Luff and Norman Fraser have a computer science background.

In the first chapter Paul Luff and Christian Heath locate screen-based activity within the social and cultural foundations of human action *per se*. They do so through an examination of the way in which a group af architects use a computer-aided design (CAD) package. Their conclusions not only add fuel to the mounting criticisms of the way in which the predominant cognitive approach in HCI has i) conceptualised social action, ii) approached user modelling, and iii) developed intentional models of language and discourse, but also question the attempt within HCI to avert the more obvious limitation of the cognitive approach, the problem that multiple users with multiple tasks and goals may work together in technological environments. Thus their findings also question the 'distributed model of cognition' which argues that artifacts such as the indicating dials in an aeroplane cockpit mediate between the different goals and knowledge and expertise of workers in that environment.

The 'improvised', *ad hoc* nature of human activity and the socially organised basis of cooperative work, as manifest in the work activities of the architects they study, lead Luff and Heath to reject the way in which, within HCI, user knowledge has been conceptualised. These conceptualisations are unable to account for the worldly, situated use of computers as revealed in their study, and they thus conclude that, instead of emphasising the conceptualisations of the knowledge a user has of a system, it may be more productive to examine how that knowledge is deployed in the actual use of systems.

In previous work, Paul Luff has championed the use of descriptions of the social organisation of conversation generated by conversation analysis in the development of natural language interfaces. Together with colleagues from the 'Social and Computer Sciences Research Group' in the department of sociology at the University of Surrey he has worked on the ESPRIT Sundial (Speech UNderstanding and DIALogue) project, and in the second chapter in this section Robin Wooffitt and Norman Fraser examine one problem that has been tackled by this project. They are concerned with a problem in modelling ordinary verbal interaction and with how a conversation analytic approach may help to illuminate its dimensions.

The attempt to produce intelligent speech interface systems has been guided by the principle that the system should be designed so as to be sensitive to the communicative competencies of its users. However, Wooffitt and Fraser argue that this begs the question 'what are these competencies?'. They ask: 'how can system designers know how people will react to computers prior to the development of an experimental system, and how can an experimental system be developed prior to an understanding of users' behaviour and requirements?' In order to address this order of problem, Wizard of Oz (WOZ) simulations have been conducted in which, as the name implies, a human being pretends to be a computer in a simulated encounter between a human and a machine. Most of these simulations have had a quantitative focus, yielding information about the construction of lexicons, grammars, and syntax for dialogue. Wooffitt and Fraser, however, report on a WOZ simulation that is based upon the qualitative analysis of talk between subjects who thought they were 'talking' to a computer and persons pretending be to that computer. The result of this analysis is that subjects can be observed to use interactional resources drawn from the world of everyday face-to-face interaction to pursue specific goals in particular, locally occasioned circumstances. It is argued that traditional quantitatively based simulations could not reveal this, but that now, the occasioned, everyday-resource-based nature of subjects' interactions with a simulated system having been revealed, designers may be recommended to build systems that take account of behaviour that is generated using these resources.

In the last chapter in this section Harry Collins continues an interest in natural language use as a way of interfacing with computers. Unlike the other studies in this section which are observationally grounded, his is based on a 'thought experiment'. However, his conclusions are as practical as the conclusions formed in the previous chapters. Collins is concerned to explore what a machine would have to do to be able to 'converse' with a human satisfactorily vs. what it would have to do to 'converse' indistinguishably from a human. In order to address this issue he adapts Block's idea of an imaginary machine that can imitate the conversational responses of humans in a Turing test. The idea is to investigate whether, in principle, 'there are any limits to memory-based imitation of human socialisation'.

On the face of it the conclusion that Collins reaches is at odds with the sentiment that runs through the previous chapter by Wooffitt and Fraser, for he argues that, with foreseeable machines, it is not possible to mimic human conversational competence. However, his argument is not with the idea of engineering a natural language interface but is concerned with the practicalities of language use and with understanding what it is necessary to do in order to 'converse' with a machine. On the basis of his arguments a machine could provide acceptable and informative responses, it could provide the sorts of information that the system in the previous chapter is concerned with, but it could not pretend to be human. However, Collins' point is that that is all we need – a machine that can satisfactorily provide informative responses. To think that it is possible to build machines that can 'converse' indistinguishably from humans may well, as suggested elsewhere (Button 1990), lead up a blind alley.

10

SYSTEM USE AND SOCIAL ORGANISATION

Observations on human–computer interaction in an architectural practice

Paul Luff and Christian Heath

The 'bricoleur' is adept at performing a large number of diverse tasks; but, unlike the engineer, he does not subordinate each of them to the availability of raw materials and tools conceived for the purpose of the project. His universe of instruments is closed and the rules of his game are always to make do with 'whatever is at hand'; that is to say with a set of tools and materials which is always finite and is also heterogeneous because what it contains bears no relation to the current project, or indeed to any particular project, but is the contingent result of all the occasions there have been to renew or enrich the stock or maintain it with the remains of previous constructions or destructions.

(Lévi-Strauss 1962: 17)

Despite its relative importance within the field of Human–Computer Interaction, there seems to be growing scepticism about the ability of cognitive science to enrich our understanding of the use of complex technologies. At the practical level, for example, it has been suggested that the designs and evaluation techniques used by actual designers of computer systems owe little to the models developed within cognitive science (Carroll 1990; Barnard 1991). Moreover, theoretically, cognitive science has been subject to wide-ranging criticism concerning, for example, its conceptualisation of social action (Winograd and Flores 1986; Lave 1988; Coulter 1989), its approach to user modelling (Suchman 1987; Gilbert 1987), and its intentional models of language and discourse (McIlvenny 1990; Frohlich and Luff 1990). In line with these criticisms, several researchers have argued that studies should move away from plan-based, goal-orientated models of system use and begin to consider the social and cultural foundations of screen-based actions and activities (Suchman 1987; Robinson 1990; Frohlich and Luff 1990; Norman and Thomas 1990).

In the following chapter we attempt to make some preliminary observations of the social and situated organisation of human–computer interaction. The observations demonstrate the *ad hoc* and improvisational properties of computer use and suggest that more conventional characterisations of the interaction between a human and computer tend to conceal, rather than illuminate, the practical reasoning and competences that ordinary users bring to bear in undertaking screen-based actions and activities. Although the bulk of our observations are directed towards the individual use of the workstation, the chapter attempts to demonstrate how seemingly individual screen-based activity is embedded in real-time collaboration with colleagues undertaking related tasks within the organisation milieu.

The materials upon which the observations are based consist of video-recordings of 'naturally occurring' computer use and collaboration in a provincial architectural practice in England. The architects are based in an open-plan office and use a computer-aided design (CAD) package to construct drawings on personal workstations. At various stages during the course of a particular commission, the architects will be given the responsibility to undertake drawings of a particular section or details of the building. Despite this division of labour however, it is necessary for the architects to collaborate continually in order to produce a consistent set of drawings.

Notwithstanding the intrinsic sociological interest of the work of the architects, the materials at hand are also of relevance to current initiatives in research on human–computer interaction. First, the CAD system used by the architects incorporates a direct manipulation interface and a direct metaphor. There has been a considerable amount of research into these ideas (Hutchins, Hollan, and Norman 1986; Norman 1988; Ankrah, Frohlich, and Gilbert, 1990), primarily because they are considered useful and good properties and yet it is unclear, precisely, what the character of these properties is. Second, analysis of the collaboration required to produce a set of drawings even when produced on individual machines may later inform the design of computer systems to support collaborative work (CSCW systems), and in particular those systems designed to support shared drawing between people in separate locations (e.g. Bly 1988; Minneman and Bly 1991; Ishii 1990).

HUMAN–COMPUTER INTERACTION IN AN ARCHITECTURAL PRACTICE

With their aim of modelling the knowledge of users of computer systems, cognitive scientists concerned with human–computer interaction frequently presuppose that different behaviours reflect differing levels of expertise. Thus, subjects for experiments are commonly divided into 'experts', 'intermediates', and 'novices', the category chosen based on the frequency of use of a particular application or computer system and familiarity with the task the user is being asked to perform (e.g. Mayes *et al.* 1988). Similarly, evaluations of computer systems are typically carried out using subjects with different 'levels of expertise' (e.g. Doane *et al.* 1990). Recently, Young, Howes, and Whittington (1990) have begun to explore more deeply the knowledge users have of a computer interface, analysing this knowledge in terms several classes, users having differing combinations of knowledge from these classes. They use the terms 'expert', 'intermediate', and 'novice' to identify notional users having particular configurations of knowledge from the classes.

In a previous study we undertook, individuals were asked to produce overhead projector slides using a specialised Macintosh application called PowerPoint[1] (Luff and Heath 1991). From recorded materials of naturalistic use of this system it was difficult to associate the behaviours proposed by Young, Howes, and Whittington for their notional classes of users. Rather than characterising skill in terms of knowledge and expertise, it was more fruitful to examine the common practices that underlay the use of the system. As with many applications it is difficult to find 'expert' or 'frequent' users, defined in either of the ways mentioned above, of a package for producing overhead projector slides. Such a package is designed for 'occasional' users. However, there are other similar text and graphics packages that are used frequently: computer-aided design (CAD) packages, for example. For this and other reasons we chose to study the use of computers in an architectural practice.

The practice we studied is small to medium sized, employing about fifteen architects, town planners, and graphic designers. It is an unusual British practice in that it uses computers extensively throughout the process of designing a building, including: showing clients what prospective buildings will look like and how they will fit within the local landscape; producing the working drawings for building contractors; and even drawing sketches of original designs. The setting is particularly suitable for our research because each architect has a Macintosh computer, the system we used in our earlier exercise and in other studies of human–computer interaction (e.g. Mayes *et al.* 1988; Young, Howes, and Whittington 1990).

The architects use a package called MiniCad,[2] each architect working on a different set of drawings. The materials collected are principally concerned with the principal project in which the practice was involved. This was to produce the working drawings for a large public building originally scheduled to take about ten months. The original designs had been produced by another architectural practice and the work involved producing drawings that were both detailed and consistent for the building contractors to use. This project consisted of two parts: the demolition and redevelopment of portions of an old, existing building and the design of a completely new building linked to the old one. As well as producing plans, sections, and elevations of these buildings[3] the architects had to work on detailed drawings of complex parts of the design, these included the staircases and the large, high windows of the new building. Both the number of architects involved in the project and the number of drawings varied throughout the course of the project. During the period of data collection, around six architects were working full-time on the building. The project was divided in terms of the drawings that had to be produced: one worked on the old building, one on the plans for the bottom six levels of the new building; one on the plans for the top five levels; one on the sections, one on the elevations, and one on the staircases. Another architect was concerned with managing this and other of the practice's projects and an eighth worked on drawings of the windows as well as other projects.

The collected materials consist of field-notes and video-recordings of individual work, 'interactions' with the computer, and collaborative work between architects.

All the architects on this project used the MiniCad package. As a Macintosh application it shares many features with other applications for that system. Figure 10.1 shows the overall screen layout when MiniCad has been opened for the first time.

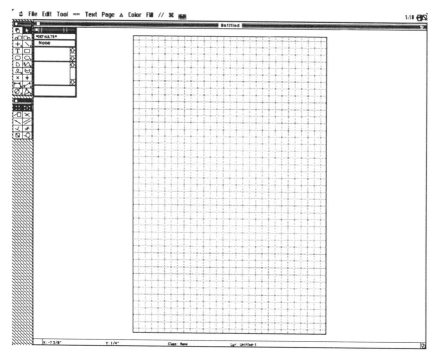

Figure 10.1 The MiniCad screen layout when opened

The main window is labelled 'Untitled' until the drawing has been named. MiniCad's tools are provided on two palettes, initially on the left-hand side of the screen. The top one contains drawing tools allowing users to type text, draw rectangles, polygons, arcs, and special, recurring symbols such as double doors and desks. The bottom palette is for a set of tools that allow the user to constrain the placing of certain objects on the screen, for example, constraining one line to be perpendicular to another or ensuring that two objects fit precisely together. The data palette is initially available above the main window and provides users with the facilities for naming objects they have drawn and assigning textual information to those objects. Below the main window is a 'data display bar' that provides information about that status of the drawing at a particular time. Above the main window is a menu bar. Figure 10.2 shows the menu bar and the contents of the individual menus.

In addition to the Apple menu available on all Macintosh applications, there are eleven MiniCad menus. The File and Edit menus have similar options to those in other Macintosh applications for opening, printing, saving, and closing files and for simple editing operations. These menus also include options for smoothing, mirroring, and reshaping objects. The Tool menu collects together several miscellaneous functions including joining objects together, combining several lines into a polygon, breaking up a polygon into several lines, and changing surfaces for later three-dimensional manipulation. MiniCad allows the user to create a drawing in layers. These act rather like tracing paper, except that the user not only has control over which layers of a drawing can be seen at any time, but also how each layer can be used, so certain layers can be invisible, greyed out, visible but unchangeable, or visible and changeable. Options for manipulating layers are given in the menu labelled '=='. The Text menu offers a range of ways of changing the style, font, size, and layout of text. The Page menu allows the user to view the drawing in various ways. Another way of viewing a plan is to change it into some 3D representation; the Delta menu labelled 'Δ' provides users with a multitude of possibilities for creating such a drawing. The Color menu provides 'pens' for drawing and shading objects on the screen in different colours and the Fill menu offers a range of shadings (or hatchings) for objects. The Line Weighting menu, labelled '//', gives a variety of styles of lines in differing thicknesses, differing dashing patterns, and with differing arrowheads. Finally, MiniCad also provides for the user to associate spreadsheets (or 'worksheets') with drawings. The rightmost menu, the command menu, provides options for manipulating these.

From the facilities offered on the menus it can be seen that MiniCad is a complex application containing a wide range of facilities. The architects' appear to use most of these, including the spreadsheet for managing the progress of projects. The major component of the package they do not use

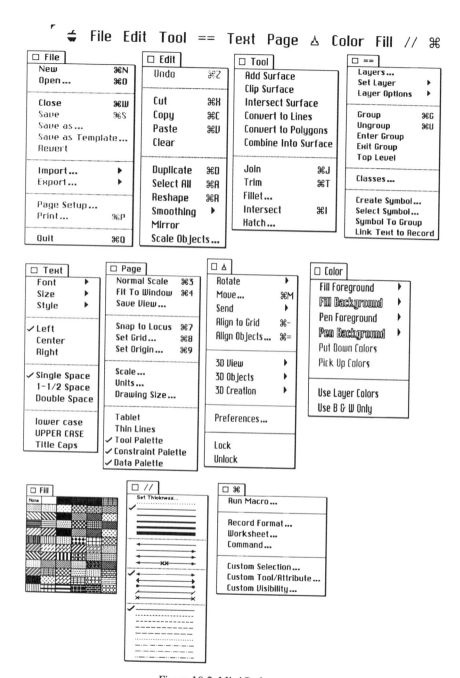

Figure 10.2 MiniCad menus

is that for converting plans into 3D. Although one of the architects does create 3D drawings of the building and others they are working on, this is done using another Macintosh application. Before considering the architects' interaction with the computer in more detail, it is worth mentioning the three principal mechanisms that MiniCad provides for moving around a drawing. These are zooming, panning, and moving between layers. Zooming in and out of a particular portion of a drawing is performed by selecting the Zoom In and Zoom Out tools in the drawing palette (on the second row). To zoom in on a portion of the drawing, the Zoom In tool is selected with the mouse, the user specifies the area to zoom in to by shaping a dashed box, called a 'Marquee', over the appropriate area with the cursor and then releasing the mouse. Moving around a drawing that is too big to fit on the screen; is possible by panning around the drawing either by using the panning tool on the drawing palette or by pressing the appropriate arrow key on the keyboard. The user can move between the layers of a building in three ways: using the Layer menu; selecting the 'Lyr' section of the data display bar at the bottom of the screen or pressing the Command key and either the up or down arrow at the same time.

THE PRACTICE USING MENUS

Previous analysis of individuals producing overhead projector slides revealed that in the course of this activity the nature of their use of menus changed from moment to moment (Luff and Heath 1991). Although designing a building using a CAD package is quite a different activity, the architects' uses of menus are similar in many ways. For example, in the following instance the architect is working on an elevation of the old building.[4]

   (1) 4B MV 5124
    1   ↓ Fill::::::::::::::::::::::::::::::::::::
    2   Color::: Fill Foreground:::: (0.5)
    3   Color (Fill Foreground) (Fill Background) (Pen Foreground)
    4   (Pen Background) Use Layer Colors::::↑
    5   (5.7)
    6   ↓ File::: New (Open) ↑
    7   (2.3)
    8   '⌘ s'

He opens the Fill menu, holds it down for over 3 seconds (line 1), then goes down the adjacent Color menu (line 2), back up to the title bar, and then down again, selecting 'Use Layer Colors' (lines 3–4). After five seconds he briefly peeps at the File menu (line 6) before typing the command key and the 's' key together (line 8).[5] It might be possible to characterise the first use of the menus (lines 1–4) as a 'search' for a particular item (i.e. 'Use

Layer Colors') or as steps towards solving a problem related to filling and colouring the drawing. Similarly, the second use (line 6) could be viewed as a search for the appropriate key command for saving a file displayed on the File menu.

Although neither of these is a behaviour that would be associated with 'expert' or 'frequent' users in the conventional menu literature, they could be seen to support the findings of Mayes *et al.* (1988). Mayes *et al.* found that 'frequent users' had difficulty in recalling even the 'gross details' of an interface. Thus, they propose, experts may have better 'semantic' knowledge of, for example, the existence of functions and therefore may not need to remember the 'lexical' knowledge of the names of particular functions. Good interface designs, like the Macintosh they were experimenting with, are those of which users do not need to remember the details. This argument ties in with other recent work in cognitive science which has begun to explore the relationship between 'knowledge in the head' and 'knowledge in the world' (Norman 1988). Utilising this distinction, Young, Howes, and Whittington (1990) have begun to develop a cognitive model of this relationship in terms of classes of knowledge that different users have when using an interface. Although being significantly more complex than those models that view actions as steps in a task or towards a goal, this work still concentrates on modelling the 'knowledge in the head' of an individual user. By being concerned with the 'interaction' between the internal knowledge of the user and the external knowledge in the artifact, Young, Howes, and Whittington suggest that their model explores 'situated' action. This conception of situated action is significantly different from that in the social sciences; characterising the user's activity in such a way ignores crucial aspects of the nature of the activity.

In the following instance, the architect is working on a particular box on a plan.

(2) 6B MV 4302
1 ↓ //:::: ((Line thickness 1))::: ((Line thickness 2)):::::
2 Fill::::::
3 Color:::::::::::: Put Down Color::: Use B&W Color: ↑

Once again, this activity does not appear to be that conventionally associated with experts using menus. It is also difficult to view it as a search for a solution to a particular problem, the line menu offering quite different possibilities for action to the Fill and Color menus. Instead, the nature of the activity of the user when engaged with the menus appears to develop in the course of using them. Although appearing to go to select a particular line width, the nature of the user's activity transforms as he is using the menus. A cognitive model of the type proposed by Young, Howes, and Whittington (1990) would presumably account for this in terms of an interaction between the task the user is carrying out, the knowledge the user has of the system, and what the system displays to the user. Yet such transformations of activity recur in the data, both in the materials collected in the architects' practice and in that of PowerPoint users (Luff and Heath 1991). They do not appear to be associated with the user's familiarity with the application or system. Characterising such activity as an interaction between knowledge in the head of the user and knowledge on the menus focuses analysis on developing some mechanism or causal connection linking the two together and ignores the innovatory, improvisatory, and, almost, ambivalent nature of the activity. Furthermore, by concentrating on individuals carrying out pre-designed tasks on systems, mainly in experimental settings, studies operate with a relatively constrained conception of screen-based activity. In the following sections a broader view of situated action will be taken. By analysing naturalistic materials from real-world settings we will begin to explore aspects of the social organisation of human–computer interaction.

DIRECTLY MANIPULATING PLANS

Much of the architects' day-to-day activity is involved in making detailed changes to the working drawings of the building. These changes are made using the CAD package. It is worth examining in detail an instance of this screen-based activity. In the following fragment an architect is making changes to a staircase in a drainage tunnel that leads away from underneath the building. Figure 10.3 is a sketch of the plan of the staircase.
The user has just been moving around the plan, both panning across it and

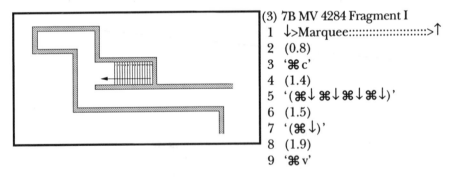

(3) 7B MV 4284 Fragment I
1 ↓>Marquee:::::::::::::::::::::::::>↑
2 (0.8)
3 '⌘ c'
4 (1.4)
5 '(⌘↓ ⌘↓ ⌘↓ ⌘↓)'
6 (1.5)
7 '(⌘ ↓)'
8 (1.9)
9 '⌘ v'

Figure 10.3 The tunnel staircase
(line 1, fragment 3)

selecting various layers of the drawing. He shapes a box (called a Marquee) over the region of a staircase (line 1), this marks the objects contained within the box as 'selected'. He then types the command and 'c' keys simultaneously (line 3). He moves down five layers (lines 5–7) by holding

192

down the command key and pressing the down arrow key. He then types the command and 'v' keys simultaneously (line 9). Together the actions in line 1 to 9 are commonly characterised as a 'cut and paste' or, more accurately, a 'copy and paste'. The architect copies a portion of staircase from one layer and pastes it onto another (see Figure 10.4). The architect goes on to manipulate the amended plan

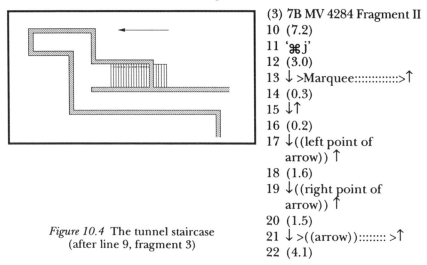

(3) 7B MV 4284 Fragment II
10 (7.2)
11 '⌘ j'
12 (3.0)
13 ↓ >Marquee::::::::::::>↑
14 (0.3)
15 ↓↑
16 (0.2)
17 ↓((left point of
   arrow)) ↑
18 (1.6)
19 ↓((right point of
   arrow)) ↑
20 (1.5)
21 ↓ >((arrow))::::::::: >↑
22 (4.1)

Figure 10.4 The tunnel staircase
(after line 9, fragment 3)

He types 'command-j' (line 11), this 'joins' the new portion of staircase to the old. After marking out an area of the staircase that contains all the numbers of the individual stairs (line 13), the architect clicks in the area above the staircase (line 15). He then selects each end of the arrow and then moves it upwards and rightwards (lines 17–21). After positioning a construction line using the '+' drawing tool and removing an indent in the wall below the staircase, the architect first moves the vertical wall to the end of the staircase (line 29) and then extends the horizontal wall (line 31). Figure 10.5 is a sketch of the plan at this point.

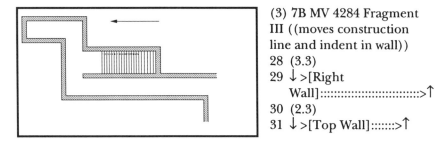

(3) 7B MV 4284 Fragment III ((moves construction line and indent in wall))
28 (3.3)
29 ↓ >[Right
   Wall]:::::::::::::::::::::::::::>↑
30 (2.3)
31 ↓ >[Top Wall]:::::::>↑

Figure 10.5 The tunnel staircase
(after line 31, fragment 3)

The user removes all the numbers on the stairs and a portion of stairs at the left end of the staircase and then selects the right- and left-hand sides of the arrow (line 35 and 37). After appearing to group the ends of the arrow together (by the 'command-g' combination, line 39) he moves it into a new position on the stairs (line 41).

(3) 7B MV 4284 Fragment IV
((removes numbers and stairs))
35   ↓ ((right point of arrow)) ↑
36   (1.5)
37   ↓ ((left point of arrow)) ↑
38   (1.4)
39   '(⌘ g)'
40   (2.9)
41   ↓ > ((arrow)):: > ↑

This fragment is extracted from an extended flow of activity. It is possible, *post hoc*, to view these actions as steps towards a goal that the architect had before commencing it or as part of sub-tasks that make up some overall task he had to accomplish. In order to extend the staircase, the user first has to copy the extended portion, consisting of a new flight of stairs from somewhere else, add this to the end of the staircase, then move the existing walls to surround this new portion and finally adjust the new staircase, removing any extraneous stairs at the bottom of the flight and changing the numbers that label each stair. Making fine alterations could then be characterised as local adjustments necessary to accomplish an overall goal.

It could be expected that a mundane activity such as extending a staircase would, for an architect, be a routine, general procedure that, with minor alterations, could be instantiated for particular cases at hand. Yet, in the fragment above, and throughout the corpus of data, it is hard to discover such a procedure. Although it is possible to construct a *post hoc* 'plan' for an architect's manipulation of a drawing, even for other manipulations of staircases, there appears to be no generality to these 'plans'. Rather, the architect's activity appears to be locally managed. When the new portion of staircase is pasted onto the old there are a range of actions to perform and a range of possible ways of performing them including: moving the walls and stairs; renumbering the stairs; and grouping, ungrouping, and constraining the movement of the various objects displayed on the screen. As the architect manipulates the plan there remains a range of further and different possibilities for action. As with the use of menus mentioned earlier, the nature of the screen-based activity that the user engages in is continually changing throughout the articulation of that activity. The selection of the numbers of the stairs using a marquee (line 13) and then the subsequent click of the mouse button that deselects them (line 15) could be seen as the commencement of a new course of activity, such as moving or deleting those numbers, that is immediately aborted. Making a selection also brings into view a set of objects that can be manipulated. This alters the range of relevant next activities for the archi- tect, the click away removes the marking, making another action, like selecting the left end of the arrow, possible (line 17). Rather than the activity being divided into segments, each concerned with a separate sub- task, an action is linked to the prior action and makes possible a range of next actions. Although architects utilise systematic procedures, or packages of actions, for getting their work done, they cannot be said to 'follow' these procedures. Rather, the architects orientate to these procedures, using them innovatively to accomplish a task at hand.

Hutchins, Hollan, and Norman (1986) explain the properties of direct manipulation interfaces, such as MiniCad, in terms of the mappings between an individual's goals and the physical tasks required to operate a system. They suggest that there are two aspects to the notion of directness of an interface; distance and engagement: distance accounting for the translation necessary from goals into physical tasks; engagement accounting for the 'qualitative feeling' of manipulating the objects of interest. Direct manipulation interfaces make the distance shorter by, for example, avoiding the semantic translation necessary to construct type- written commands and increase engagement by employing visual meta- phors of objects related to the user's task on the screen. Other researchers have attempted to further clarify aspects of direct manipulation by, for example, exploring the differing roles of direct metaphor and direct man- ipulation (Ankrah, Frohlich, and Gilbert 1990), and characterising the properties of screen objects in terms of their affordances (Gaver 1991). Though direct manipulation interfaces such as desktop environments, spreadsheets, and CAD packages appear to be successful, being easy to use and learn, it has been difficult to explain this usability in terms of a cognitive model. This may be because such work tries to explain a direct activity in terms of intermediate and unseen processes. The recordings of architects reveal them engaged in using the tools of MiniCad and directly manipulating the objects that they have created, and yet it is hard to draw mappings between the corresponding 'real-world' tools, actions, and objects and those they use on the screen. In (3) the architect is directly manipulating plans on the screens using tools for moving and copying boxes and lines, positioning construction lines, constraining angles, and joining objects together. In terms of metaphors with the 'real-world' tools of pen, eraser, ruler, set square, and tracing paper, the MiniCad interface appears to be rather indirect. Also, it is difficult to imagine how a particular box on the screen 'affords' being moved. Yet, the user appears to do these activities quite unproblematically. It may be useful to explore the archi- tects' practices of using these screen-based tools.

Obviously, the positioning and sizing of objects is a crucial aspect of the work of the architects. Not only are they working on drawings to be used by building contractors that need to be accurate to about 5mm, but also the placement of objects must fit precisely across layers in a drawing and across separate drawings. In (3) the architect organises his activity so the location to which objects are to be moved is specified before he moves the object. The join command (line 11) does not just connect together two disconnected objects, it makes one object of two distinct objects. In the case of walls, the join command removes intermediary lines between two connected walls. So, the architect's 'paste' of the new portion of staircase (line 9) is carefully designed for subsequent actions. The architect still has to make adjustments to the positioning of objects on the drawing, especially to related ones, but his manipulation of those objects could be better characterised as slotting them into a particular position rather than sliding or pushing them around the drawing. It is not the tools and the objects on the screen that are essential to the way the architect orientates to his activity, but it is also the space on the screen. In (3), the user moves the arrow on the staircase up and to the left (line 21). This position is nicely out of the way of the staircase, which the user goes on to manipulate, and also is vertically above the new location of the staircase. In the following instance the user is redrawing a plan of a toilet. (Figure 10.6 is a sketch of the plan before he has altered anything.)

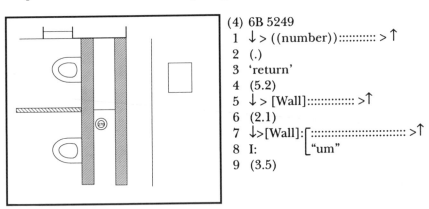

Figure 10.6 Toilet (line 1, fragment 4)

After moving a number on the drawing (line 1), he deselects the number (line 3) then moves the left vertical wall to the right (line 5). (Figure 10.7 is a sketch of the plan at this point.)

The architect then moves another wall, originally in the same position as the wall he just moved, to the right-hand side of the drawing (line 7). He then goes on to work in the space he has now left to the right of the urinals. As in (3) the walls are moved into a space, clear but related to the area in

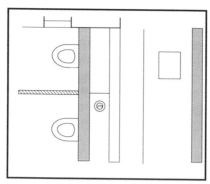

Figure 10.7 Toilet (line 9, fragment 4)

which the architect is to work, though, in this case, one, and probably both, of these walls are no longer required for the plan. It is as if the walls, whose size and shape are still consistent with the rest of the drawing, are being preserved as a resource for further work. Such preservation of objects recurs throughout the corpus of data. There are also related instances where a copy of an object is moved into an area of free space and manipulated there. This manipulation could be characterised as a side activity: working out the precise shape of the object or trying out operations on it. The MiniCad package in particular, and the Macintosh system in general, facilitates the preservation of objects and the production of such side activities.

So far we have considered solely the uses of local spaces; in the next section we will begin to consider wider aspects of direct manipulation in a CAD package.

NAVIGATING AROUND DESIGN

As mentioned earlier, MiniCad provides three ways of moving around a drawing: panning across a drawing; zooming into and out of an area of a drawing; and moving between layers of the drawing. In the following instance the architect uses all three (shown schematically in Figure 10.8).

After working on the title in the bottom right-hand corner of a set of elevations, the architect shuffles the drawing up twice by moving the cursor over the edge of the drawing (lines 1–3) and then across to the left (line 5). He types 'command-4' (line 7), fitting the entire drawing onto the screen. He then zooms out further using the Zoom Out tool on the Drawing Tools palette and marks the area on the screen where he wants the less detailed drawing to go (lines 9–11). By selecting the top window bar of the window and dragging it down to the bottom of the screen he effectively moves the current set of elevations out of view and reveals another elevation (line 13).

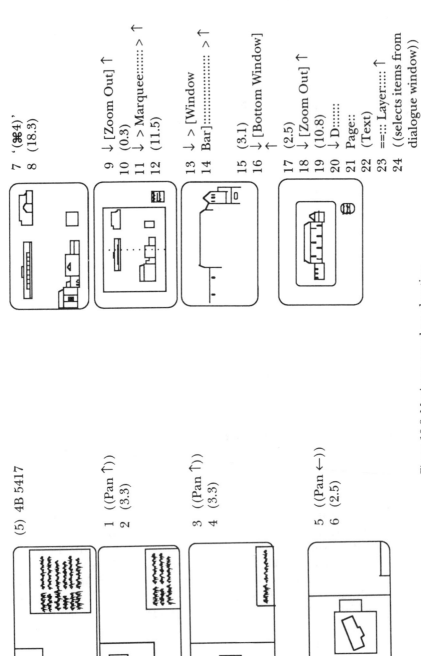

(5) 4B 5417

1 ((Pan ↑))
2 (3.3)

3 ((Pan ↑))
4 (3.3)

5 ((Pan ←))
6 (2.5)

7 '(⌘4)'
8 (18.3)

9 ↓ [Zoom Out] ↑
10 (0.3)
11 ↓ > Marquee:::::: > ←
12 (11.5)

13 ↓ > [Window
14 Bar]:::::::::::: > ↑

15 (3.1)
16 ↓ [Bottom Window] ↑

17 (2.5)
18 ↓ [Zoom Out] ↑
19 (10.8)
20 ↓ D::::::
21 Page::
22 (Text)
23 ===::: Layer:::: ↑
24 ((selects items from dialogue window))

Figure 10.8 Moving around an elevation

He clicks on this elevation (line 16), zooms out of this elevation (line 18), goes to the menus to select the layers of the drawings to display (lines 20–4), and he then goes on to alter the title block of this drawing.

The architect not only moves from one drawing to another in three different ways, he accomplishes this by moving the mouse, using an accelerator, the menus, and the Zoom Out tool. Just as in previous instances, it is possible to consider this movement as a path from one title block to another: zooming out of the first plan, jumping across to the other drawing, and then zooming in on that. But once again this ignores the development of the activity from moment to moment. In the following instance, the user has just finished altering some walls at the right-hand end of the service tunnel (shown schematically in Figure 10.9).

He pans left across the top of the tunnel six times (lines 1–9), then down three times (lines 11–15) by pressing the appropriate arrow keys. He adds some layers to the drawing (lines 17–20), pans down again (line 23), then pans diagonally down to the right (line 25–26).

The service tunnel is a bent 'T-shape' and enters the main building at its base. The architect pans across and down the plan following the service tunnel into the building. He also paces his activity with the system's re-drawing of the plan. It is possible to press keystrokes in quick succession, avoiding redrawing intermediate plans along the way. By slowing down the frequency of pressing of the arrow keys as he nears the centre of the service tunnel the architect is able to monitor the system, redrawing the plan. Progression down the tunnel is slower and only after he passes the crook in the tunnel (line 15) does he add layers to the drawing and then proceed into the female staff room in the new building. There are other ways in which the user could move between the staircase at the right end of the tunnel and the female staff room: for example, zooming out to a plan of the whole drawing and then zooming into the relevant area. Yet, this activity rests on the architect's skill of manipulating this particular plan and the system in general. MiniCad takes longer to draw the entire 'level 0' plan than to draw many plans of details. It also takes longer to draw such details if it has to draw several layers each time. Thus, the activity in (6) is organised and shaped by a range of contingencies including the architect's pacing of his own actions with the system's operations, the projected speed of the system, and the very shape and position of the tunnel on which the architect is working. This is a different form of direct manipulation to that normally considered in the literature. 'Direct navigation' of this sort is facilitated by the contingent manipulation of objects.

Navigation around the plan can also be seen as contingent on aspects of architectural practice in general. The building the architects are working on has certain consistencies and symmetries. The architects can make use of these in their drawings, for instance, copying portions of a plan from one area to another. It also means that work on one localised area of a plan has

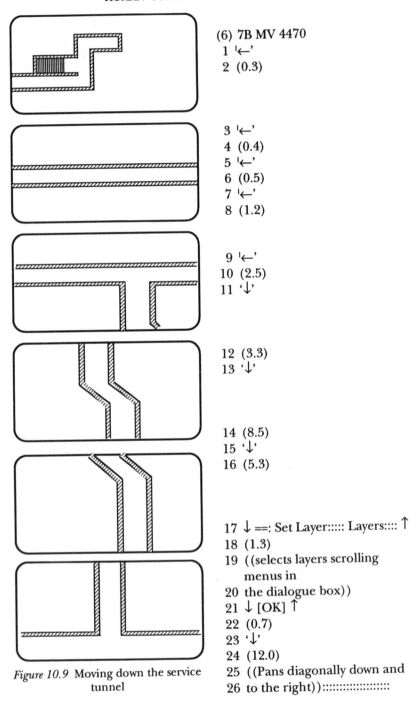

(6) 7B MV 4470
1 '←'
2 (0.3)

3 '←'
4 (0.4)
5 '←'
6 (0.5)
7 '←'
8 (1.2)

9 '←'
10 (2.5)
11 '↓'

12 (3.3)
13 '↓'

14 (8.5)
15 '↓'
16 (5.3)

17 ↓ ==: Set Layer::::: Layers:::: ↑
18 (1.3)
19 ((selects layers scrolling
      menus in
20 the dialogue box))
21 ↓ [OK] ↑
22 (0.7)
23 '↓'
24 (12.0)
25 ((Pans diagonally down and
26 to the right))::::::::::::::::::::

Figure 10.9 Moving down the service
tunnel

important implications for changes that need to be made to other areas. For example, changes to an internal staircase on one level will involve similar, but not identical, changes to other staircases on that level. In the materials there are numerous instances of movements back and forth between spatially distant areas of the plan. These movements rest on the architects' skills of 'interacting' with the computer, drawing this particular plan, and the everyday, architectural skills of drawing buildings.

PRACTICES IN SUPPORT OF MULTIPLE ACTIVITIES

As in other practices, changes that the architects need to make to the drawings are 'marked up' on paper. There is one set of these mark-ups made on a recently plotted version of the drawings. The architects also keep paper versions of the drawings on which they are individually working. These paper versions have a range of advantages, especially, as they are over a metre in length, making it possible to see more of the drawing than on a 30cm wide screen. These paper drawings also need to be organised, plotted, and marked. Similarly, the architects have other artifacts around their desk with which they have to work, including reference books, manuals, and calculators. Thus, their interaction with the machine is embedded within a range of other activities.

In the following instance, the architect selects a menu item to export a file into a different format (line 3). He then types the new file's name into a field in a dialogue box (line 7).

(7) 14B JVC 3500 2:20:18 Transcript I
1   ↓ == Set Layer::::::::::::::: Layers . . .
2   Layer ↑
3   ↓ File::::::::: Export::: (Item1) (Item2:) (Item3::) ↑
4   (2.3)
5   >'((file name)):::::: >
6   (0.8)
7   '((new file name)):::::::::::::::::::::::'
8   (1.0)
9   ↓ [OK] ↑

Prior to this activity the architect is marking up a paper plan. As he lifts his pen from the paper he looks towards the screen to his right. Just after his glance reaches the screen, he moves towards the workstation and reaches out for the mouse. He then selects the item from the menu. This brings up a dialogue box that has a default file name in it which he drags the mouse over (line 5). This allows him to replace the default name with a new one (line 7). After he selects the 'OK' button in the dialogue box he goes back to the drawing. The following figure maps out the architect's visual conduct and some of his other activities.[6]

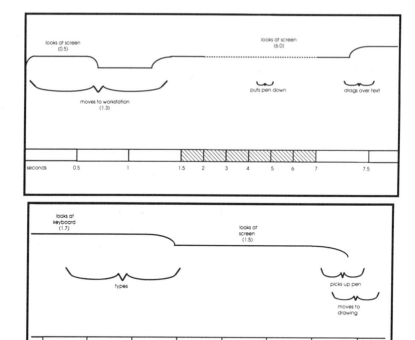

Figure 10.10 (7) 14A JVC 3596 Transcript II

The architect's use of the computer is embedded in the other activities in which he is engaged. On glancing at the screen he moves over to the system and then starts interacting with it. After selecting 'OK' he glances down from the screen and moves back to his drawing. Such tight interleaving of two activities is not always possible. Instead, as in Figure 10.10, the architect may have to monitor the screen while engaged in another activity.

So in fragment (8) Figure 10.11, although engaged in an activity of folding up a plan, the architect is continually glancing at the screen. In this instance, the architect was opening a file of a particular drawing. As the drawings the architects are working on are complex, saving, opening, closing, and plotting operations can take the system a long time to perform. It is often the case that the architects engage in another activity that ties into the speed of operation of the machine. It should be noted that a plan of the entire building that fits on the screen is very dense. When opening the drawing it is difficult to see from the drawing when the operation has been completed. It appears that the architects look for other aspects of the interface, such as the title bar or the existence of a dialogue box to monitor when the system is 'available'.

202

Miyata and Norman (1986) consider some work in psychology that may support the understanding of multiple activities, such as research on memory, attention, and the processing of tasks. In particular, they suggest a distinction between foregrounded, backgrounded, and suspended activity. They go on to suggest the advantages and disadvantages of windows to support such activities. In the corpus of data we are considering there are occasions when the architects use more than one window, such as in Figure 10.11, to contain alternative drawings with which to work or to compare an elevation to a plan. More interestingly, the architects can use other devices and tools provided on the computer system innovatively to support activities that do not take place on the screen, and switch from one of these activities to another from moment to moment. In such a flow of activity, the architects manage for themselves the assignment of foregrounded and backgrounded activities and the movement between the two.

SHARED DRAWING

Not only must a single drawing be internally consistent so that items such as staircases between the same floors have equal number of stairs, but also the different types of drawings (i.e. plans, sections, elevations, and details) must be consistent with each other. As different architects are responsible for these drawings, consistency demands collaboration. The architects also collaborate in other ways: they have to organise and order the work of the practice; they have to monitor the progress and collect together the work on the building; and they have to solve particular problems with the design of the building. The individual's use of the computer is embedded within the surrounding domain of activity in the office.

The mark-up sheets are one of the ways that changes to the plans are communicated to one another. They also draw small details on 'Post-it' stickers and pass these to one another, they keep a spreadsheet of the progress of all the drawings for the project, and, from time to time, pass computer files to each other. In fact, a number of procedures have emerged in the practice to facilitate the communication of plans. The practice has a policy for naming computer files that relates the name to the type of drawing it contains, its scale, and the architect who is responsible for it. When files are copied from one machine to another this name is changed to avoid problems having two different drawings with the same name. Each drawing is positioned on a grid that is common to all drawings. This makes it easier to position portions of drawings taken from other files. Also, the architects try to avoid redundancy in their plans (i.e. plans sharing common details) as this increases the possibility of inconsistencies. However, none of these procedures ensure consistency. Rather, consistency is achieved by the ways in which the architects monitor each other's work. For example, in the following fragment the architect working

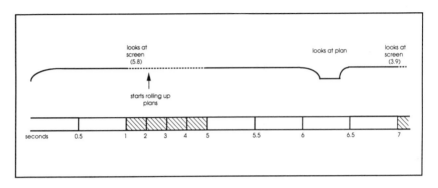

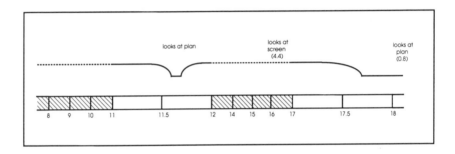

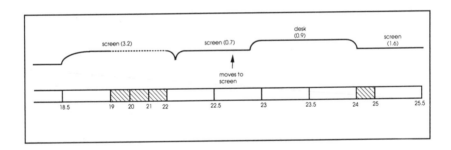

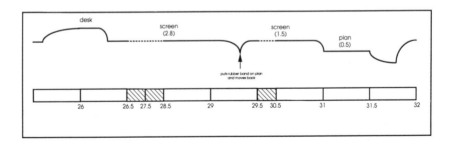

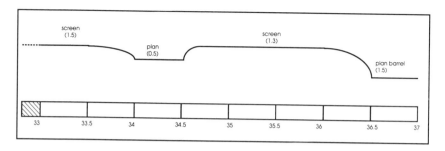

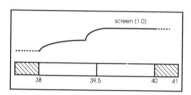

Figure 10.11 (8) 14A 3277

on the details of the staircases (R) is looking at the mark-up sheets while the architect drawing the plans (P) sits to his right working on his computer.

(9) 8A JVC 3094 Fragment I

```
 1  R:   are you su:re you're flipping the right one arou:nd ↓ Pe:te.
 2       (0.2)
 3  P:   yeah
 4       (2.5)
 5  P:   your flipping (0.5) look on level one
 6       (1.1)
 7  R:   you you just told me that you have flip>flipped that one arou:nd
 8       (0.6)
 9  P:   Yeah (0.3) I ⌈ ()
10  R:            ⌊ it must be that one () what
11  P:   I've only just made these corrections now (0.9) these red marks
12       (0.5)
13  R:   why do>does the red marks (.) go in different directions then
         the black?
14       (0.8)
15  P:   no ⌈ you want the red (0.4) this is correct
16  R:      ⌊ (there)
17       (1.9)
18  P:   and this one I'm changing (0.2) you see this one goes up the
         other way ↑
```

About 1.4 seconds after he answer's R's question, T turns towards the plans and they start to discuss the 'mark-ups' on the plans. Because of large-scale changes to the overall design of the building a room has been moved onto a new split level towards the top of the building. The staircase to this room cannot just be extended up from an existing level. For access to the new room to be convenient the staircase has to go in the opposite direction. Turning (or flipping) the staircase around at the top level requires turning all the other stairs at lower levels. It is the mark-ups relating to this change that the architects are discussing, in particular, the differing statuses of mark-ups made in black and red ink. A little later the architects are discussing the details of the staircases.

(9) 8A JVC 3094 Fragment 2

```
 1  P:   you see (0.3) um:
 2       (0.6)
 3  P:   there this is the outside level
 4       (1.0)
 5  R:   umm ↓
 6       (1.3)
 7  P:   and it can start
 8       (0.7)
 9  P:   part of the drawing we're on now
10       (2.3)
11  P:   righ(t) yeah
12       (1.4)
13  P:   youve done a section through (.2) this guy here right?
14       (0.6)
15  R:   yep
16       (.)
17  P:   thats the stair of the section I had ↓(0.3) too: give myself
18       () and he has set back these () and he has to start back here
         (0.4)
19       and go up ↑
```

The talk in fragment 9 is accompanied by a considerable amount of visual conduct and gestures by the participants, particularly as they orient themselves to plans on the screen and on the paper. P begins to turn to his screen as he says 'um:' (line 1) and, on uttering 'there' (line 3) he points to a place on the bottom of a section on the screen, sketched in Figure 10.12.

P's pointing does not secure R's gaze towards the screen. Only as P utters 'side' of 'outside level' does R gaze up to the screen. About 0.5 seconds after his utterance, P moves his finger along the bottom of the section on the screen. Both P's utterance and his movement secure a response from R (line 5), but R remains orientated towards the plans on the desk. P then

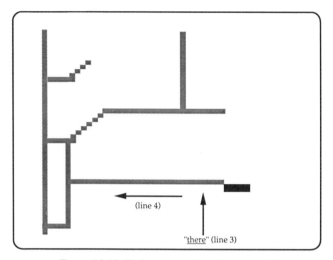

Figure 10.12 Staircase section (fragment 9)

presses a key-chord zooming out of the section as he says 'of the' in 'part of the drawing' (line 9). R then begins to orient himself towards P's screen and moves behind P as P is saying 'youve done a section through' (line 13). Then P points back to the plans (on 'this guy here right?' – line 13). R gazes back at the plans and says 'yep' (line 15). Meanwhile P gazes back at the screen and when he says 'too:', R also looks at the screen (line 17).

Although this is only a brief outline of the vocal, visual, and screen-based conduct in (9), it reveals a sequential relationship between these activities. P's talk, gaze, and body movement secure R's alignment first to the screen, then to the paper plans, and then back to the screen. P's own activity is also tied to his. His key-command results in the system displaying a complete view of his drawing, consisting of many tiny sections displayed on the screen. P says 'right yeah' just after this appears on the screen (line 11). As he says 'had' in 'thats the stair of the section I had' (line 17) he zooms into one of the sections which appears while he is saying 'too:'. The gap and the extension of 'too:' appear to draw R's gaze to the screen. Particular visual alignments can be engendered through perturbations in talk: a restart, pause, extension, or shift of gaze aligning another to a particular object (Goodwin 1981; Heath 1986). Here it appears that visual conduct and talk are also tied to the activity on the system, the irregularities or perturbations in the talk and the shifts of gaze and body movement being tied to the irregular pacing of the system's operations and the variability of the contents of the screen. Although the system in fragment (9) is being used by a single individual, the zoom out and the zoom in, from one section to another, is thoroughly embedded within the interaction between the two architects. It is unclear how a cognitive model could account for this activity.

In this fragment, P uses both the screen and paper-based drawings as a resource in his interaction with R. Various developments in CSCW have aimed to provide shared drawing tools for users, allowing them to collaborate over distances on the same drawing (Bly 1988; Ishii 1990; Minneman and Bly 1991). Analysis of video materials can point to some essential requirements for such systems to be useful in architectural settings concerning the visibility, size, and orientation of displays. For example, it would appear necessary for the displays to be large and flat on the desk (or only slightly tilted). It would also be useful if they could interact with their plans in much the same way they interact with the present paper documents. Experiments with such 'desktop' interfaces where both images of electronic documents are projected onto the desk and paper documents are scanned through cameras are already currently under way at EuroPARC (Wellner 1991; Newman and Wellner 1992). Video analysis can also reveal some of the practices with which architects orient to the same object on the screen or on paper, practices that may not be supported solely by providing multiple pointers on the screen. Some of the difficulties faced by designers of distributed drawing systems are just those that are concerned with how to embed the use of such devices within the talk and visual conduct of the users. Recent developments with video images and audio connections appear to be a way of addressing this issue (Tang and Minneman 1991).

SUMMARY

The work of architects depends not only on the work of others in the office, but also on a range of other individuals in different organisations. These include structural engineers, drainage engineers, building contractors, fire officers, and the clients. In fact, all the instances considered above can be directly related to the changing 'requirements' of outside organisations: the tunnel staircase had to be extended because of instructions to deepen the tunnel by the drainage engineer (fragment 3); the staircases had to be turned around because of the requirement for a new room from the client (fragment 9); and one of the justifications for drawing details of the toilets in the old building is to give the drainage engineer something to work with so that he can design a drainage system (fragment 4).

Recently, Hutchins (1985) has proposed a distributed model of cognition which attempts to take into account the differing goals of individuals in various technological environments (e.g. on the bridge of an aircraft carrier and in the cockpit of a plane, Hutchins 1990; Hutchins and Klause 1990). He proposes that particular artifacts, such as maps, charts, and dials, mediate between individuals with differing tasks, goals, knowledge, and expertise. Presumably, the architects' drawings are such mediating artifacts between the architects and between the architects and other individuals.

Even this relatively radical reconceptualisation of the relationship between the individual, his or her activity, and the computer system does not appear to capture the situated and socially organised character of cooperative work revealed in the instances above.

In this chapter we have attempted to describe aspects of the human–computer interaction in a real-world, organisational setting. Even a cursory glance at the ordinary use of such systems within ordinary work tasks, as we have undertaken here, begins to reveal characteristics of computer use which cannot be incorporated comfortably into more conventional descriptions of the interaction between human and computer. For example, attempts to distinguish conceptually and empirically the internal and external knowledge of users unfortunately neglect the innovative and improvisational character of systems' use and the ordinary competences upon which individuals rely in undertaking screen-based activities in 'practical situations of choice'. Perhaps part of the difficulty in utilising more conventional cognitive models to characterise real-world computer use derives from their concern with conceptualising the knowledge a user has 'of' a system, rather than 'how' knowledge is used within the situated accomplishment of a range of social actions and activities. Users, and, in this particular case, architects, bring a range of resources to bear in producing and rendering intelligible screen-based actions and activities, and more detailed analysis of the procedures, practices and reasoning involved in the accomplishment of technologically informed architectural work might well provide a more satisfactory characterisation of certain aspects of human–computer interaction. However, the naturalistic analysis of individual screen-based activity does raise important methodological problems and it is not at all clear that at the present time the work discussed here, or related studies, has been able to provide satisfactory solutions to those difficulties. Despite these difficulties, and placing to one side the various programmatic reasons for undertaking naturalistic studies of computer use, it would seem that preliminary observations of the use of complex technology by individuals in real-world situations raises significant questions for some of the more important assumptions and conceptualisations which underlie a range of current work on human–computer interaction.

NOTES

We should like to thank Marina Jirotka, and colleagues at Rank Xerox Cambridge EuroPARC for their discussions and comments on an earlier draft of the chapter. Part of the research reported here was undertaken under the auspices of a Joint Cognitive Science Initiative (ESRC/MRC/SERC) Research Grant concerned with the Social Organisation of Human–Computer Interaction.

1 Macintosh is a trademark of Apple Computer Inc. and PowerPoint is a trademark of the Microsoft Corporation.
2 A trademark of Graphsoft Inc.

3 Plans cut through a building horizontally about 1.5m above floor height, sections cut through vertically, usually at places where there are significant changes to the shape of the building, and elevations show the sides of the building viewed from the outside and capturing all its possible faces.

4 Faced with the complexity of the conduct revealed in the video-recordings of screen-based activity, it was necessary to develop a transcription system to be used alongside the recordings. The titles of menus, for example 'Fill', are used to show when they are selected by the user and highlighted on the screen. They are written down the page whereas when the user highlights particular menu items they are written to the right of the menu title. Colons are used to capture the timing of the activity, each colon for one tenth of a second. Pauses between activities are given in seconds in parenthesis. Up and down arrows represent when the user presses or depresses the mouse button; the bracketed heading such as '[Untitled]' is for the region of the screen over which the mouse button was clicked. Users' 'self talk' is shown in double quotes and follows the orthography of Jefferson (1972). A fuller description of the transcription system is given in Luff and Heath (1990).

5 As with many other applications for the Macintosh, MiniCad offers users what are called 'accelerators' as quick alternatives to selecting items from menus. These are performed by typing combinations of keys simultaneously (called 'chording'). In (1), the user types the command key labelled '⌘' and the 's' key together. This performs the same operation as selecting 'Save' from the File menu. These chords are often displayed on the menu to the right of the appropriate item.

6 A transcription notation for visual conduct is described in Goodwin (1981) and Heath (1986). For the purpose of presentation in this chapter, gaze movement is shown by a line above which is the name of the object the architect is glancing at (e.g. screen, desk, or paper plan).

11

WE'RE OFF TO RING THE WIZARD, THE WONDERFUL WIZARD OF OZ [1]

Robin Wooffitt and Norman Fraser

CHICKENS AND EGGS AND THE WIZARD OF OZ

In recent years much research has been done to try to model ordinary verbal interaction with computational tools to produce intelligent speech interface systems. Conventionally, it is felt that to produce systems that are 'user-friendly' they must be designed to be sensitive to the communicative competencies which human users will bring to bear in their exchanges with intelligent speech systems. This requirement, however, entails a 'chicken and egg' type of problem: how can system designers know how people will react to computers prior to the development of an experimental system, and how can an experimental system be developed prior to an understanding of users' behaviour and requirements? That is, in advance of the actual system being built and operational, there is little knowledge about the way people will interact with it to inform the design of the system so that it facilitates easy use by a human.

Simulation experiments provide a way into this otherwise closed circle. So-called 'Wizard of Oz' (WOZ) simulations, which involve a person pretending to be an intelligent computer, are becoming increasingly popular as designers attempt to anticipate the behaviour of human users in their dealings with interactive systems (Fraser and Gilbert 1991). The name of the simulation technique is derived from Baum's novel *The Wizard of Oz* (1900), in which the 'great and terrible' Wizard is revealed to be no more than a device operated by an ordinary man hiding behind a screen. Similarly, WOZ simulations require an accomplice (the 'wizard') to play the role of a projected technological artifact using whatever measures are necessary to effect the disguise, while the experimental subjects are led to believe that they are interacting with a piece of existing technology.

Most WOZ simulation experiments which have been carried out so far have involved typed, rather than spoken, natural language dialogues. For example, typed WOZ simulations of natural language information systems have been conducted by Beun and Bunt (1987) simulating a train and plane timetable system; Dahlbäck and Jönsson (1989) simulating a variety of information provision systems; and Whittaker and Stenton (1989) simulating an artificial art expert. The lessons learned from these typed studies cannot be generalised to spoken interactions since a considerable body of empirical evidence is available to demonstrate that significant differences exist between spoken and written language, at least in the context of human–human dialogues (for example, Chapanis 1981).

Several WOZ studies have also been carried out in which the user communicates with the system by means of natural language and the system communicates with the user by means of text displayed on a video screen. The metaphor for these experiments is that of the 'listening typewriter' (for example, Gould et al. 1983; Newell 1987). In the context of an electronic mail system, Hauptmann and Rudnicky (1988) compared speech input to a human operator with speech input to a simulated computer (in fact, the operator remained the same and was unaware of which role he was playing at any time). All operator output was typed. Significant linguistic differences were found in subjects' talk under the different conditions, thus demonstrating that the ascribed 'species' of the dialogue partner is a significant factor in the organisation of utterances in talk.

To date, only a few WOZ simulations have been carried out in which both participants use speech. Examples include Guyomard and Siroux's Yellow Pages information system simulation (1988); French train timetable system simulations by Morel (1986, 1987) and Luzzati and Neel (1989); and British train timetable system simulations by Richards and Underwood (1984a, 1984b). A number of interesting facts about talk to (supposed) intelligent computer systems have emerged from analyses of simulation corpora. However, most of these analyses have been quantitative, focusing on the construction of lexicons and grammars for syntax and dialogue. Our work constitutes the first attempt to conduct qualitative analysis of samples of talk in which subjects believed they were talking to an intelligent computer.

Quantitative studies provide basic information about gross trends in talk. For example, a number of researchers (including those mentioned above) have observed that, typically, fewer words are used in human–computer dialogues than in human–human dialogues on the same subject. This is an interesting observation and one that begs further investigation. However, it is difficult to see how an explanation for this phenomenon could be constructed on the basis of purely quantitative study. Qualitative study, on the other hand, seeks to elucidate what is being transacted in the talk. It recognises that utterances do not just occur – they occur with social significance. For example, qualitative analysis may reveal that speakers do not hold computers accountable for their behaviour in talk in the same way that they hold other people accountable. This, in turn, may contribute to the lower word counts recorded for human–human dialogues. It is our belief that qualitative analysis of simulated dialogues can shed light on observations which emerge from quantitative studies. More importantly, it can also bring to light facts which would not otherwise be revealed.

THE SURREY WOZ SIMULATION PROCEDURE

A randomly selected session of telephone calls to British Airways' flight information service was tape-recorded, and the first 100 calls were transcribed. This corpus was analysed to generate 'scenarios' corresponding to a representative sample of calls. A scenario is simply a story which includes all of the major task parameters of the enquiry from which it was derived. For example, the following dialogue appeared in the corpus.

(1) T1:SA:146 ('A' is the British Airway's agent, 'C' is the caller.)[2]

```
 1  A    ·hh good ↑morning british airways flight
 2       infor↑mation:
 3  C    ·h umm I wonder if you could help me
 4       please=could you check flight bee ay nine oh three:,
 5       it's due in tomorrow ↑morning from frankfurt.
 6       tuh ↑heath↑ro:w,³·h an' I just want t⌈o co-
 7  A                                         ⌊oh tomorrow,
 8  C    °yes please° (.) I ju⌈st want to confirm
 9  A                         ⌊sorry,
10  C    what ti:me it is due in ⌈( )
11  A                            ⌊YEs certainly
12       >hold on<
13       (5.5)
14  A    Er:: nine oh three frankfurt ↓london?
15       (.7)
16  C    ye⌈s
17  A      ⌊that flight is scheduled fuh(r) ↓twe:lve noon
18       tomorrow
19  C    A:nd which terminal
20  A    sorry?=number one
21  C    thank you very much
22  A    thanky⌈ou
23  C          ⌊bye bye
```

On the basis of this dialogue, the following scenario was generated.

Scenario 1

Your boss is due to fly back from Germany tomorrow morning and you have to meet him off the plane. His flight number is BA 903 and the flight departs from Frankfurt and arrives at Heathrow airport.

To control for effects introduced by the wording or parameter ordering of the scenarios, alternative formulations of the same tasks were produced.

Scenario 1a

Find out what time the Frankfurt–Heathrow flight (BA903) gets in tomorrow morning. You'll have to meet your boss who's returning from Germany on it.

Ten subjects were obtained, of whom six were female and four male. All were volunteers drawn from a student population and were aged between 18 and 35 years. The subjects were placed in a room alone, and given ten scenarios and a pre-experimental questionnaire containing the following five questions.

Pre-experimental questionnaire
1. Are you male or female?
2. What is your age?
3. Which of the following best describes your experience of using computers? {none, a little, moderate, quite a lot, expert}
4. Have you ever used a telephone answering machine?
5. Do you think it is possible to have an intelligent conversation with a computer?

It must be stressed that the use of questionnaires was not motivated by an assumption that they would provide us with valuable information; rather they were used specifically to facilitate subjects' understanding that they were participating in an experiment to test a real computer system. However, subjects were not explicitly told that they would be talking to a computer. The following instructions were given to subjects, and, other than the telephone number to dial, no further information was provided.

Instructions to subjects

Your task in this experiment is to enquire about the flights mentioned in some scenarios. You will be given ten scenarios, each on a separate piece of paper. You can if you wish add more information to each scenario so long as it does not contradict information in the scenario; for example, if you are asked whether a flight arrives at Gatwick or Heathrow and the scenario says nothing about the destination

214

airport, then you could answer that it arrives at Gatwick or Heathrow or that you don't know. Of course, you may be told that your information is incorrect!

Carefully read the first scenario. Then pick up the receiver and make your enquiry. When you have finished, put the receiver down and move on to the next scenario.

Subjects' calls were answered by the wizard, whose speech was filtered through a vocoder in order to flatten out the prosodic variation, thereby making the speech sound synthetic. The wizard also produced slightly slowed speech. This improved intelligibility and, according to subjects who took part in a pilot study, it helped make the speech sound more artificial.

At every possible opportunity, the wizard used exactly the same linguistic forms as those produced by the British Airways agents in the dialogues on which scenarios were based. In order to generate a corpus which is not too far out of step with foreseeable developments in speech recognition, speech production, and computational linguistics, the wizard asked for utterances of more than about twenty words to be reformulated, asked for some randomly chosen utterances to be repeated, and deliberately misunderstood a small number of user utterances, thus facilitating failure–repair sequences. On the whole, however, subjects were allowed to formulate utterances in the ways that they chose. A total of 100 recorded trials was collected.

After the simulation, subjects completed a second questionnaire. The most important questions for the purposes of this paper were:

Post-experimental questionnaire

1. Were you able to ask questions the way you wanted to?
10. Do you think it is possible to have an intelligent conversation with a computer?

Subjects were also informally interviewed in order to gauge their reactions to the design of the experiment, and, more importantly, to determine if they had any suspicions at all that they had been talking to another human merely pretending to be a computer.

All subjects answered 'yes' to the question 'Were you able to ask questions the way you wanted to?' They had no perception of being led through a menu, or of having constraints imposed upon their linguistic behaviour. All but two subjects answered 'yes' to the pre-experimental question 'Do you think it is possible to have an intelligent conversation with a computer?' Identical responses were given in the post-experimental questionnaire. However, even the two subjects who answered 'no' clearly believed that they had been talking to a machine. In answer to the post-experimental question, one of them wrote, 'No. Only in this context, where

215

it [the system] has the information and just gives it to you. It can't express its own opinion.' The other subject wrote 'I'm impressed by the amount it seemed to understand' and 'I thought the system worked well'. All subjects were enthusiastic about the 'system' and offered more information than was requested in the post-experimental questionnaire and in the informal interview. There can be no doubt, then, that they all believed they had been conversing with a computer, including those who had claimed some previous experience with computers.

CONVERSATION ANALYSIS IN THE STUDY OF HUMAN–(SIMULATED) COMPUTER INTERACTION

As we mentioned earlier, materials generated through previous studies of the interactions between humans and WOZ simulations have been examined through the use of primarily quantitative methodological techniques. We have decided to examine our data using a conversation analytic approach, and it is appropriate here to explain why this analytic methodology has been adopted, and to describe why we think it will yield information of benefit to the broader project of designing interactive speech interfaces.

Conversation analysis has emerged in the past twenty years as one of the pre-eminent approaches to the study of naturally occurring conversational interaction. The goal of analysis is to describe and explicate the communicative competencies which underpin mundane, everyday interaction. Such studies have produced a substantial and cumulative body of findings about various dimensions of conversational organisation. These findings provide an invaluable store of information to which we can refer to inform our understanding of human interaction with simulated and, eventually, actual interactive[4] speech interfaces.

More relevant to the present study, however, are recent attempts to examine spoken interaction which occurs in various institutional settings. There are now a number of studies which point to the ways that features of the organisation of everyday conversation are modified in specific contexts and settings (Atkinson 1984; Atkinson and Drew 1979; Drew and Heritage forthcoming; Greatbatch 1988; Heath 1984, 1986; Heritage and Greatbatch 1986; Hutchby 1991). One upshot of these findings is that everyday communicative competencies can be treated as having a foundational or 'bedrock' status in relation to talk which occurs in institutional contexts. Furthermore, this research suggests that there is no deterministic relationship between contexts and language use which takes place within those contexts. Rather, it emphasises that, through local modifications of specific conversational practices, participants display their orientation to, and thereby instantiate and reproduce, the institutional dimensions of the settings in which interaction occurs.

216

With this in mind, we can begin to analyse data generated from simulation studies to explicate which conversational resources, rooted in the domain of everyday talk-in-interaction, are marshalled in exchanges with computerised artifacts. Furthermore, in the exploration of the ways that communicative resources are so modified to meet the practical contingencies of actual dealings with artifacts, we can start to sketch the organisation and operation of interactional resources through which human–computer interaction, as a series of institutionalised communicative arrangements, is constituted and rendered distinctive from other instances of talk-in-interaction.

For present purposes we wish only to sketch some preliminary analytic observations,[5] and thereby to illustrate some themes emerging from our studies of the WOZ simulation corpus. Our empirical remarks are derived from examination of circumstances in which there are signs of trouble in the exchange between the user and the wizard. This focus is motivated by two concerns. First, conversation analytic studies have revealed a complex organisation of strategies and procedures through which participants in conversation can identify and address difficulties as they emerge in the course of the exchange, and thereby ensure the smooth trajectory of the interaction. System designers should be sensitive to the kinds of resources and their organisation that people will bring to bear in their dealings with intelligent artifacts.

A more mundane point, but one relevant to designers of interactive systems, is that prototype systems are, by their nature, likely to crash, hiccup, develop bugs, and generally produce a range of curious outpourings to perplex the user. It is in anticipation of this projected array of problem sources that we have decided to turn our attention to the examination of the ways that conversationalists identify and address difficulties in their exchanges with the simulated artifact in the WOZ corpus.

We focus loosely on two features of the wizard's speech production which appear to lead to difficulties in the exchange: the (sometimes lengthy) silences between a user's utterance and the wizard's subsequent turn; and the problems encountered as a consequence of the use of technical resources to disguise the wizard's voice.

(NOT ALL) SILENCE IS GOLDEN

It has already been reported that, in order to foster the impression that the subjects were indeed talking to a computer, the wizards tended to speak with a slow, staccato delivery. It was felt that this kind of delivery would give the impression of computational processes operating to formulate what to say next. Moreover, the wizards left lengthy pauses between the end of a caller's turn and their own reply. These speech delivery patterns are illustrated in the following extract.

(2) Dialogue 3:8: Scenario 2a.[6]

```
 1  W   flight (.2) information (.5) can (.) I help (.) you
 2              (.5)
 3  U   yes I'd (.) like to: confirm when ·h the
 4          flight from warsaw arrives ·h at heathrow
 5          terminal two tomorrow evening=I think
 6          it's at nine thirty (.) pee em
 7          could you confirm that please
 8              (4)
 9  W   please (.) wait
10              (22.5)
11  W   there (.) are (.) no (.) british (.) airways (.)
12          flights (.) from (.2) warsaw
13              (1)
14  W   please (.) try (.2) pol(and) (.2) airlines
15              (1)
16  U   thank you
17              (2.2)
18  W   thank you (.) good (.) bye
```

This extract reveals some lengthy silences in the exchange. For example, 4 seconds elapse after the user's request formulation before the wizard provides any acknowledgement, and then there is a 22.5-second silence between the wizard's acknowledgement and the subsequent answer.

Previous research indicates that the occurrence of such lengthy gaps in exchanges could be a source of trouble. Jefferson (1989) suggests that there is a standard metric of approximately one second in conversational interaction. Her analysis of instances of silences falling within a 0.8 to 1.2 second boundary reveals that speakers orientate to this metric as a 'tolerance interval' (Jefferson 1989: 170) which marks the acceptable length of absence of talk in conversational interaction. That is, after silences of the duration between approximately 0.8 to 1.2 seconds, speakers can be observed to begin talking so as to terminate the silence. This suggests that silences which reach beyond this maxim are being treated as signs of trouble in the conversation. Furthermore, conversation analytic research has shown that silences in conversation are monitored closely, and that such monitoring is consequential to the inferences that participants may arrive at concerning the significance of the co-participants' behaviour.

(2) (TW:To,M,85)

```
Child:   Have to cut the:se Mummy
             (1.3)
Child:   Won't we Mummy
```

(Atkinson and Drew 1979: 52)

In this instance, after the child asks a question, the mother does not answer and there is an absence of talk for 1.3 seconds. However, the child does not merely repeat the question, but provides a truncated utterance which abbreviates the previously formulated question. The child's subsequent turn is therefore informed by an analysis of the absence of talk as indicating not 'Mummy didn't hear', but 'Mummy heard but didn't answer'. The child's behaviour in this fragment is clearly informed by normative requirements associated with paired action sequences (Schegloff and Sacks 1973). But for our purposes we need only note that the child addresses a 'trouble' – the absence of the conditionally relevant answer – after a silence which reaches the outer edge of the tolerance boundary.

In the light of this observation, consider the following extract from the WOZ corpus.

```
(3) Dialogue 1:6: Scenario 13
 1  W   flight (.) information (.4) british (.) airways
 3      (.5) good day (.7) can I help you
 4          (.6)
 5  U   ·h yes- (.) I'm enquiring about em the flights
 6      coming from crete ·h there's one due in: (.) to
 7      gatwick (.2) approximately ten o'clock this morning
 8      ·h but I've heard (.) there's some problems (.) do
 9      you know if there's any flight delays
10          (4)
11  W   please wait
12          (27)
13  W   please (.3) repeat (.) the (.) point (.) of
14      departure⁷
15          (1.2)
16  U   ·hh well >th-< the- it's flying from crete
17          (4.3)
18  U   to gatwick
19          (1.2)
20  U   arriving at gatwick
21          (4.3)
22  W   I'm (.) sorry (.7) british (.) airways (.5) do not
23      have (.) any (.) flights (.5) from (.) crete (.3)
24      arriving (.) this (.) morning
```

We shall focus on the sequence in lines 16 to 20 which is prompted by the wizard's request for a partial repeat of the initial query.

Note that the user has been asked to provide specific information concerning only one parameter of the relevant flight, and that she complies with this request. Equally, after the word 'crete' the user makes no non-lexical sounds ('err', 'erm', and the like) which might indicate that there is more to come; neither is the word 'crete' itself elongated, as it might be if the user wanted to display that it was not the last thing that she was going to say in that turn. It would appear that at the point where the user completes the word 'crete' she has, for all practical purposes, completed her turn.

The user's completion of the turn passes the floor to the system.[8] There are a variety of relevant responses which the system could produce here: it could acknowledge that the information has been received, announce that the inquiry is now being dealt with, ask the user to wait, or pursue some further information to enable it to address the flight request. But there are no responses of any kind, and after 4.3 seconds, the user begins to speak again, saying first 'to gatwick' and then providing a minor reformulation of this information 'arriving at gatwick'.

In one of his early lectures Sacks considered the delicate issue of no one starting to talk when someone has demonstrably completed a turn (Sacks winter 1969, lecture 9: 15). He focused on one strategy by which conversationalists can address this problem, namely, to treat the silence not as 'nobody's talking', nor as an absence of the talk of the last person to speak, but as a *pause* within one person's talk. He states that this can be done by turning whatever is said *next* into a recognisable continuation of what was said *prior* to the silence. And this is exactly what 'to gatwick' does: it stands as a continuation of the turn 'it's flying from crete'. However, if it is the case that the turn in line 18 is done as a completion for the turn in line 16, then we can also say that it proposes that the early turn was incomplete. 'To gatwick' thus retrospectively 'de-completes' 'well >th-< the- it's flying from crete'.

Before we examine this sequence in more detail we want to sketch some broader dimensions of this strategy. First, continuations are produced after lapses in the talk which approach or extend beyond the tolerance boundary of approximately 0.8 – 1.2 seconds. In the following example the turn 'and which terminal' continues the initial request after a silence of 1 second.

(4) Dialogue 1:3 Scenario 3
```
 7  U   I wonder if you could tell me the time of arrival
 8      (.) ·h and also which (.) london airport it will b-
 9      arrive at
10              (1)
11  U   and which terminal
12          (2.5)
13  W   bee ay (.3) two (.) nine (.) six
```

There may be more than one attempt to continue the initial turn. In the following extract the user provides two additional continuation components. Note that both continuation utterances are produced after silences which extend into the vicinity of the 1-second tolerance level.

(5) Dialogue 1:7 Scenario 7

```
18  W     please (.) repeat (.) your (.) request
19              (1.3)
20  U     ·h I'm enquiring about the (.) the flight
21        (.) ·h bee ay two
22        eight six
23              (1)
24  U     flying in later today (.) ·h from san        [1]
25        francisco
26              (.7)
27  U     ·h and I want to know which                  [2]
28        airport (.4) it's arriving at (.3) and
29        which terminal (.) ·hh and also what
30        time (.3) please h
31              (3)
32  W     please wait
```

(6) Dialogue 1:6 Scenario 13

```
33  U     and do you know if any other companies hhh (.8) w-
34        do have any schesuls (.) scheduled flights flying
35        into gatwick
36              (1.3)
37  U     this morning                                 [1]
38              (.8)
39  U     from crete                                   [2]
40              (6)
41  W     this (.) flight (.2) may be handled (.) by another
42        (.2) carrier
```

In those cases in which users produce two continuations, as in extracts (5) and (6), the length of the silence between the original turn and the first continuation is longer than the silence between the first and the second continuation. The duration of the silences are, respectively, in extract (5), 1 second and 0.7 of a second, and in extract (6), 1.3 seconds and 0.8 of a second. In extract (3) there is only one continuation, but then the user provides a minor reformulation of this information. The duration of the silences between the initial turn and the continuation utterance and between the continuation and the reformulation are, respectively, 4.3 seconds and 1.2 seconds.

A final point is that while there are examples of users producing a second continuation utterance after a first, there is no case of a speaker then producing a third. In each instance, the users wait for the agent to respond, even if the length of an absence of any talk between the end of the second continuation and the wizard's utterance clearly breaches the 1.2/3 second tolerance boundary. In extract (3) there is a 4.3 second silence after the second continuation; in extract (5) there is a 3-second silence before the wizard's acknowledgement of the request, and in extract (6) there is a 6-second silence. During these silences the users make no effort to extend further the initial turn. Thus there may be constraints operating to circumscribe the kinds of circumstances in which users will initiate remedial actions via the production of continuation utterances.

These observations point to some organisational dimensions to the production of continuation utterances. While these features themselves warrant further inspection, we introduce them here only to illustrate the emergence of recurrent properties of users' exchanges with the system. For the rest of this section we wish to explicate an example of the kind of interactional and sequential work mediated through the production of continuation utterances, and with this in mind, we can return to the target sequence from extract (3).

```
Dialogue 1:6: Scenario 13
16   U    ·hh well >th-< the- it's flying from crete
17                  (4.3)
18   U    to gatwick
19                  (1.2)
20   U    arriving at gatwick
```

The silence of 4.3 seconds (line 17) is treated by the user as a problem. By continuing a turn prior to the silence, we can see that the user is not treating the absence of talk as a consequence of a technical glitch in the lines of communication, or any kind of system failure. Such assumptions would motivate attempts to assess whether the telephone line was still working, or questions directed to the system which focus explicitly on its continued participation. The production of a continuation is premised on the system's *current* participation in that it portrays the absence of system contribution as a consequence of a *temporary* non-participation.

The user provides a continuation which characterises her prior turn as being unfinished. Furthermore, this furnishes additional information concerning the flight about which the inquiry is being made. The continuation utterance therefore proposes that the pre-silence turn was incomplete. Furthermore, insofar as it specifies another parameter of the relevant flight, it proposes that the prior utterance was incomplete with respect to precisely this kind of information. 'To gatwick' therefore displays the users' reasoning as to the cause of the problem silence and simultaneously constitutes its remedy.

Insofar as the user provides a continuation which furnishes additional details of the relevant flight, she proposes that, in the absence of talk, the system *should* have made some contribution, but that it could not do anything until she had furnished further information. Thus, the responsibility for the absence of talk is identified as the system's inability to participate. And insofar as the user does work to remedy this, she demonstrably colludes in (what is now taken to be) the system's 'indication' that the turn 'it's flying from crete' was not complete.

'To gatwick', then, both characterises the nature of, and provides a resolution to, a problem. The source of the problem is portrayed as the insufficient information in the user's initial turn in this sequence; and the additional information is an attempt to remedy this. Through this pragmatic work, then, the user can be seen to be *aligning* herself with what has been inferred as the source of the systems' temporary non-participation.

In his lecture, Sacks mentions some 'virtues' which accrue from the provision of turns which continue turns prior to spates of silence, and we may consider these here. First, some inferential virtues. We have noted already that the design of the continuing turn proposes, broadly, the user's alignment to, or agreement with, what the system's problem is taken to be. But with regard to specific details of this sequence, there is a more concrete upshot of this strategy, in that it allows the user to propose that the request had been misheard. That is, the provision of the additional information 'to gatwick' portrays the caller as being in the position of 'coming to realise' that it was departure *and* arrival place that was required, and thereby establishes her 'current understanding' that her own prior turn had not ended. This in turn corroborates a sense of alignment achieved by the user, in that it characterises the user as 'coming to realise' that she has made a mistake. Furthermore, and this is an observation taken from Sacks' lecture, it proposes that the co-participant, or, in this case, the system, was correct not to participate at this moment, because the turn in which such talk could have started was not at that point complete: had the system started to contribute to the exchange, it would have been an 'interruption' in the user's turn.

There are some sequential virtues also. The significant feature of this sequence is that the system did not begin to participate upon the completion of the utterance 'well >th< the- it's flying from crete'. The provision of a continuation furnishes another opportunity for the system to begin in that it projects a further turn transition relevance place (Sacks *et al.* 1974). Furthermore, a continuation utterance can be so designed to identify and deal with a trouble source as a feature of the ongoing exchange, thereby diminishing the likelihood and necessity of a sequence of explicit repair or clarification.

SOME CONSEQUENCES OF DEHUMANISING A HUMAN VOICE

In the following extract the exchange runs into difficulty in lines 12 and 13.

(7) Dialogue 7:5: Scenario 4
  1 W   flight information can I help you

```
2                  (1.5)
3   U    yes I wanted to get the number:
4        the flight number for the british airways
5        flight (.) lea:vi:ng to↑morrow from gatwick
6        to barcelona. (.3) leave in the morning.
7                  (5)
8   W    please (.) wait
9                  (38)
10  W    british (.) airways (.4) has (.) no flight(s) (.5)
11       from gatwick to (.) barcelona
12                 (1.3)
13  U    er: perhaps it's another airline >would you
14       be able to check> (.) if: if there's
15       flights from gatwick to barcelona: on
16       say any other airline leaving tomorrow morning
```

The user appears to encounter some kind of difficulty in formulating what to say after the wizard's turn in lines 10 and 11. There is a silence of 1.3 seconds, which is curtailed by the user's hesitation marker, 'er:'. We propose that the silence in line 12 indicates the user's procedural difficulty, and that this in turn rests upon an ambiguity as to what next action the system's turn projects for the user.

While it is clear that the system cannot deal with the request as formulated, it is not entirely obvious what the problem is. It may be the case that British Airways has no services to Barcelona, or it may be that British Airways does carry services to Barcelona, but from Heathrow Airport, and not from Gatwick Airport. This ambiguity is in part a consequence of the technical protocol of the experiment: remember that the wizard's voice is distorted so that the user has no intonational clues by which to interpret, and perhaps disambiguate, the informational content of the wizard's utterances. But more significantly, it impedes the user's tacit analysis of what kind of next turn is appropriate. So, if the system's turn is designed to indicate that it simply cannot deal with the request, then the user is faced with the option of exiting from the exchange, or asking the system to provide an alternative source for the required information.[9] Alternatively, the system may have been indicating (albeit ambiguously) that the user had incorrectly formulated a relevant flight parameter in the original request, in which case the user has the option of pursuing the information through a suitably amended request formulation.

The first part of the user's subsequent turn addresses these kinds of sequential issues. 'Perhaps it's another airline' is informed by the user's understanding that the flight about which she has inquired is not run by British Airways. Moreover, it displays an acceptance of that problem and, as such, portrays the user's alignment with what is inferred to be the significance of the system's prior turn. However, the identification of the trouble source does not here become the topic of the exchange: there is no explicit reference to a mistake being made. Instead, the reference to the airline as a problematic parameter is designed as an *upshot* of the system's prior turn. This facilitates the user's pursuit of the required information. Furthermore, insofar as she identifies and proposes a solution for the source of the system's apparent difficulty, the user here is doing a form of 'self-repair'. This in turn indicates her analysis that the system's previous contribution initiated the relevance of, and projected a place for, such repair.

We have noted that the user's turn is designed to take account of what is inferred to have been the import of the system's prior turn, and to pursue the required information. As such, aspects of its design may display an orientation to a potential impropriety: asking an agent of the British Airways flight information service about the flights of another airline is to ask about a *competitor*. There is an element of 'impertinence' associated with asking for information about a competitor's services. We may note that these improprieties are sensitive issues for those callers to the actual British Airways flight information service who are subsequently informed that the flight about which they are inquiring is carried by another airline. For example:

```
(8) T4:SA:1860
 1  A    british airways may I ↑help you
 2  C    yes can you tell me please if air ukay three
 3       ni:ne↑ty is coming in at fifteen twenty
 4       five still
 5  A    I'm sorry we're british airways (we) don't
 6       handle air u↑kay (.4) ⌈ (        )
 7  C                         ⌊ er: >well it just
 8       says in the book <heathrow seven five
 9       nine two five two five two five
10  A    that's british airways heathrow
```

In line 7 the caller begins to explain that he has called this number because it is the one provided in the (phone) book. He thus furnishes an account for calling what has been revealed to be the wrong service. Insofar as it has a defensive character, this account mitigates the impropriety of the caller's error. Accounting practices such as this are regular features in circumstances in which required or projected behaviour does not occur (Heritage 1988).

To conclude this section we wish to make some remarks on the way that some features of the user's turn in lines 13 to 16 in extract (7) display an orientation to this impropriety.[10]

We may note firstly that the request 'would you be able to check' is produced at a faster rate than the surrounding talk. Remember that the user's previous utterance 'perhaps it's another airline' has formulated the source of the system's difficulty. Given the nature of this difficulty, it is possible that the system is simply unable to help (and, eventually, this indeed turns out to be the case). So at the point after the system's negative turn, there is a chance that the exchange may be entering a terminal phase prior to the user's exit. The production of 'would you be able to check' as a spate of accelerated speech may indicate the user's sensitivity to the potential onset of a terminal phase of the exchange.

The appropriateness of this pursuit, however, is in part warranted in the manner in which the user has displayed her analysis of the nature of the system's difficulty with the original request. We have observed that 'perhaps it's another airline' formulates the user's upshot of the system's prior turn. Furthermore, it portrays the user's acceptance that this indeed is a problem, and thereby constitutes her alignment with the system's difficulty. However, the accomplishment of alignment has the consequence of making the user's turn hearable as offering a candidate *solution* for that difficulty. This in turn constitutes the problem not as an 'intractable condition', which implies the closure of the exchange, but as 'just another contingency' in the process of locating the required information.

CONCLUSION

As our analysis is still at a preliminary stage we will refrain in this chapter from making specific and detailed recommendations about the design implications of the observations we have presented; rather, we will address some more general issues generated from our use of the WOZ methodology.

Consider the circumstances of our WOZ simulation. Our 'subjects' were led to believe that they were participating in an experiment to test a speaking machine; they were isolated in a room, provided with a set of scenarios and instructions, and asked to converse, through a telephone, with a person whose voice was disguised so that it sounded not unlike a 'Dalek' from the BBC television series *Dr. Who*. Plainly, the actual exchanges between the users and the wizard were obtained in a contrived and artificial environment.

In the light of the circumstances from which the data were generated, it seems almost perverse to consider the utility of an analytic methodology that emerged from the observation and description of *naturally occurring* interaction, in which the participants have no imposed or even agreed conversational agenda. However, despite the apparent incompatibilities of a conversation analytic investigation of partially orchestrated interaction, we believe that the WOZ simulation procedure furnishes a rich environment for the detailed description and analysis of the competencies that underpin human–computer exchanges.

Perhaps the most striking observation is the extent to which ordinary communicative competencies were deployed by the subjects in the experiment. A simple instance of this (although not one focused upon here) was the occurrence of politeness tokens such as 'please' and 'thank you'.

(9) Dialogue 3:8: Scenario 2a
14 W   please (.) try (.2) pol(and) (.2) airlines
15   (1)
16 U   thank you

It is by no means unusual to find subjects saying 'please' and 'thank you' in their exchanges with what they thought was a machine. In one sense this is comparable to thanking a kettle for boiling. But we mention this not to mock the people who took part in the study, but to introduce the point that, on some occasions, the design of users' turns was informed by the kinds of interpersonal concerns which pervade, and to some degree provide the motor for, the detail and arrangement of human–human interaction. This was particularly clear in the examination of turns which were designed, broadly, to constitute the user's alignment with what was inferred to have been the source of the system's difficulty.

In one respect this observation should come as no surprise, because the kind of competencies that appear to inform the users' turns are simply the kinds of cultural resources which in part stand as criteria of what it is to be 'human'. In this sense it would have been an unexpected result had the users demonstrated radically new sets of communicative competencies in their exchanges with what was supposed to be an intelligent artifact. But there is another point. It is not simply that we are claiming that the users behaved as if they were interacting with a human agent, for such an observation furnishes little insight to the detail of the users' conduct. Rather, we have tried to show that interactional resources, grounded in the everyday domain of face-to-face interaction, were deployed in the *strategic* pursuit of circumscribed goals, namely, flight information. Furthermore, we have argued that these goals were pursued in specific, *locally occasioned* circumstances, namely, when users had analysed the system's immediately prior turns (or lack of them) and inferred that there was a problem with some aspect of the request. Moreover, in the case of the user's production of continuation utterances, we have explicated how interactional and sequential work was accomplished through some seemingly robust properties of a domain of conversational organisation. And we believe that is it the provision of precisely these kinds of insights about the users' practical tasks which confirms the utility of a conversation analytic approach to the examination of simulated human–computer interaction.

Finally, perhaps the most salient point is that the qualitative analysis of human–(simulated) computer interaction provides the kinds of insights which remain resolutely unavailable from more quantitative studies. We have observed, for example, the display of some delicate interactional sensitivities in the users' dealings with the Wizard, especially in the way that difficulties in the exchange were identified and addressed. One issue for system designers, then, is the construction of machines so that they avoid producing the kinds of behaviour which human users take to be indications of the onset of problematic stages in the exchange. The technology of interactive speech systems is already such that systems capable of running in 'real time' are not far away; thus it is unlikely that future users of actual systems will have to negotiate instances of relatively long silences of the kind which appeared in our data. But users will face other difficulties. Rather than using informed guesswork or a priori speculation to formulate the nature of these difficulties, perhaps it is more productive simply to examine instances of actual troubles generated through human interaction with a simulated system.

APPENDIX: TRANSCRIPTION SYMBOLS

The following symbols are used in the data.

(.5)	The number in brackets indicates a time gap in seconds.
(.)	A dot enclosed in brackets indicates pause in the talk less than two tenths of a second.
·hh	A dot before an 'h' indicates speaker in-breath. The more h's, the longer the in-breath.
hh	An 'h' indicates an out-breath. The more 'h's the longer the breath.
-	A dash indicates the sharp cut-off of the prior word or sound.
:	Colons indicate that the speaker has stretched the preceding sound or letter. The more colons the greater the extent of the stretching.
( )	Empty parentheses indicate the presence of an unclear fragment on the tape.
(guess)	The words within parentheses indicate the transcriber's best guess at an unclear fragment.
.	A full stop indicates a stopping fall in tone. It does not necessarily indicate the end of a sentence.
,	A comma indicates a continuing intonation.
?	A question mark indicates a rising inflection. It does not necessarily indicate a question.
Under	Underlined fragments indicate speaker emphasis.
↑↓	Pointed arrows indicate a marked falling or rising intonational shift. They are placed immediately before the onset of the shift.
CAPITALS	Capital letters indicate a section of speech noticeably louder than that surrounding it.
° °	Degree signs are used to indicate that the talk they encompass

	is spoken noticeably more quietly than the surrounding talk.
> <	'More than' and 'less than' signs indicate that the talk they encompass was produced noticeably more quickly than the surrounding talk.
=	The 'equals' sign here indicates that one component within a turn has been 'latched' on to another.
[	Square brackets between adjacent lines of concurrent
]	speech indicate the onset and end of a spate of overlapping talk.

A more detailed description of these and other transcription symbols commonly used in conversation analytic research can be found in Atkinson and Heritage (1984: ix–xvi), and Button and Lee (1987).

NOTES

1 The work presented here was undertaken as part of the ESPRIT Project P2218, Sundial (Speech UNderstanding and DIALogue). We would like to thank our colleagues on the project, and our colleagues in the Social and Computer Sciences Research Group, for their encouragement and support. We would also like to thank British Airways for making available tape-recordings of calls to their flight information service.

2 The transcription symbols used here are common to conversation analytic research, and were developed by Gail Jefferson. These symbols are explained in the Appendix.

3 The British Airways flight information service deals primarily with enquiries about BA flights to and from the two main London airports, Heathrow and Gatwick.

4 We leave here the debate about the extent to which eventual systems can properly be called interactive, or can be said to display some measure of conversational competence. (For a discussion of these issues see Button 1990; Gilbert, Wooffitt, and Fraser 1990; Fraser and Wooffitt 1990.) There are already in operation rudimentary speech-based systems which are interactive in the sense that they respond to users' spoken input. The wizard's contributions were organised to reflect in part the capabilities of such machines. We feel, therefore, that the data generated from the simulation study, and the analytic observations subsequently derived from our inspection of these data, can indeed make a contribution to contemporary issues in the design of computer interfaces.

5 The present collection focuses on a broad array of issues in the application of sociology to technological development. We feel, therefore, that illustration of the sort of analytic gains which result from a conversation analytic examination of simulated HCI material is more appropriate than a detailed and thorough analysis.

6 'W' represents the wizard, and 'U' represents the caller or user.

7 It should be noted that the wizard's attempt to elicit a repeat of the point of departure is not based on the ways that the British Airways agents actually pursued this task. The wizard's turns were organised like this merely to facilitate the impression of a speaking machine.

8 We use the word 'system' to refer to the wizard when we are trying to

characterise how the users' responses have been organised with respect to what is assumed to be an artifact.

9 The scenarios were organised to encourage the subjects to experiment with the system and, if they felt inclined, to discover if it could provide an alternative contact number for information which it could not provide.

10 It may be objected that these concerns are not relevant to subjects in conditions as contrived as those in the WOZ simulation. However, we consider that the WOZ simulation is simply another environment in which culturally available, tacit practices and knowledge can become momentarily salient, and thereby inform in various ways users' conduct. Consequently, we consider it legitimate to explore this somewhat commercial dimension of cultural competence in our simulation data.

12

THE TURING TEST AND LANGUAGE SKILLS [1]

H. M. Collins

This is a strange kind of inquiry into human machine interaction because it is based on a thought experiment. The conclusion, however, is quite practical. Among other things, I consider what a machine would have to do to communicate either satisfactorily as a conversational partner or indistinguishably from a human. In the first case the answer is not very much; in the second the answer is more than any foreseeable machine based on existing principles can do. The conclusion is: aim for the former, that's all we need.

I want to explore the imaginary outer limits of what we, and machines, could say and do by virtue of being told things and compare this with what we can say and do by virtue of our socialisation. In the thought experiment I relax the constraints imposed by the typical lifetime of a human being and even the size of the universe. I allow a machine to be told everything that it is possible to tell in English in a finite time. Though this has no direct bearing on any real computer programs it is, I believe, revealing of the nature of skill and socialisation and the problem of being told rather than being socialised. It reveals, then, something of the predicament, not only of computers, but also of spies, those who learn foreign languages from books rather than conversation, philosophers of science, and all those who learn about the world from words rather than their own experience.

The thought experiment starts with an idea discussed by Ned Block. Block (1981) describes an imaginary machine that, he claims, can imitate the conversational responses of any human being in a Turing test of finite length. The design of the machine is based on the fact that the number of typed strings of symbols that can be exchanged in a test of fixed length is finite and the number of possible typed conversations is a subset of these strings. Therefore, in principle, all possible conversations can be memorised in advance. I generalise this idea in order to find out if there are, in principle, any limits to memory-based imitation of human socialisation. I allow the machine to have a memory as large as desired so long as it is finite. The machine has to perform as well as a human in the hard case (for the human) of the Turing test (Turing 1950). One might say, one is testing the ultimate plausibility of Searle's Chinese Room hypothesis.[2] My version of the machine is a little more ambitious than Block's model and is equipped to pass Turing tests with more stringent protocols than Block had in mind.

I would describe the machine as being designed to reproduce the behavioural coordinates of conversational action (Collins 1990). It is like a record-and-playback device for conversational interchange. Though every conversation that is put into the machine's memory must be made explicit, knowledge of sentence structure, conversational turn taking, and so forth – the things we acquire without conscious effort – are entered without needing to be explicated. If human conversational competence could, in principle, be completely reproduced by storing only its behavioural coordinates, then it seems to follow that there is nothing in a skill that cannot be reproduced by finite, if very large, ramification of a rule base. This point of principle is worth exploring even though it tells us nothing about the actual human organism and little about the practicalities of writing programs. At first sight the program I describe does seem to mimic all our tacit conversational skills. Its residual failures are, however, the illuminating thing.

THE BLOCK MACHINE[3]

In a Turing test the parties interact via typewriter keyboards. Imagine that the test is, say, one hour in length. Ignore the control for the time being and let all the interaction be between the interrogator and the machine. If they both type fast they might type 20,000 characters between them in an hour. Call such a collection of 20,000 symbols a 'symbol-string'. If the dialogue is in English each character will be one of about 100 possibilities – twenty-six letters of the alphabet, their capitalised equivalents, numbers, various punctuation marks and other miscellaneous symbols, the space, and a return symbol to signify the end of a conversational turn. Thus, given an hour, the number of different strings of characters that might have comprised the interchange – that is the number of symbol-strings that there are – is about 100 raised to the power of 20,000, or $10^{40,000}$. This is a finite number albeit a Very Very Large Number (the number of particles in the known universe is about 10^{125}). One can adapt the argument for a test of any finite length.

Most of these strings would not be sensible conversations. For example, there would be one comprising 20,000 'a's, one comprising 20,000 spaces, one comprising a long passage from *A Midsummer Night's Dream* but with the word 'frobscottle' in the middle of one of Titania's speeches while another contained the word 'fribscottle' instead. Another excruciating string would make complete sense except that the very last letter was an 'f' instead of an 'e' – and so forth.

Some of the symbol-strings would consist of sensible conversations. Chance would guarantee that in some strings all the spaces, letters, punctuation marks, and return symbols would be arranged to make a sensible English interchange. Call such a string a 'conversation string'. Each conversation string consists of a series of turns separated by the return symbol. Every possible conversation string would be included somewhere in the Very Very Large Number of strings in the complete set of combinations of symbols. That is, everything sensible that it is possible for two people to type to each other in an hour would be included somewhere (mixed up with the nonsense strings). For example, all possible hour-long quotations from *Alice in Wonderland* and Shakespeare, all the songs ever sung by Liverpool Football Club supporters, everything that Edward VIII said to Mrs Simpson and Profumo said to Christine Keeler and Mandy Rice-Davies would be included and so would everything you said between 11 p.m. and midnight last night. There would also be conversation strings representing all hour-long conversations which have never happened but which have the potential to take place so long as the basic set of symbols in the English language remains the same. There is nothing you or I can type that is not included somewhere in the set of conversation strings.

Now, suppose we generate every possible symbol-string by some mechanical means and type them all out. We hand the printed list to a programmer. The programmer is told to discard all the nonsense strings extracting just the conversation strings which make sense. He or she (hereafter 'he') has to winnow out the conversation strings from the symbol-strings.

Now, selecting sensible strings is a complicated business. The programmer will not extract every conversation string because he will not recognise certain strings for the sense that they are. The strings that the programmer extracts will depend upon what he counts as a reasonable interchange. For example, if he is not a philosopher, he might miss some of Wittgenstein's 'Remarks' for they would not seem to make sense. Likewise, some programmers – those not familiar with A.A. Milne – would miss the meaningfulness of the term 'Pooh sticks' while others would not recognise that passages of, say, *Studies in Ethnomethodology* comprise sensible interchanges in the English language. Even if the programmer ignores all strings that contain turns that he does not recognise as sense, the number of conversation strings that a typical programmer would select from the Very Very Large Number of symbol-strings would still be much larger than the number of particles in the universe; the number of strings in the average programmer's set of selected conversation strings will be a 'Very Large Number'.

The Very Large Number of conversation strings is then encoded into the memory of the Block machine. (It should be clear by now that this can never be more than a thought experiment.) We may now imagine the machine exposed to a Turing test. The machine works in the following way: the interrogator types in a conversational turn. The machine compares this with all the first turns of the strings in its memory. It selects from the memory the many, many, conversation strings which begin with this turn. It picks one of these strings at random and replies with the conversational turn that happens to come next in that conversation string. The interrogator responds. The machine now compares these three turns with its memory, selecting the many conversation strings that begin in the same way. Again it selects one of these conversation strings at random and responds with the fourth turn in that particular string. Continuing in this way, at the end of an hour, the machine and the interrogator have reproduced one complete conversation from the memory store and, since all conversations in the store are reasonable, the computer's performance ought to be indistinguishable from that of a real human being such as the one sitting in the control cell. Block's description (1981) is apt. He says the machine acts as a conduit for the programmer's intelligence.

> If one is speaking to an intelligent person over a two-way radio, the radio will normally emit sensible replies to whatever one says. But the radio does not do this in virtue of a capacity to make sensible replies that it possesses. The two-way radio is like my machine in being a conduit for intelligence, but the two devices differ in that my machine has a crucial capacity that the two-way radio lacks. In my machine, no causal signals from the interrogators reach those who think up the responses, but in the case of the two-way radio, the person who thinks up the responses has to hear the question. In the case of my machine, the causal efficacy of the programmers is limited to what they have stored in the machine before the interrogator begins.
>
> (Block 1981: 22)

Block says of his machine that 'All the intelligence it exhibits is that of its programmer' (1981: 21). The intelligence is captured in the programmer's choosing the set of conversations that appear sensible to him and excluding the others.

THE MACHINE'S STRENGTHS

In spite of its essential simplicity of design, the Block machine is very good indeed. It can answer any technical question that its programmer can answer and its interrogator knows how to ask. It can appreciate and tell jokes and it can write or understand any poem that its human programmer can understand.[4] It can cope with all the tricky questions such as 'Do you love me?', 'What does it feel like to hate?', 'How does it feel to eat an onion?', 'How did you learn to ride a bike?', and 'Continue the sequence "2,4,6,8"' in a variety of spoken contexts. It could also have just as good a conversation about chess as its programmer.[5] In so far as a successful conversation machine needs to hypothesise about the internal states of its conversational partners, or build a model of its user, the Block machine will effectively do it. It will appear to grasp every nuance of every form of words, and every implication of social context that its interrogators are able to express through the medium of the typed word at the time it was programmed.

The machine would also be a super expert system in any field of competence covered by the programmer so long as all that was required was written advice or instruction.

The same argument applies to a person skilled or experienced in an art or craft. A human pretending to be skilled in a Turing test is likely to be caught out by an interrogator who is skilled. An inexperienced human will not know enough to generate the full range of relevant conversations; it is just a matter of logistics. But a Block machine would not be caught out because it can be programmed with every conversation in which a skilled person could take part.

Note that the Turing test is not a test of a skill but only a test of what you can say about a skill. That is why the Block machine, though it has never touched a piece of wood, could pretend to be a carpenter and, though it had never touched a brush, could pretend to be an artist. Having a skill involves more than talking about it, however. As I will go on to show, that does turn out to be important in the Turing test.

THE MACHINE'S WEAKNESSES

Earlier, when I suggested that the programmer would not select all sensible strings because he might not recognise passages of Wittgenstein, A.A. Milne, or Harold Garfinkel as sense, I ignored a problem. The problem is that the programmer cannot anticipate what every interrogator might say. If an interrogator's conversational turn included something that the programmer thought was an impossible passage, the program would grind to a halt. There is, however, a technical solution to this problem. The programmer can be liberal with what he counts as potential interrogator turns; he can include almost everything. To make the program work he will select strings that contain these turns followed by turns along the lines of, 'Sorry, I don't know what you mean by that'. It does not matter if the programmer includes interrogator turns that no interrogator would ever actually use because they will simply never arise during a Turing test. Strings including those turns will never be selected from memory during a run.

Now let us examine the programmer's task in more detail. Imagine the programmer sitting down with the long list of symbol-strings and reading each of them through. He selects those that do represent reasonable conversations and rejects those that do not. In making the decision his first concern is whether the responses that the machine will make represent what he could have said in response to the same putative interrogator turns.

Suppose the programmer is reading through some strings which contain a single political comment and response. For example $string_i$ contains interrogator $turn_n$, which reads, 'I prefer conservative politicians'. This is followed by machine $turn_n$ which reads, 'I prefer more progressive types'. Since the programmer is himself a 'leftish' type, there is no reason for this machine turn to seem anything other than reasonable and he will continue to check the rest of the string for sense. Now suppose he finishes with that string and some time later starts on another, $string_j$, which is identical to $string_i$ except that machine $turn_n$ in this string reads, 'I prefer left-wing politicians myself'. The programmer's decision will be the same as before; this variation is equally consistent with what he might say in response to interrogator $turn_n$. Indeed, there are a very large number of possible comments that express a politically 'leftish' sentiment that could be substituted for the original machine $turn_n$ without causing trouble and the set of symbol-strings contains conversations which include all of them.

Now suppose the programmer comes upon a string, which is identical to $string_i$ up to and including the interrogator turn above but the machine turn reads, 'Yes, me too. I'm glad to meet another conservative.' This is not the sort of response that the programmer would normally make. Should he include it?

Now, the programmer is supposed to be including only what could count as sensible conversations in English. This cannot simply mean grammatically sensible conversations for there are many such conversations that do not make sense. Any conversation that contained too many statements along the lines of 'green elephants sleep furiously' would give the game away. The only safe course of action is for the programmer to include just those replies that he would be likely to utter himself. His first instinct, then, on encountering a politically unsympathetic machine turn will be to reject the whole string. Call this the restrictive strategy. If he continues this way, the machine turns, it might be thought, will represent his own conversational repertoire reflecting, among other things, his political personality.

The trouble is that the set of strings that remain will not really represent his conversational repertoire. There will be no strings at all expressing conservative sentiments yet the programmer will probably be able to think of occasions or contexts when he could make such a response. For example, he might do this if he had a whim to pretend to be a conservative, or if he felt there was danger in expressing left-wing sentiments, or if he wanted to play devil's advocate in an argument. If he rejects all strings which contain 'rightish' sentiments he will not produce a machine that has his full conversational potential. In a Turing test the interrogator now has an advantage. If he bets that conversational partners who always produce woodenly predictable political responses are machines, he would be likely to win his bet in the long term. In this case the program has not mimicked the full range of human competences.

An alternative strategy for the programmer, the liberal strategy, is to include strings that contain politically conservative machine turns. Now, for each grammatically accurate conversation string that contains a left-wing sentiment among the machine turns there is a conversation string that contains a right-wing sentiment. The programmer might express his left-wing sentiments in many ways and when he plays devil's advocate or whatever, he has just as many ways to express right-wing sentiments. Therefore, if he wants to express the full range of his conversational potential he must include just as many strings containing right-wing sentiments as strings containing left-wing sentiments. This follows solely from the flexibility of the English language and the rules of selection under which the programmer operates; he must include all conversations that make sense to him.[6]

Under this liberal strategy there are as many strings expressing right-wing sentiments as left-wing sentiments in the memory of the Block machine. When the machine is interrogated it selects all the strings that are consistent with the conversation that has taken place so far and then selects the string containing the next turn at random. This means it is just as likely to select a string containing a conservative response as a progressive one.

Thus, even though the programmer was unambiguously a progressive thinker, the actual political preference expressed by the program would be unpredictable. The ratio of conservative to progressive responses within strings would be the same as the ratio of conservative to progressive comments in the English language rather than the same as the ratio in the conversational performance of the programmer. This ratio would hold at every machine turn expressing a political sentiment in the entire string, for the programmer might have decided to play devil's advocate at any time.[7]

Under the liberal strategy the interrogator who bets that the machine is the politically inconsistent respondent[8] will win the bet in the long term.[9] One way of expressing the problem is to say that the machine's memory contains the programmer's conversational capacity but not the programmer's conversational propensities. Capacity without propensity does not model a human being.

The same arguments apply to non-political preferences and, indeed, to all cases where we can imagine that a conversational partner might decide to break the rules of normal conversational interchange. Thus, consider another form of rule-breaking action – 'nonsense talk'. Block says that some of the strings that represent possible conversations would include turns such as, 'Let's talk nonsense for a while', with some nonsense turns following, but this gives rise to a variation of the problem we have just encountered. The set of speakable strings which include nonsense-containing turns is much larger than the set of strings which contains only what we normally think of as sense. This is because nonsense includes many more arrangements of the 100 available characters than standard English. The set of nonsense-containing strings is so much less limited than the sensible strings because nonsense can be so freely created; there are fewer cultural restrictions on what counts as nonsense because nonsense involves breaking normal cultural boundaries.

Now imagine a conversation between speakers 'A' and 'B' which does contain a bit of nonsense and would therefore be included in the Block machine's memory under a liberal interpretation of what constitutes conversational competence:

1A: Hello Jim, nice weather today.
1B: Needle niidle noo.
2A: You naughty boy.
2B: Aaaaaaaaaaaaeeeeeeeeeeooooooooooogh! ———That's better.

Though there are some restrictions on their form, '1B' and '2B' are but single examples of a large number of possible continuations to '1A'. [10] For example, while retaining the general form and rhythm, '1B' might read 'Needle noddle noo', 'Needle niddel noo', 'Noddle niidel noo', 'Needle niidle nog', 'Noggle needle niing' . . . and so on for a very long time indeed. Given a liberal strategy, all these continuations will have to be included in the Block machine's repertoire of continuations to '1A'. This is because, if it is to be indistinguishable from a certain class of humans, it will have to use nonsense itself from time to time in a spontaneous way; it will have to be as potentially inventive in its use of spontaneous nonsense as a human.

Now let us imagine that the interrogator begins with '1A' – 'Hello Jim, nice weather today.' The Block machine will look through the large number of strings in its memory which start in this way and choose one with its associated second turn. It might find a conversation string with a sensible continuation such as, 'Yes, not bad for the time of year', or 'I got a bit wet on the way to the test actually', or 'Why are you calling me Jim?'. But there will be a much larger set of strings with nonsensical continuations because of the freedom that nonsensical inclusions gives to the way letters can be combined. Thus, when the machine selects a single string at random from the range of possibilities there is an overwhelming chance that it will come back with a nonsense continuation. The problem of nonsense turns out to be even worse than the problem of political sentiment because the ratio of nonsense turns to sense turns is much higher than 1:1 and therefore the number of potential conversations containing nonsense is much larger than those containing only sense. This is so despite the fact that actual written human conversation rarely contains nonsense because humans don't have a great propensity to use it. It is their capacity to use it that wrecks the Block machine.

To reiterate, while there will be no string in the machine's memory which contains more than the amount of nonsense than can be supported in a foreseeable conversation among humans, it is overwhelmingly likely that unobjectionable nonsense will figure early and often in the machine's conversational repertoire. Though the programmer's typical hour-long conversations contain bits of nonsense, say, only one time in 1,000, the machine would almost always talk some nonsense whatever is said to it. Again, this shows the interrogator the way to bet.[11]

These problems might look like mere technicalities but they are really instances of the profound difficulties arising out the attempt to replace a socialised sense of context, which tells one when and how often to break rules, with predetermined behaviour. Going back to Block's metaphor, the programmer is like a conduit. What he appears to convey to the program as he selects the sensible strings from the nonsense is his social competence in separating reasonable interchanges from unreasonable ones. But the promise is not fulfilled. The machine is unable to recognise the moment for the introduction of a piece of innovative social behaviour.[12]

Another problem is that the machine can only be programmed with what counts as acceptable conversation at a particular historical moment. Thus a programmer like me would include strings containing 'Twas brillig and the slithey toves did gyre and gimble in the wabe' and some bits of Goon Show-type dialogue but I could not include the works of the next Lewis Carroll or the next equivalent of the Goons. Suppose the next lot of 'Goons' turned up shortly after the machine was programmed. A whole lot of new responses would suddenly become widely legitimate but the machine would not know about them. Of course, all those possible future Goon-like and Lewis Carroll-like responses can be found among the Very Very Large Number of symbol-strings and I have already shown that the programmer has no problem if he includes them all among the interrogator turns. But, if the machine is to imitate a human, such responses would have to be included in the machine turns too. This is a different sort of problem altogether because an illegitimate machine turn will be executed if it is in the memory even though an illegitimate interrogator turn will not. If the programmer cannot anticipate what might become legitimate speech in English at the time the machine is exposed to interrogation, he will not know what to include. Imagine the impossible. Imagine the programmer is as much of a creative genius as Anthony Burgess and can foresee the possibility of a whole new style of dialogue of the sort that Burgess invents for his novel *Clockwork Orange*. The trouble is that the language of *Clockwork Orange* has not, in fact, caught on. Invention of new languages may be the prerogative of individual geniuses but legitimation of new languages is the prerogative of the cultural collectivity. Languages are the property of communities not individuals.

Because the programmer cannot anticipate the future of language, for the machine to work lastingly, he will have to be on hand all the time, continually updating and changing the memory store so that it corresponds to the social changes taking place around him. He will have to act as a permanent socialisation conduit. In that case, however, the machine can be dispensed with – the programmer might as well speak directly to the interrogator just as in the two-way radio to which Block compares his device. Of course, exactly the same is true of the control. If the control is locked away from society once the test has begun, he too will never learn the novelties of the changing social repertoire. But we are not interested in comparing machines with prisoners or social isolates, only with the most human-like of humans.

SKILL, THE TURING TEST, AND INTERPRETATIVE ASYMMETRY

Nonsense is only one example of non-standard English. The less standard the English, the greater are the creative possibilities and the greater the problem for the Block machine. For example, the phonetic transcriptions of naturally occurring speech, beloved of conversational analysts, show just how much work we do in understanding what is said to us. As an unintended consequence the transcripts also show us just how well we can repair and make sense of unusual printed representations of the language. Take the following quotation from Lynch (1985a: 220):

> Th'thing is's thee ehm
> This is garbaijhe.
> Wehh I dunnuh
> Nuhh doesn' look like vesiculs
> Hhlooks more like a spine er s'm

Just as there were many possible versions of the nonsense phrase, 'needel niidel noo', there are many possible versions of this kind of phonetic representation. For example, the words in the second line of the transcript (I hypothesise) might on other occasions be better represented as 'This is garbaijje' or 'Thisis garbaijhe'. At issue is not the accuracy of Lynch's transcripts but the flexibility of speech as opposed to regular written language.[13] This means that phonetic transcripts of speech are far more flexible than their standard written counterparts. If all these possibilities are included in the memory cf the Block machine then, in the counterpart of the nonsense problem, we would see the machine resorting to phonetic spelling with unwarranted frequency. Both this and the nonsense problem are symptoms of the inability of the machine to deal with our everyday creativity in the use of language.

This argument leads us to a much more important generalisation. As has been said above, the feature of the Turing test that loads it in favour of the machine and allows a design like the Block machine to be a contender is the restricted channel of communication. Written communication can transmit only articulated knowledge – it can transmit only what can be said about a skill, not the skill itself. Therefore the interrogator cannot test the scope of the machine's tacit knowledge in a direct way, he can only test if the machine can say everything that an expert could say about a skill. For example, while the machine could tell us all about the skills of golf, it cannot be asked to demonstrate them. So, while the Turing test is a good test of human-like capability in so far as it is a test of interactional competence, it is a poor test because interactions involving skills are not possible.[14] It is not possible to check to see if the machine can do things by virtue of its tacit knowledge, only whether it can articulate whatever its programmers can articulate by virtue of what they can do.

And yet there is one skill that we can test directly even in the restricted circumstances of the Turing test; this is the skill of making written conversation. The nonsense problem, and the phonetic spelling problem, are examples of failures in conversational skill. The machine cannot, after all, handle language. For computers that interact with us through the written word (most of them), the language interface is the point at which either our skills or the computer's skills are required to digitise the world. If the computer is ever to become genuinely intelligent it will cease to require our help; it will learn to digitise the world for itself in the same way as we do. It will have to learn our inductive propensities. This new ability will become visible at its interface with us. That is the point at which it has the chance to display a skill. The development of the printing press led to standardisation of the written English language. In the Turing test the restriction of the channel of communication normally has the effect of making all legitimate conversational turns expressible only in the subset of standard English that comprises English as 'defined' by the conventions of printing. This is English in which the words have been digitised and it is the digitisation that makes it possible for us even to imagine that we could capture all possible hour-long conversations in a program.

Computerised dictionaries reveal the problem in miniature. Such a dictionary contains a digitised subset of the language. Offer the computer something outside the subset – such as 'niddle' – and it asks if you really mean something else. You then have to decide whether to include a strange and temporary usage in your personal dictionary. If you do not include it the computer's dictionary will always query it every time it appears in a text.[15] If you do include it the dictionary will never query it again even if you

241

put it in by mistake. The dictionary cannot solve the problem of when to accept a creative usage. The Block machine is an attempt to overcome this problem by creating a vast dictionary of huge 'words'. Instead of words, the dictionary contains whole conversations. That is why the machine is so big.[16] In the end, however, nothing is solved.

I have suggested that we test machines such as the Block machine by looking for their ability to handle the equivalent of pre-printing-press English, including phonetic spelling and nonsense with all their implications of non-standardised openness and creativity. To handle this, the computer will have to learn our inductive skills. A general conclusion about Turing testing follows from the argument. Language handling is not an esoteric skill, it is spread widely among the population at all ability levels. It is, for example, a skill that we regularly exercise when we treat the output of computers with respect, as when we make allowances for the curious mistakes of ELIZA-like programs, or when we hear poor voice output as like human speech, or read the limited vocabulary of ordinary package programs. It is our ready willingness to repair such deficiencies that allows current computers to work with us. It is the invisibility of this repair work – because of its pervasiveness even in ordinary human speech – that makes us able to mistake machines for humans. However, if, in conditions of doubt or in Turing test-like circumstances, we exploit interpretative asymmetry and instead of repairing the computer's awkward speech we look for its ability to repair ours, we will discover whether we are communicating with an entity that has skills. If we ever make a computer that can handle the full range of conversational skill – including correcting our deficiencies – then even if it does this via a keyboard, it will merit the title 'Intelligent Machine' or 'Artificial Expert'. Such a machine will share our culture.

CONCLUSION

The argument suggests that it is not possible, with foreseeable machines, to mimic human conversational competence.[17] It also shows why it is that when AI is thought of as engineering rather than science, it is not hard to make an acceptable conversational partner. The aim should be to give us the maximum scope to do the 'repair work' in our conversations rather than expect the machine to do it. A memory-based machine would simply have a liberal strategy for interrogator turns – allowing the interrogator to say anything and then querying what was not understood – and a restrictive strategy for machine turns – producing a wooden but quite acceptable and informative response. The machine would be very useful for any task that one might want to use a conversational machine for, except pretending to be a human. But why does anyone want to make a machine that can pretend to be a human. The only legitimate reason is scientific research; the other reasons seem a lot less respectable.[18]

NOTES

1 This is an adapted version of Chapter 14 of my book *Artificial Experts: Social Knowledge and Intelligent Machines*, MIT Press, 1990.

2 The 'Chinese Room' is able to reproduce conversation in Chinese via a human who uses a code book and a set of file cards to produce written answers to written questions without understanding the language himself. Searle (1981) uses the argument to show that understanding and reproducing conversational competence are not the same thing. I argue that the conversational competence could not be reproduced without the understanding. In discussing Block's ideas in this way I am doing violence to the author's intentions. Block wanted to use the idea to distinguish between intelligence and a 'conduit' for intelligence in which all the intelligence exhibited by the machine was possessed by the programmer. For this purpose the machine need only perform once at a satisfactory level. It seems Block had something similar to Searle's argument in mind in writing his paper. I think that Searle's hypothesis directs attention away from the interesting questions of artificial intelligence. In the same way, I am not interested in Block's argument but only in his design. I believe his design cannot do all that he claims for it. His imaginary program cannot mimic the performance of humans as thoroughly as he thinks. Showing why this is so is interestingly and revealingly difficult

3 I adopt the name 'Block machine' for my refined version in deference to Block's original design of 'string searcher'.

4 In Collins (1985: 23) I used a joke relying on onomatopoeia as an example of an impossible task for a speech transcriber. The Block machine would have no trouble with the joke so long as the programmer understood it.

5 A machine of the power of the Block machine could be a perfect 'chess' player if programmed deterministically – there are only about 10^{120} possible moves in chess!

6 In Block's original article he simply has programmers allowing responses that 'Aunt Bertha' might make, without thinking through the ramifications of this. If only a single set of possible responses is catered for, without allowing any conversational variation, then the machine can produce only quasi-human behaviour – that is, conversational behaviour that is wooden and repetitive.

7 Remember that even a left-winger's complete conversation will be full of right-wing sentiments, under certain circumstances, or half full, or three-quarters full, or whatever. For a left-winger the probability that these versions will come up in actual conversations is low, but the possibility is unavoidable. All grammatical versions of the possibility have to be catered for, and this means that the number of strings completely full, half full, three-quarters full, etc., of right-wing sentiments will be equal to the number of strings equivalently full of left-wing sentiments.

8 Either within a run or between separate runs.

9 Whenever I have presented these ideas members of the audience have invariably come up with clever modifications that seem to overcome the problems I outline. For example each string could be labelled with the probability of its use within the personality being modelled. Thus, while there would be as many strings expressing conservative sentiments as expressing progressive sentiments, where the programmer was a progressive thinker each conservative string would have a very low probability of selection attached to it so that the chance of selection of a conservative string summed across all the conservative strings would be very low. The problem is that this requires that we know the relevant probabilities. That is, if I am the programmer, I have to be able to

articulate, in the form of a set of statistics, the characteristics of my potential conversational performance. But if I can do that the major problems of artificial intelligence are already solved. Innovatory rule-breaking behaviour will have turned out to be just a matter of statistics. Another way round the problem is simply to equip the machine with a set of defensive responses. Thus, the machine simply need not make political statements at all – all strings that include a political sentiment on the part of the machine are excluded, while political expressions by the interrogator are met with responses such as 'I never discuss politics'; strings which contain nonsense expressed by interrogators (see below) are met with defensive responses such as 'I don't really follow that'. Undoubtedly such a strategy would make for an acceptable conversational partner but not one that could mimic everyone's competence. For example, it would not be able to mimic a trained Turing-test interrogator or an exciting conversationalist. All the technical fixes of this type that I have encountered require either that we make explicit our tacit knowledge of how to carry on conversations, returning us to the problem that the Block design so cleverly sidesteps, or they fail to reproduce conversational competence.

10 Actually, the general form of this piece of nonsense is taken from the British BBC Radio series of the 1950s *The Goon Show*. The piece is not entirely free of form, therefore. For example, 60 'x's would not represent a turn, and in fact '1B' has only certain permissible rhythms.

11 As before, we could 'hack' around this problem by dividing the memorised strings into sensible ones and nonsense-containing ones and introducing a rule about the frequency with which the nonsense-containing ones can be sampled. This, however, is open to all the previous objections against hacking round the political preference problem.

12 Since innovative social behaviour may involve being grammatically inaccurate from time to time it is not even clear any longer that we can capture grammatical capacity in the machine without being unduly restrictive.

13 The same argument applies to onomatopoeia. Though I have argued that the machine could cope with a joke that depended on onomatopoeia, the fact that onomatopoeic representation of sounds is less restricted than standard English spelling means that the joke and its minor variants would be repeated rather more frequently among the conversation strings than corresponds to its frequency of repetition in ordinary English. This means the machine would have rather more of a tendency to tell onomatopoeic jokes than a normal person!

14 This is what leads Neumaier and other critics to undervalue the test and consider 'extended Turing tests', involving robots and so forth. I will argue that there is no need for such elaboration. The performance of a skill can be examined even via teletypes.

15 I am now predicting what will happen when I spell-check this chapter. I am now confirming that the prediction was correct. Unsurprisingly, the spell-checker had a lot of trouble with all the non-standard words in this chapter.

16 A dictionary of acceptable pairings of words would be much bigger than a regular dictionary and so forth. The Block machine is much less puzzling when it is thought of as a giant 'sense-checker' and its mistakes are compared to those of a regular spell-checker.

17 Though I have dealt only with a memory-based machine, the argument applies just as much to 'learning' machines such as neural nets. There is not the slightest reason to suppose that neural nets will develop context sensitivity as a result of their essentially behaviourist training.

18 I have heard the developers of AI machines stating, with straight faces and serious looks, that they are worried about their machines being mistaken for humans. Worry not! Just make the machines make a sound like a frog every ten seconds. The machines will still do the job perfectly adequately, but no one will mistake them for humans.

REFERENCES

Abel, M. (1990) 'Experiences in an exploratory distributed organisation', in J. Galegher, R.E. Kraut, and C. Egido (eds) *Intellectual Teamwork: Social and Technological Foundations of Cooperative Work*, Hillsdale, NJ: Lawrence Erlbaum, pp. 489–511.

Amann, K. and Knorr-Cetina, K. (1990) 'The fixation of (visual) evidence', in M. Lynch and S. Woolgar (eds) *Representation in Scientific Practice*, Cambridge, MA: MIT Press, pp. 85–122.

Anderson, R.J., Heath, C., Luff, P., and Moran, T.P. (forthcoming) 'The social and the cognitive in human computer interaction', *Journal of Man-Machine Studies*.

Anderson, R.J., Hughes, J.A., and Sharrock, W.W. (1989) *Working for Profit: The Social organisation of Calcuability in Entrepreneurial Decision Making*, Aldershot: Avebury.

Anderson, R.J., Hughes, J.A., Shapiro, D.Z., Sharrock, W.W., Harper, R., and Gibbens, S. (1990) 'Flying planes can be dangerous: work skills and traffic management in air traffic control', unpublished manuscript, Rank Xerox EuroPARC.

Ankrah, A., Frohlich, D.M. and Gilbert, G.N. (1990) 'Two ways to fill a bath, with and without knowing it', in *Proceedings of Interact '90 – Third IFIP Conference on Human–Computer Interaction*, Cambridge, August, pp. 73–8.

Atkinson, J.M. (1984) *Our Master's Voices: The Language and Body Language of Politics*, London: Methuen.

Atkinson, J.M. and Drew, P. (1979) *Order in Court: the Organisation of Verbal Interaction in Judicial Settings*, London: Macmillan.

Atkinson, J.M. and Heritage, J.C. (eds) (1984) *Structures of Social Action: Studies in Conversation Analysis*, Cambridge: Cambridge University Press.

Baccus, M. D. (1986) 'Multipiece truck wheel accidents and their regulation', in H. Garfinkel (ed.) *Ethnomethodological Studies of Work*, London: Routledge, pp. 20–56.

Bainbridge, L. (1974) 'Analysis of verbal protocols from a process control task', in E. Edwards and F.P. Lee (eds) *The Human Operator In Process Control*, London: Taylor & Francis.

Bannon, L. and Schmidt, K. (1991) 'CSCW: four characters in search of a context', in J.M. Bowers and S.D. Benford (eds) *Studies in Computer Supported Cooperative Work: Theory, Practice and Design*, Amsterdam: Elsevier, pp. 3–17.

Banta, A., Dorward, P.H. and Scampini, S.A. (1985) 'New cardiograph family with ECG analysis capability', *Hewlett Packard Journal*, September.

Barker, J. and Downing, H. (1985) 'Word processing and the transformation of patriarchal relations of control in the office', in D. MacKenzie, and J. Wajcman (eds) *The Social Shaping of Technology*, Milton Keynes: Open University Press, pp. 147–64

Barnard, P. (1991) 'Bridging between basic theories and the artifacts of human–computer interaction', in J. M. Carroll (ed.) *Designing Interaction: Psychology at the Human–Computer Interface*, Cambridge: Cambridge University Press.

Baum, F. (1900) *The Wizard of Oz*, London: Collins, 1974.

Becker, H.S. (1973) *The Outsiders*, New York: The Free Press.

Benson, D. (1990) 'Science, science policy and ethics', in A. Elzinga (ed.) *In Science We Trust?*, Lund: Lund University Press.

Benson, D. and Hughes, J. (1991) 'Evidence and inference', in G. Button (ed.) *Ethnomethodology and the Human Sciences*, Cambridge: Cambridge University Press, pp. 109–36.

Berger, P. and Luckmann T. (1966) *The Social Construction of Reality*, New York: Anchor Books.

Beun, R.J. and Bunt, H.C. (1987) 'Investigating linguistic behaviour in information dialogues with a computer', *IPO Annual Progress Report* 22.

Bijker, W., Hughes, T.P., and Pinch, T. (eds) (1987) *The Social Construction Of Technological Systems*, Cambridge, MA: MIT Press.

Birdwhistell, R.L. (1970) *Kinesics and Context: Essay in Body-Motion Research*, Philadelphia: University of Pennsylvania Press.

Bittner, E. (1968) 'Police discretion in emergency apprehension of mentally ill persons', *Social Problems* 14: 278–92.

Bjerknes, G., Ehn, P., and Kyng, M. (eds) (1987) *Computers and Democracy*, Aldershot: Avebury.

Block, N. (1981) 'Psychologism and behaviourism', *The Philosophical Review* XC: 5–43.

Bloor, D. (1976) *Knowledge and Social Imagery*, London: Routledge & Kegan Paul.

Bly, S. A. (1988) 'A use of drawing surfaces in different collaborative settings', in *Proceedings of CSCW '88*, 26–28 September, Portland, Oregon, pp. 250–6.

Borning, A. and Travers, M. (1991) 'Two approaches to casual interaction over computer and video networks', in *Proceedings of CHI '91*. New Orleans, Louisiana, pp. 13–19.

Bowers, J.M. and Benford, S.D. (1991) *Studies in Computer Supported Cooperative Work: Theory, Practice and Design.* Amsterdam: Elsevier.

Braverman, H. (1974) *Labour and Monopoly Capital*, New York: Monthly Review Press.

Brun-Cottan, F. (1991) 'Talk in the workplace: occupational relevance', *Research on Language in Social Interaction 1991*, guest editor R. Hopper, pp. 277–95.

Bull, P. (1983) *Body Movement and Interpersonal Communication*, Chichester: Wiley.

Burian, R.M. (1991) 'Underappreciated pathways toward molecular genetics', paper given at Boston University Colloquium for the Philosophy of Science, Boston, MA, April.

Burrows, J. and Dumbell, P.C. (1990) 'PCs for PCs', *Policing* 6.

Button, G. (1990) 'Going up a blind alley: conflating conversation analysis and computational modelling', in P. Luff, G.N. Gilbert, and D.M. Frohlich (eds) *Computers and Conversation*, London and New York: Academic Press, pp. 67–90.

Button, G. and Lee, J.R.E (1987) *Talk and Social Organisation*, Avon: Multilingual Matters.

Callon, M. (1986) 'Some elements of a sociology of translation', in J. Law (ed.) *Power, Action and Belief.* London: Routledge & Kegan Paul, pp. 196–233.

Callon, M., Law, J., and Rip, A. (eds) (1986) *Qualitative Scientometrics: Studies in the Dynamic of Science*, London: Routledge.

Cambrosio, A. and Keating P. (1988) '"Going monoclonal": art, science, and magic in the day-to-day use of hybridoma technology', *Social Problems* 35: 244–60.

Cambrosio, A., Keating, P., and MacKenzie, M. (1990) 'Scientific practice in the courtroom: the construction of sociotechnical identities in a biotechnology patent dispute', *Social Problems* 37: 275–93.

Cantor, C., Caskey, T., White, R., and Kosland D. (1989) 'Driving toward an intersection in New Jersey', The AAAS Observer Roundtable, *The AAAS Observer* 8 (November): 8–9.

Carroll, J.M. (1990) *Infinite Detail and Emulation in an Ontologically Minimized HCI,* Proceedings of CHI '90, Seattle, April, pp. 321–7.

Chapanis, A. (1981) 'Interactive human communication: some lessons learned from laboratory experiments', in B. Shackel (ed.) *Man–Computer Interaction: Human Factors Aspects of Computers and People,* The Netherlands: Sitjhoff & Noordhoff.

Clarke, R. and Hough, S. (1984) *The Effectiveness of Policing,* Aldershot: Gower.

Cockburn, C. (1985) 'Caught in the wheels: the higher cost of being a female cog in the male machinery of engineering', in D. MacKenzie and J. Wajcman (eds) *The Social Shaping of Technology,* Milton Keynes: Open University Press, pp. 55–65.

Collins, H.M. (1985) *Changing Order: Replication and Induction in Scientific Practice,* London: Sage.

Collins, H.M. (1990) *Artificial Experts: Social Knowledge and Intelligent Machines,* Cambridge, MA: MIT Press.

Comrie, M.A. and Kings, E.J. (1975) 'Studies of urban workloads: a final report', *Home Office Research Services Unit.*

Cosnier, J. and Kebrat-Orecchioni, K. (1987) *Decrire la Conversation,* Lyons: Publicité Université Lyons.

Coulter, J. (1973) *Approaches to Insanity: A Philosophical and Sociological Study,* London: Martin Robertson.

Coulter, J. (1979) *The Social Construction of Mind: Studies in Ethnomethodology and Linguistic Philosophy,* London: Macmillan.

Coulter, J. (1983) *Rethinking Cognitive Theory,* London: Macmillan.

Coulter, J. (1989) *Mind in Action,* Polity Press/Basil Blackwell: Cambridge/Oxford.

Dahlbäck, N. and Jönsson, A. (1989) 'Empirical studies of discourse representations for natural language interfaces', *Proceedings of the 4th Conference of the European Chapter of the Association for Computational Linguistics,* pp. 291–8.

Dennis, D. (1990) 'The black box: on representations of DNA-forensic typing', paper given at 85th Annual Meeting of the American Sociological Association, Washington, DC, August.

Doane, S.M., Pellegrino, J.W., and Klatzy, R.L. (1990) 'Expertise in a computer operating system: contextualization and performance', *Human–Computer Interaction* 5.

Doue, J.C. and Vallance, A.G. (1985) 'Computer-aided ECG analysis', *Hewlett Packard Journal* September.

Douglas, J. (ed.) (1971) *Understanding Everyday Life.* London: Routledge & Kegan Paul.

Drew, P. and Heritage, J. (eds) (forthcoming) *Talk at Work.* Cambridge: Cambridge University Press.

Dreyfus, H.L. and Dreyfus, S.E. (1986) *Mind Over Machine,* New York: The Free Press.

Egido, C. (1990) 'Teleconferencing as a technology to support cooperative work: its possibilities and limitations', in J. Galegher, R.E. Kraut, and C. Egido (eds) *Intellectual Teamwork: Social and Technological Foundations of Cooperative Work,* Hillsdale, NJ: Erlbaum, pp. 351–73.

Ehn, P. (1988) *Work Orientated Design of Computer Artifacts*, Stockholm: Arbetslivscentrum.

Ekman, P. and Friessen, W.V. (1969) 'The repertoires of nonverbal behaviour: categories, origins, usage and coding', *Semiotica* 1: 49–98.

Erickson, F. and Schultz, J. (1982) *The Councillor as Gatekeeper*, New York: Academic Press.

Erlich, H.A. (ed.) (1989) *PCR Technology: Principles and Applications of DNA Amplification*, New York: Stockdon Press.

Fine, B., Kinsey, R., Lea, J., Piccotto, S., and Young S. (1979) *Capitalism and the Rule of Law*, London: Hutchinson.

Fish, R.S., Kraut, R.E. and Chalfonte, B.L. (1990) 'The videowindow system in informal communication', *Proceedings of the Conference on Computer Supported Collaborative Work*, Los Angeles, California, pp. 1–11.

Fleck, L. (1979) *The Genesis and Development of a Scientific Fact*, Chicago: University of Chicago Press.

Forbes, K. (1991) 'The complex sheet', Department of Anthropology, University of California, Berkeley, unpublished manuscript.

Foucault, M. (1979) *Discipline and Punishment*, New York: Random House.

Fraser, N.M. and Gilbert, G.N. (1991) 'Simulating speech systems', *Computer Speech and Language* 5: 81–99.

Fraser, N.M. and Wooffitt, R.C (1990) 'Orienting to rules', *American Association for Artificial Intelligence, Proceedings of the Workshop on Complex Systems, Ethnomethodology and Interaction Analysis*, Boston, MA.

Friedman, A. and Cornford, D.S. (1989) *Computer Systems Development*, New York: Wiley.

Frohlich, D.M. and Luff P. (1990) 'Applying the technology of conversation to the technology for conversation', in P. Luff, G.N. Gilbert, and D.M. Frohlich (eds) *Computers and Conversation*, London and New York: Academic Press, pp. 189–222.

Fujimura, J. (in press) 'Crafting science: standardized packages, boundary objects, and "translation"', to appear in A. Pickering (ed.) *Science as Practice and Culture*, Chicago: University of Chicago Press.

Fyfe, G. and Law, J. (eds) (1988) *Picturing Power: Visual Depictions and Social Relations*, London: Routledge.

Gale, S. (1989) 'Adding audio and video to an office environment', *Proceedings of the First European Conference on Computer Supported Cooperative Work*. London, pp. 121–33.

Garfinkel, H. (1967) *Studies in Ethnomethodology*, New York: Prentice-Hall.

Garfinkel, H. (ed.) (1986) *Ethnomethodological Studies of Work*, London: Routledge.

Garfinkel, H. (1991) 'Evidence for locally produced, naturally accountable phenomena of order, logic, reason, meaning, method, etc. in and as of the essential haecceity of immortal ordinary society (I) -an Announcement of studies', in G. Button (ed.) *Ethnomethodology and the Human Sciences*, Cambridge: Cambridge University Press, pp. 10–19.

Garfinkel, H. and Sacks, H. (1970) 'On formal structures of practical actions', in J.C. McKinney and E.A. Tiryakian (eds) *Theoretical Sociology*, New York: Appleton Century Crofts, pp. 338–66.

Garfinkel, H. and Wiley, N. (1980) Transcribed tape-recording of a discussion of Agnes and social construction, transcriber unknown.

Garfinkel, H., Lynch, M. and Livingston, E. (1981) 'The work of a discovering science construed with materials from the optically discovered pulsar', *Philosophy of Social Science* 11: 131–58.

Garfinkel, H., Livingston, E., Lynch, M., Macbeth, D., and Robillard, A. (1989)

'Respecifying the natural sciences as discovering sciences of practical action, I&II: doing so ethnographically by administering a schedule of contingencies in discussions with laboratory scientists and by hanging around their laboratories', unpublished paper, Department of Sociology, University of California, Los Angeles.

Gaver, W.W. (1991) 'Technological affordances', *Proceedings of CHI '91*, April–May, New Orleans, pp. 79–84.

Gilbert, G.N. (1987) 'Cognitive and social models of the user', in H.J. Bullinger and B. Shackel (eds) *Human–Computer Interaction – Interact '87, Proceedings of the Second IFIP Conference*, September, Stuttgart, Amsterdam: North-Holland, pp. 165–72.

Gilbert, G.N., and Mulkay, M. (1984) *Opening Pandora's Box: An Analysis of Scientists' Discourse*, Cambridge: Cambridge University Press.

Gilbert, G.N., Wooffitt, R.C., and Fraser, N.M. (1990) 'Organizing computer talk', in P. Luff, G.N. Gilbert, and D. Frohlich (eds) *Computers and Conversation*, London: Academic Press, pp. 235–57.

Ginzton, L.E. and Laks, M.M. (1984) 'Computer aided ECG interpretation', *MD Computing* 1 (3).

Goffman, E. (1959) *The Presentation of Self in Everyday Life*, Harmondsworth: Penguin.

Goffman, E. (1971) 'The territories of the self' in *Relations in Public*, New York: Harper & Row, pp. 28–61.

Goodwin, C. (1981) *Conversational Organisation: Interaction between a Speaker and Hearer*, London: Academic Press.

Goodwin, C. and Goodwin, M. (forthcoming) 'Formulating planes: seeing as a situated activity', in Y. Engestrom and D. Middleton (eds) *Communication and Cognition at Work*, New York: Cambridge University Press.

Gould, J.D., Conti, J., and Hovanyecz, T. (1983) 'Composing letters with a simulated listening typewriter', *Communications of the Association for Computing Machinery* 26: 295–308.

Greatbatch, D. (1988) 'A turn taking system for British news interviews', *Language and Society* 17 (3).

Greif, I., (ed.) (1988) *Computer-Supported Cooperative Work: A Book of Readings*, San Mateo: Morgan Kaufman.

Grosjean, M. (1989) 'L'Annonce Sonore', Secretariat, Departement du Developpement Prospective, Paris, unpublished research report.

Guillaume, M. (1987) 'The metamorphosis of epidemia', *Zone* 1/2: 58–69.

Guyomard, M. and Siroux, J. (1988) 'Constitution incrémentale d'un corpus de dialogues oraux coopératifs', *Journal Acoustique* 1, pp. 329–37.

Hacking, I. (1983) *Representing and Intervening: Introductory Topics in the Philosophy of Natural Science*, Cambridge: Cambridge University Press.

Harper, R.R. (1988) 'Not any old numbers: an examination of practical reasoning on an accountancy environment', *The Journal of Interdisciplinary Economics* 2: 297–306.

Harper, R.R., Hughes, J.A., and Shapiro, D.Z. (1989) *The Functionalities of Flight Data Strips*, London: CAA.

Harper, R.R., Hughes, J.A., and Shapiro, D.Z. (1991) 'Working in harmony: an examination of computer technology in air traffic control', in J.M. Bowers, and S.D. Benford (eds) *Studies in Computer Supported Cooperative Work: Theory, Practice and Design*. Amsterdam: Elsevier.

Harper, R.R., Hughes, J.A., Randall, D, Shapiro, D., and Sharrock, W.W. (forthcoming) *Order in the Skies*, London: Routledge.

Hauptmann, A.G. and Rudnicky, A.I. (1988) 'Talking to computers: an empirical investigation', *International Journal of Man-Machine Studies* 28: 583–604.

Heath, C. (1984) 'Talk and recipiency: sequential organisation in speech and body movement', in J.M. Atkinson and J. Heritage (eds) *Structures of Social Action: Studies in Conversation Analysis*. Cambridge: Cambridge University Press.

Heath, C. (1986) *Body Movement and Speech in Medical Interaction*, Cambridge: Cambridge University Press.

Heath, C. and Luff, P. (1991) 'Collaborative activity and technological design: task coordination in London Underground control rooms', *Proceedings of the Second European Conference on Computer-Supported Cooperative Work*, Amsterdam, The Netherlands, pp. 65–80.

Heritage, J. (1988) 'Explanations as accounts: a conversation analytic perspective', in C. Antaki (ed.) *Analysing Everyday Explanation: A Casebook of Methods*, London: Sage, pp. 127–44.

Heritage, J. and Greatbatch, D. (1986) 'Generating applause: a study of rhetoric and response at party political conferences', *American Journal of Sociology* 92 (1): 110–57.

Hopkin, V.D. (1979) 'The controller versus automation', in A. Benoit (ed.) *A Survey of Modern Air Traffic Control*, AGARDograph, No. 209, AGARD.

Hughes, J.A., Shapiro, D.Z., Sharrock, W.W., Anderson, R.R., Harper, R.R., and Gibbons, S. (1988) *The Automation of Air Traffic Control*, SERC/ESRC Grant No. GR/D/86157.

Hughes, J.P. (1985) 'Edison and electric light', in D. MacKenzie, and J. Wajcman (eds) *The Social Shaping of Technology*, Milton Keynes: Open University Press, pp. 39–52.

Hutchby, I. (1991) 'The organisation of talk on talk radio', in P. Scannell (ed.) *Broadcast Talk*, London: Sage, pp. 119–37.

Hutchins, E.L. (1985) 'The social organisation of distributed cognition in an airplane cockpit', unpublished paper, Department of Cognitive Science, University of California, San Diego.

Hutchins, E.L. (1990) 'The technology of team navigation', in J. Galegher, R.E. Kraut, and C. Egido (eds) *Intellectual Teamwork: The Social and Technological Foundations of Cooperative Work*, Hillsdale, NJ: Erlbaum, pp. 191–221.

Hutchins, E.L., and Klause, T. (1990) 'Distributed cognition in an airline cockpit', unpublished manuscript, University of California, San Diego.

Hutchins, E.L., Hollan, J.D. and Norman, D.A. (1986) 'Direct manipulation interfaces', in D.A. Norman and S.W. Draper (eds) *User-Centered System Design*, Hillsdale NJ: Erlbaum, pp. 87–124.

Innis, M.A., Gelfand, D.H., Sninsky, J., and White, T.J. (1990) *PCR Protocols*, New York: Academic Press.

Ishii, H. (1990) 'Teamworkstation: towards a seamless shared workspace', *Proceedings of CSCW '90*, October, Los Angeles, pp. 13–26.

Jackson, A. and Onslow, G.J. (undated) 'The replay technique: the concept, initial experience and proposed developments', *RSRE Memorandum* 3827.

Jefferson, G. (1972) 'Side sequences' in D. Sudnow (ed.) *Studies in Social Interaction*, New York: Free Press, pp. 294–338.

Jefferson, G. (1974) 'Error correction as an interactional resource', *Language in Society* 2: 181–99.

Jefferson, G. (1984) 'Notes on a systematic deployment of the acknowledgement tokens "yeah" and "mm hm"', *Papers In Linguistics* 17: 197–206.

Jefferson, G. (1989) 'Preliminary notes on a possible metric which provides for a "standard maximum" silence of approximately one second in conversation', in D. Roger and P. Bull (eds) *Conversation*, Clevdon and Philadelphia: Multilingual Matters, pp. 166–96.

Jordan, B. (in preparation) *Technology and Social Interaction: Notes on the Achievement of Authoritative Knowledge in Complex Settings*, Xerox, Palo Alto Research Centre and Institute for Research on Learning, Palo Alto, CA.

Jordan, K. and Lynch, M. (in press) 'The sociology of a genetic engineering technique: ritual and rationality in the performance of the plasmid prep', in A. Clarke and J. Fujimura (eds) *The Right Tools for the Job: Materials, Techniques, Instruments and Work Organization in Twentieth Century Life Sciences*. Princeton, NJ: Princeton University Press.

Kay, L. (1991) 'Life as technology: representing, intervening, and molecularizing', paper given at Boston University Colloquium for the Philosophy of Science, Boston, MA, April.

Kendon, A. (1990) *Conducting Interaction: Patterns of Behaviour in Focussed Encounters*, Cambridge: Cambridge University Press.

Kinsey, R., Lea, J., and Young, J. (1986) *Losing the Fight against Crime*, Oxford: Blackwell.

Kitsuse, J.I and Cicourel, A.V. (1963) 'A note on the use of official statistics', *Social Problems* 11: 131–9.

Knorr-Cetina, K.D (1981) *The Manufacture of Knowledge*, Oxford: Pergamon.

Knorr-Cetina, K.D. and Mulkay, M. (eds) (1983) *Science Observed: Perspectives On the social study of science*, London: Sage.

Kuhn, T.S. (1962) *The Structure of Scientific Revolutions*, Chicago: University of Chicago Press.

Lack, J., Morris, D.J. and Marshall, A.J. (1989) 'An assessment of computerised electrocardiograph analysis', *Cardiology in Practice* 7 (8).

Latour, B. (1987) *Science in Action*, Cambridge MA: Harvard University Press.

Latour, B. (1988) *The Pasteurization of France*, trans. A. Sheridan and J. Law, Cambridge, MA: Harvard University Press.

Latour, B. (1990) 'Drawing things together', in M. Lynch and S. Woolgar, (eds) *Representation in Scientific Practice*, Cambridge, MA: MIT Press, pp. 19–68.

Latour, B. and Woolgar, S. (1979) *Laboratory Life: The Construction of Scientific Facts*, Princeton, NJ: Princton University Press, 2nd ed., 1976.

Lave, J. (1988) *Cognition in Practice*, Cambridge: Cambridge University Press.

Law, J. (ed.) (1986) *Power, Action and Belief*, London: Routledge & Kegan Paul.

Law, J. (1987) 'Technology and heterogeneous engineering: the case of Portuguese expansion', in W. Bijker, T.P. Hughes, and T. Pinch (eds) *The Social Construction of Technological Systems*, Cambridge MA: MIT Press, pp. 113–34.

Lévi-Strauss, C. (1962) *The Savage Mind*, London: Weidenfeld & Nicolson.

Livingston, E. (1986) *The Ethnomethodological Foundations of Mathematics*. London: Routledge & Kegan Paul.

Livingston, E. (1987) *Making Sense of Ethnomethodology*, New York: Routledge & Kegan Paul.

Luff, P. and Heath, C.C. (1990) 'The first steps towards a transcription system for analysing the social organisation of human–computer interaction', Laboratory Notebook, EuroPARC.

Luff, P. and Heath, C.C. (1991) 'The practicalities of menu use: improvisation in screen based activity', Laboratory Notebook, EuroPARC.

Luff, P., Gilbert, N., and Frohlich, D. (eds) (1990) *Computers and Conversation*, London: Academic Press.

Luzzati, D. and Neel, F. (1989) 'Dialogue behaviour induced by the machine', *Eurospeech '89* Paris, pp. 601–4.

Lynch, M. (1982) 'Technical work and critical inquiry: investigations in a scientific laboratory', *Social Studies of Science* 12: 499–534.

Lynch, M. (1985a) *Art and Artifact in Laboratory Science*, London: Routledge & Kegan Paul.

Lynch, M. (1985b) 'Discipline and the material form of images: an analysis of scientific visibility', *Social Studies of Science* 15: 37–66.

Lynch, M. (1988) 'The externalized retina: selection and mathematization in the visual documentation of objects in the life sciences', *Human Studies* 11: 201–34; reprinted in M. Lynch and S. Woolgar (eds) *Representation in Scientific Practice*, Cambridge, MA: MIT Press, 1990, pp. 153–86.

Lynch, M. (forthcoming) *Ethnomethodology and the Sociology of Science: Toward a Post-Analytic Ethnomethodology*, New York: Cambridge University Press.

Lynch, M., Livingston, E., and Garfinkel, H. (1983) 'Temporal order in the laboratory', in K.D. Knorr-Cetina and M. Mulkay (eds) *Science Observed*, London: Sage, pp. 205–38.

McGrath, J. (1990) 'Time matters in groups', in J. Gallagher, R.E. Kraut, and C. Egido (eds) *Intellectual Teamwork: Social and Technological Foundations of Co-operative Work*, Hillsdale, NJ: Erlbaum, pp. 23–62.

McIlvenny, P. (1990) 'Communicative action and computers: re-embodying conversation analysis?' in P. Luff, G.N. Gilbert, and D.M. Frohlich (eds) *Computers and Conversation*, London and New York: Academic Press, pp. 91–134.

MacKenzie, D. and Wajcman, J. (eds) (1985) *The Social Shaping of Technology*, Milton Keynes: Open University Press.

Maniatis, T., Fritsch, E.F., and Sambrook, J. (1982/1989) *Molecular Cloning: A Laboratory Manual*, Cold Spring Harbor Laboratory.

Mannheim, K. (1936) *Ideology and Utopia*, New York: Harvest Books.

Mayes, J.T., Draper, S.W., McGregor, A.M. and Oatley, K. (1988) 'Information flow in a user interface: the effect of experience and context on the recall of MacWrite screens', in D.M. Jones and R. Winder (eds) *People and Computers IV, Proceedings of the Fourth Conference of the BCS HCI Specialist Group*, University of Manchester, September, pp. 275–89.

Minneman, S.L. and Bly, S.A. (1991) 'Managing à trois: a study of a multi-user drawing tool in distributed design work', *Proceedings of CHI '91*, April–May, New Orleans, pp. 217–24.

Miyata, Y. and Norman D.A. (1986) 'Psychological issues in support of multiple actvities', in D.A. Norman and S.W. Draper (eds) *User-Centered System Design*, Hillsdale, NJ: Erlbaum, pp. 265–84.

Montaigne, M. Eyquem de (1952) *Essays, Book II, no' 12* trans. C. Cotton, Chicago: Encyclopedia Britannica.

Morel, M.A. (1986) 'Computer–human interaction', NATO Research Study Group on ASP and CHI in Command and Control: Structures of Multimodal Dialogue Including Voice, Venaco, France.

Morel, M.A. (1987) 'Computer–human communication', in M.M. Taylor, F. Neel, and D.G. Bouwhuis (eds) *The Structure of Multimodal Dialogue*, Amsterdam: North Holland.

Mumford, E. and Henshall, D. (1979) *A Participative Approach to Computer System Design. A Case Study of the Introduction of a New Computer System*, London: Associated Press.

Murray, F. and Woolgar, S. (1991) 'Social perspectives on software: a preliminary report', unpublished paper, Centre for Research into Innovation, Culture and Technology, Brunel University.

Neumaier, O. (1987) 'A Wittgensteinian view of artificial intelligence', in R. Born (ed.) *Artificial Intelligence: The Case Against*, London: Croom Helm, pp. 132–73.

Newell, A.F. (1987) 'Speech simulation studies – performance and dialogue specification: recent developments and applications of natural language understanding', Unicom Seminar, London, December.

Newing, J. (1988) 'The future PNC', *Policing* 3 (4).

Newman, W. and Wellner, P. (1992) 'A desk supporting computer-based interaction with paper documents', *Proceedings of CHI '92*, pp. 537–42.

Nickerson, R. S. (1981) 'Some characteristics of conversation', in B. Shackel (ed.) *Man–Computer Interaction: Human Factors Aspects of Computers and People*, The Netherlands: Sitjhoff & Noordhoff, pp. 53–65.

Norman, D.A. (1988) *The Psychology of Everyday Things*, New York: Basic Books.

Norman, M. and Thomas, P. (1990) 'The very idea: informing HCI design from conversation analysis', in P. Luff, G.N. Gilbert, and D.M. Frohlich (eds) *Computers and Conversation*, London and New York: Academic Press, pp. 51–66.

Olson, G.M. and J.S. Olson (1991) 'User-centered design of collaboration technology', *Journal of Organisational Computing* 1 (1): 61–83.

Olson, J.S., Olson, G.M., Mack, L.A. and Wellner, P. (1990) 'Concurrent editing: the group interface', *Proceedings of Interact '90 – Third IFIP Conference on Human–Computer Interaction* Cambridge, 27–30 August, pp. 835–40.

Parsons, T. (1958) *The Social System*, London: Tavistock.

Payne, S.J. and Green, T.R.G. (1986) 'Task-action grammars: a model of the mental representation of task languages', *Human–Computer Interaction* 2 (2): 93–133.

Pinch, T. and Bijker, W. (1987) 'The social construction of facts and artefacts: or how the sociology of science and the sociology of technology might benefit each other', in W. Bijker, T.P. Hughes, and T. Pinch (eds) *The Social Construction of Technological Systems*, Cambridge, MA: MIT Press, pp. 399–442.

Poster, M. (1990) *The Mode of Information: Post-structuralism and Social Context*, Cambridge: Polity Press.

Rabinow, P. (1990) 'Galton's regret', paper given at the meetings of the American Anthropological Association, New Orleans, November.

Rasmussen, J. and Jensen, A. (1974) 'Mental procedures in real-life tasks: a case study of electronic trouble shooting', *Ergonomics* 17: 293–308.

Rhees, R. (1969) *Without Answers*, London: Routledge.

Richards, M.A. and Underwood, K.M. (1984a) 'Talking to machines: how are people naturally inclined to speak?', in E.D. Megaw (ed.) *Contemporary Ergonomics*, London: Taylor & Francis.

Richards, M.A. and Underwood, K.M. (1984b) 'How should people and computers speak to each other?', *Interact '84* 33–6.

Robinson, H.M. (1990) 'Towards a sociology of human–computer interaction', in P. Luff, G.N. Gilbert, and D.M. Frohlich (eds) *Computers and Conversation*, London and New York: Academic Press, pp. 39–49.

Ryle, G. (1963) *The Concept of Mind*, Harmondsworth: Penguin.

Sacks, H. (1964–1972) unpublished transcribed lectures (transcribed and indexed by G. Jefferson), University of California, Irvine.

Sacks, H. (1974) 'An analysis of the course of a joke's telling in conversation', in R. Bauman and J. Sherzer (eds) *Explorations in the Ethnography of Speaking*, Cambridge: Cambridge University Press, pp. 337–53.

Sacks, H. and Schegloff, E. (1979) 'Two preferences in the organization of reference to persons and their interaction', in G. Psathas (ed.) *Everyday Language: Studies in Ethnomethodology*, New York: Irvington, pp. 15–21.

Sacks, H., Schegloff, E.A., and Jefferson, G. (1974) 'A simplest systematics for the organisation of turn-taking in conversation', *Language* 50 (4): 696–735.

Saiki, R.K., Scharf, S., Faloona, F., Mullis, K.B., Horn, G.B., Erlich, H.A., and Arnheim, N. (1985) 'Enzymatic amplification of ß-globin genomic sequences and restriction site analysis for diagnosis of sickle-cell anemia', *Science* 230: 1350–4.

Saiki, R.K., Gelfand, D.H., Stoffel, S., Scharf, S.J., Higuchi, R., Horn, G.T., Mullis,

K. B., and Erlich, H.A. (1988) 'Primer-directed enzymatic amplification of DNA with thermostable DNA polymerase', *Science* 239: 487–91.

Schegloff, E. (1972) 'Notes on a conversational practice: formulating place', in D. Sudnow (ed.) *Studies in Social Interaction*, New York: The Free Press, pp. 75–119.

Schegloff, E. (1979) 'Identification and recognition in telephone openings', in G. Psathas (ed.) *Everyday Language: Studies in Ethnomethodology*, New York: Irvington, pp. 23–78.

Schegloff, E.A. (1984a) 'Discourse as an interactional achievement: some uses of "uh huh" and other things that come between sentences', in D. Tannen (ed.) *Analyzing Discourse Text and Talk: Georgetown Roundtable on Languages and Linguistics*, Washington, DC: Georgetown University Press, pp. 71–93.

Schegloff, E.A. (1984b) 'Iconic gestures: locational gestures and speech production', in J.M. Atkinson and J.C. Heritage (eds) *The Structures of Social Action: Studies in Conversation Analysis*, Cambridge: Cambridge University Press, pp. 266–96.

Schegloff, E.A. and Sacks, H. (1973) 'Opening up closings', *Semiotica* 7: 289–327.

Schur, E.M. (1971) *Labeling Deviant Behavior: Its Sociological Implications*, New York: Harper & Row.

Schutz, A. (1962) *The Problem of Social Reality: Collected Papers I*, (ed.) M. Natanson, The Hague: Martinus Nijhoff.

Searle, J.R. (1981) 'Mind brains programs', in J. Houseland (ed.) *Mind Design*, Vermont: Bradford Books.

Shapiro, D.Z., Hughes, J.A., Randall, D., and Harper, R. (1991) 'Visual re-representation of database information: the flight data strip in air traffic control', *Proceedings, 10th Interdisciplinary Workshop on 'Informatics and Psychology': Cognitive Aspects of Visual Language and Visual Interfaces,* Scharding, Austria, May.

Sharrock, W.W. (1991) 'Description and re-description in sociology', unpublished paper, Department of Sociology, University of Manchester.

Sharrock, W.W. and Button, G. (1991) 'The social actor', in G. Button (ed.) *Ethnomethodology and the Human Sciences*, Cambridge: Cambridge University Press, pp. 137–75.

Smith, R.B., O'Shea, T., O'Malley, C., and Taylor, J.S. (1989) 'Preliminary experiments with a distributed, multimedia problem solving environment', *Proceedings of the First European Conference on Computer Supported Cooperative Work*, London, pp. 19–35.

Spiegel-Rosing, I. and Price, D. de Solla, (eds) *Science, Technology and Society*, London: Sage.

Star, S.L. and Griesemer J. (1989) 'Institutional ecology, "translations" and boundary objects: amateurs and professionals in Berkeley's Museum of Vertebrate Zoology, 1907–39', *Social Studies of Science* 19: 387–420.

Suchman, L. (1983) 'Office procedure as practical action: models of work and system design', *ACM Transactions on Office Information Systems*, 1 (4).

Suchman, L. (1987) *Plans and Situated Actions: The Problem of Human–Machine Communication*, Cambridge: University Press.

Suchman, L.A. (1989) 'Rediscovering cooperative work', Keynote Address, *Proceedings of EC-CSCW Conference*, Gatwick, England, September.

Suchman, L. (forthcoming) 'Constituting shared workspaces', in Y. Engestrom and D. Middleton (eds) *Communication and Cognition at Work*, New York: Cambridge University Press.

Suchman, L. and Wynn, E. (1984) 'Procedures and problems in the office', *Office: Technology and People* 2: 133–54.

Tang, J.C. and Minneman, S.L. (1991) 'Video Whiteboard: video shadows to support remote collaboration', *Proceedings of CHI '91*, New Orleans, Louisiana, pp. 315–22.

Thomas, P.J. (1990) 'Conversation analysis in interactive computer system design', unpublished PhD thesis, University of Hull.

Turing, A. (1958) 'Computing machinery and intelligence', *Mind*.

Watabe, K., Sakata, S., Maeno, K., Fukuoka, H., and Ohman, T. (1990) 'Distributed multiparty desktop conferencing system: MERMAID' *Proceedings of the Conference on Computer Supported Collaborative Work*. Los Angeles, California, pp. 27–38.

Weber, H. and Wasserman, A. (1979) *Issues in Data Base Management*, Oxford: North-Holland.

Weber, M. (1947) *Theory of Social and Economic Organisation*, New York: The Free Press.

Wellner, P. (1991) 'The Digital Desk Calculator: tactile manipulation on a desk top display', *Proceedings of the ACM Symposium on User Interface Software and Technology* (UIST '91) November.

West, C. (1985) *Routine Complications: Tasks and Troubles in the Medical Consultation*, Bloomington, IN: Indiana University Press.

Whalen, J. (1991) *9-1-1 Communications Project: Project Report to US West Technologies*, unpublished report, Department of Sociology, University of Oregon, Eugene.

Whalen, M. and Zimmerman, D. (1990) 'Describing trouble: practical epistemology in citizen calls to the police', *Language in Society* 19: 465–92.

White, L. Jr. (1978) *Medieval Technology and Social Change*, New York: Oxford University Press.

Whitfield, D. (1979) 'A preliminary study of the air traffic controllers picture', *Journal of the Canadian Air Traffic Controllers' Association*, ii (i): 19–28.

Whitfield, D. (1980) *Discussion Paper: The Air Traffic Controller and Sector Capacity*, Ergonomics Unit, University of Aston, Birmingham.

Whitfield, D. and Jackson, A. (1982) 'The air traffic controller's "Picture" as an example of a mental model', *Proceedings of the IFAC-IFIP-IFORS-IEA Conference on Analysis, Design and Evalutation of Man–Machine Systems*, Baden-Baden.

Whitfield, D., Ball, R.G., and Ord, G. (1980)'Some human factors aspects of computer-aiding concepts for air traffic controllers', *Human Factors* 22: 569–80.

Whittaker, S. and Stenton, P. (1989) 'User studies and the design of natural language systems', *Proceedings of the 4th Conference of the European Chapter of the Association for Computational Linguistics*, Manchester, pp. 116–23.

Wieder, D.L. (1974) *Language and Social Reality: The Case of Telling the Convict Code*, The Hague: Mouton.

Wilson, T.P. (1974) 'Normative and interpretative paradigms in sociology', in J.D. Douglas (ed.) (1971) *Understanding Everyday Life*, London: Routledge & Kegan Paul.

Wilson, P. (1990) *Introducing Computer Supported Cooperative Work*, CCTA Publications.

Winch, P. (1958) *The Idea of a Social Science and its Relation to Philosophy*, London: Routledge & Kegan Paul.

Winner, L. (1985) 'Do artifacts have politics', in D. MacKenzie, and J. Wajcman (eds) *The Social Shaping Of Technology*, Milton Keynes: Open University Press, pp. 26–38.

Winograd, T. and Flores, F. (1986) *Understanding Computers and Cognition: A New Foundation for Design*, Norwood, NJ: Addison-Wesley.

Wittgenstein, L. (1958) *Philosophical Investigations*, Oxford: Blackwell.

Woolgar, S. (1988) *Knowledge and Reflexivity: New Frontiers in the Sociology of Knowledge*, London: Sage.

Woolgar, S. (1991) 'The turn to technology in social studies of science', *Science, Technology and Human Values* 16 (1): 20–50.

REFERENCES

Young, K.Y., Peter, J.B., and Winters, R.E. (1990) 'Detection of HIV DNA in peripheral blood by the polymerase chain reaction: a study of clinical applicability and performance', *AIDS* 4: 389–91.

Young, R., Howes, A., and Whittington, J. (1990) 'A knowledge analysis of interactivity', *Proceedings of Interact '90 – Third IFIP Conference on Human–Computer Interaction*, Cambridge, August, pp. 115–120.

Zimmerman, D. (1971) 'The practicalities of rule use', in J.D. Douglas (ed.) *Understanding Everyday Life*, London: Routledge & Kegan Paul, pp. 221–38.

NAME INDEX

SUBJECT INDEX